THE
BALLAD-
DRAMA
OF
MEDIEVAL
JAPAN

****

Published under the auspices of
The Center for Japanese and Korean Studies
University of California, Berkeley

THE
BALLAD
DRAMA
OF
MEDIEVAL
JAPAN

****

Published under the auspices of
The Center for Japanese and Korean Studies
University of California, Berkeley

The *kōwaka* performer.

(Photograph by James T. Araki)

THE BALLAD-DRAMA OF MEDIEVAL JAPAN

✳✳✳✳✳✳✳✳✳✳✳✳✳✳✳✳✳✳✳✳✳✳✳✳✳

JAMES T. ARAKI

CHARLES E. TUTTLE COMPANY

RUTLAND, VERMONT
&
TOKYO, JAPAN

Representatives

Continental Europe: BOXERBOOKS, INC., *Zurich*
British Isles: PRENTICE-HALL INTERNATIONAL, INC., *London*
Canada: HURTIG PUBLISHERS, *Edmonton*
Australasia: BOOK WISE (AUSTRALIA) PTY. LTD.
104-108 Sussex Street, Sydney 2000

Published by the Charles E. Tuttle Company, Inc.
of Rutland, Vermont & Tokyo, Japan
with editorial offices at
Suido 1-chome, 2-6, Bunkyo-ku, Tokyo, Japan
by special arrangement with
University of California Press
Berkeley and Los Angeles, California

Copyright in Japan, 1964, by
The Regents of the University of California

Library of Congress Catalog Card No. 76-050314

International Standard Book No. 0-8048-1279-9

First Tuttle edition, 1978

0274-000440-4615
PRINTED IN JAPAN

TO

PETER A. BOODBERG

The Center for Japanese and Korean Studies of the University of California is a unit of the Institute of International Studies. It is the unifying organization for faculty members and students interested in Japan and Korea, bringing together scholars from many disciplines. The Center's major aims are the development and support of research and language study. As part of this program the Center sponsors a publication series of books concerned with Japan and Korea. Manuscripts are considered from all campuses of the University of California as well as from any other individuals and institutions doing research in these areas.

PREFACE

THE four centuries known in Japanese history as the Medieval Era were dominated politically by the society of samurai, men of a noble breed who, ideally, lived and fought in accordance with an estimable code of chivalrous conduct and loyalty. Its genesis in the mid-twelfth century was amidst the violence of war; its demise in the late sixteenth century was amidst even greater turbulence and disorder. The relatively tranquil middle years are characterized by the arts which flowered within the serene, scholarly confines of Zen monasteries or amidst the elegant setting of the court of the Ashikaga Shogun in Kyoto. Flower-arrangement, the tea ceremony, monochrome painting, dry-landscape gardening, the nō drama—these are the arts from that era in history, and which even today epitomize traditional Japanese culture. The quiet, somber mood and subdued tone of beauty set the Medieval Era distinctly apart from the cultural periods between which it stands in time. The era was preceded by the classical Heian Period (794–1185), during the efflorescence of which a culture of remarkable sensual beauty was evolved by a small society of leisured aristocrats centered around the Imperial Court, and followed by the buoyant, colorful Edo Period (1600–1867), when artistic tastes and fashion were dictated by a new pleasure-seeking class of plebeian townsmen.

The ballad-drama known as kōwaka is a legacy of the turbulent years of the Medieval Era. It was created and performed widely before a samurai audience during the middle and late sixteenth century. The stories are drawn mostly from the tumultuous early decades of the era; they treat dramatic highlights of the heroic struggle between the Genji and the Heike as well as other stirring martial adventures that make up the epic material in Japanese literature. The code of fidelity honored by samurai of later ages was, indeed, inspired in large measure by

vii

the gallantry and heroism described in such literature. Although the kōwaka was an art of major significance, favored especially by warring feudal barons and their samurai retainers, it was quickly forgotten once the warrior was transformed into the sedentary sword-bedecked aristocrat of the Edo Period. Long considered an extinct art, its existence was rediscovered only in the present century.

We would know very little about the kōwaka had it not been perpetuated in geographical isolation, relatively uninfluenced by the mainstream of social and artistic evolution. It exists today only in a hamlet called Ōe, situated deep in the provincial recesses of Kyushu. Learned acquaintances in Japan have often commented to me on the remarkable similarity between the kōwaka and some folk art they had once observed. I have analyzed the three which have been mentioned most prominently in this respect—the *daimokutate* and *Yamato manzai* of Nara and the *ennen no mai* of the Mōtsuji monastery in Hiraizumi—and have found that they are artistically of a different order from the kōwaka; and that the fragmentary similarities that do exist attest only to their being products of one culture. This status of uniqueness of the kōwaka can be challenged, of course, with the uncovering of new material. The opportunity to study the kōwaka as a performing art—a composite art comprising elements that are visual, aural, and verbal—has, nevertheless, given me the opportunity to penetrate the vagueness which has shrouded the circumstances of its flourish and decline in history.

The present study is organized in two parts. Part One is a treatment of the kōwaka as a performing art. I have described the history of the kōwaka in considerable detail, tracing and delineating all artistic elements that may have contributed to its formation. A complete and technical treatment was necessary, I felt, if the discussion were to be in any way conclusive; for explanations of origins inevitably falter with the new appearance of yet another suspected antecedent. Although I have touched upon every possible source of influence, however remote, there may be others unknown to me. In preparing the chapter on the history of the kōwaka, I have relied heavily on past studies by Japanese scholars, especially those of the late Takano Tatsu-

yuki. Their conclusions and hypotheses have in many instances
served as points of departure for further inquiry; and if I have
pointed out inconsistencies in their findings, I have been able
to do so owing largely to my advantage of having collated their
research results. The writing of the third chapter ("The Kōwaka
Today") was, of course, based on my own observations and information provided largely by the residents of Ōe Village.

Part Two, which may be read independently, is a study of the
kōwaka libretto; it consists of an analysis and description of the
texts and two complete translations. The full textual annotation is the first to appear in any language. The kōwaka text is
sixteenth-century Japanese literature, and its stylistic divergence
from contemporary Japanese approximates that between the
styles of King James and present-day English. I have tried to
reproduce the tone and style of the original—as it may appear
to the Japanese today, at least—not by resorting to archaisms but
by rendering faithfully the literary conventions which characterize the kōwaka. I have not attempted to make the texts appear
more charming in translation than they are in the original.
Lyrical passages may occasionally, but fortuitously, be cast in
meters which are discernibly English; it is hoped that in such
instances the effect will not be disagreeable. Epithets, titles, and
names have been rendered in translation if their imagistic qualities predominate over their value as utterances: thus, "Inner
Wilds" for Uchino and "Hall of the Valley" for Tani-no-dō.
Others I have transcribed: for example, *nyūdō* ("one who has
entered the [Buddhist] Way"), which on the Japanese ear seems
to register primarily as a sound symbolism rather than a di-
morphemic term of description. Colorful words in the Japanese
have not been allowed to pale in translation: so we have "bow
hand" and "steed hand" for *yunde* and *mete* rather than "left
hand" and "right hand," their meanings by implication. I have
enclosed in square brackets [ ] only words which are neither
stated explicitly nor clearly understood in the Japanese text. I
have not aimed at achieving consistency in such matters of style
with but one exception: all personal names of Japanese and Chinese are cited, as is customary, with the surname first.

I had hoped, when I began this study, to synthesize the aesthetic
effect of the performance of this ballad-drama, but I find in the

end that what I can offer amounts to little more than fragmentary descriptions of its component elements. My original intention may itself have been pretentious, though I suspect that such a total description of aesthetic meaning is what scholars of the performing arts aspire to achieve.

The esteemed Sasano Ken in 1943 compiled a valuable compendium of source material relating to the kōwaka—the *Kōwaka-bukyoku shū*, which I have used liberally—with the expressed hope that it may enable someone to write a definitive literary and historical study of the kōwaka. The present study has its obvious limitations. An acquaintance in depth with the many lesser topics discussed would have been desirable. Parts of the discussion of traditional forms of Japanese music are only as reliable as the technical studies which I have consulted. My treatment of the choreography and music of the kōwaka may more properly be termed descriptions rather than analyses. It lies beyond the scope of the present study, for instance, to treat the problem of defining the musical modes employed in kōwaka melodies, for this is something that will require a major effort by a competent musicologist. It is my hope that the present study will be of value to yet another inquirer who may be able to illuminate such relevant areas. Other shortcomings will have been due to my inability to consult a number of unpublished sources.

J. T. A.

Los Angeles, California
March, 1963

ACKNOWLEDGMENTS

THOUGH I have not been privileged to meet Mr. Sasano Ken, I should like first to acknowledge a debt of gratitude to him; for I could not have begun this study without the aid of his marvelous compendium of sources pertaining to the topic of this book. I am indebted also to Professor Donald H. Shively, who encouraged me to investigate the kōwaka as a dissertation topic; to the Fulbright Commission and the Ford Foundation for having provided me with the opportunity to carry out this study; and to Professor Ichiko Teiji of the University of Tokyo for his many kindnesses during my sojourn in Japan. I wish to express my deepest gratitude to Mr. Esaki Ushio and the many performers of Ōe Village in Kyushu who sacrificed precious hours in the midst of rice-planting in order to rehearse and perform the kōwaka for the benefit of this visiting student; and to Mr. Haruyoshi Uno, Superintendent of the Fukui-ken Diocese of the Tenrikyō Church, for conducting me on a survey of Kōwaka family sites in the area of Nishi-Tanaka Village, Fukui-ken.

I wish to acknowledge my debt to Mr. Misumi Haruo of the Tokyo National Cultural Property Research Institute for permission to analyze his tape recordings and texts of the *daimokutate*; to Professor Atsumi Kaoru, who graciously offered me copies of her tape recordings of *Heike-biwa, mōsō-biwa, Yamato manzai, Oku-jōruri,* and *shōmyō;* to Professor Ishida Ichirō and his students at Tōhoku University for tape-recording and photographing the *ennen* of Mōtsuji on my behalf; and to the Kawade Shobō for permission to quote from the *Nihon rekishi daijiten.*

I should like to thank Professors Denzel Carr, Cyril Birch, and Wayne Shumaker for their generous assistance during the writing of the original manuscript; Professors Mantle Hood and Robert A. Garfias for their suggestions in the course of my revising the sections pertaining to music; Professor Claude E. Jones for reading the revised manuscript; and Mr. Ben Sakoguchi, whose fine drawings compensate for inadequacies in my verbal descriptions. I have been especially grateful throughout for the reassuring support of the scholar and teacher to whom this study is dedicated.

CONTENTS

PART ONE

*The History and Tradition of the Kōwaka
as a Performing Art*

xiii

ILLUSTRATIONS

PLATES

FIGURES

PART
ONE

✳✳✳✳✳✳✳✳✳✳✳✳✳✳✳✳✳✳✳✳✳✳✳

*The History and Tradition of the Kōwaka
as a Performing Art*

I: INTRODUCTION

THE HISTORICAL STATUS OF KŌWAKA

> *Should man, after his fifty years,*
> *Scan the subcelestial realm,*
> *All will prove a dream, an illusion;*
> *To acquire life and perish not—*
> *This cannot be.**

THESE lines, expressing the ephemeralness of man's existence, were intoned by Oda Nobunaga (1534–1582) as he
danced the kōwaka on the eve of the Battle of Okehazama in
1560. Nobunaga's domain lay in the path of Imagawa Yoshimoto
(1519–1560), whose army appeared to be an irresistible tide of
strength as it began marching toward the capital city of Kyoto,
and it seemed foolhardy even to attempt resistance. But Nobunaga was a man destined for greatness. He danced the kōwaka,
ignoring the confusion about him, and found solace in its performance and inspiration in its words. No sooner did he finish
than he mounted his steed and headed for the battlefield, leaving
his vassals to follow as they would. By the time he neared Okehazama, all his warriors were riding behind him. Nobunaga's
meager forces attacked with inspired vigor and won a victory that
changed the course of Japanese history.

Many Japanese, students of history and laymen alike, are
familiar with this romanticized episode in the life of the man who
brought the first semblance of order to Japan after a century of
chaos, and these celebrated lines from the kōwaka text are often
quoted by Japanese writers of history and romance. But readers

* The passage is from *Atsumori*, which is translated in its entirety in Part
Two of this book.

3

have undoubtedly wondered what the kōwaka was like. Though they may have read of the profound influence which the art had on Nobunaga's view of life, they will seldom see kōwaka mentioned elsewhere and may conclude that it was simply another of many archaic and insignificant forms of entertainment. A closer look at history reveals, however, that the first two Edo shoguns, Tokugawa Ieyasu (1542–1616) and his son Hidetada (1579–1623), were also known to have been patrons of the kōwaka—a fact bespeaking its possible importance as a performing art in this historical period.

The kōwaka evidently ceased to attract notice as a performing art and was consigned to oblivion long before the advent of the Modern Era. Fortunately, the librettos were preserved for posterity in the *Texts for Kōwaka Dances (Mai no hon)*, an anthology of thirty-six standard kōwaka compiled in the early seventeenth century and published as prose tales to be enjoyed in reading. Many of them present stirring tales that recount the heroics and tragedies of the war between the Genji and the Heike, the warrior clans whose epic struggle for supremacy in the latter half of the twelfth century made this the Heroic Age in Japanese history.

When this anthology was reprinted in 1900, Ueda Kazutoshi, in the editor's preface, provided tantalizing bits of information hinting at the possibility that the kōwaka was a performing art that had, indeed, been the equal of the nō drama in its importance to the culture of medieval Japan. Evidence available at that time indicated that the kōwaka had been named after Kōwakamaru, who was alleged to have been its originator and the author of its texts. Kōwakamaru was said to have been the childhood name of Momonoi Naoaki (1393?–1470?),[1] a grandson of the illustrious warring daimyo, Momonoi Naotsune (1307–1371?),[2] whose martial exploits are recounted in the *Chronicle of the Grand Pacification (Taiheiki)*, the celebrated romantic war chronicle of the fourteenth century. The renown of Kōwakamaru was said to have been such that he was summoned to the Imperial Court to perform before the emperors of his time.

During the years of political turbulence and widespread military strife at the close of the Medieval Era, the kōwaka found a receptive audience in the warring samurai. This was also the age in which the nō attained its heights of restrained artistic elegance amidst the luxurious setting of the court of the Ashikaga shoguns in Kyoto. Many of the lesser daimyos in the provinces cultivated a liking for the nō because of the solace and enjoyment it provided during moments of respite between wars and, also, because of the satisfaction they derived from emulating the elegant ways of the residents of the capital. The provincial daimyos and their chivalrous but often unlettered samurai retainers established themselves as the aristocracy of Japan during the late sixteenth century. These men prized the kōwaka as an art to be enjoyed equally by viewing and by participating. The master performers of the kōwaka came to be esteemed as "artists," untinged for the most part by the stigma associated with the label of professional entertainer; they were granted fiefs, wore two swords—the symbol of the samurai—and often fought in battle alongside the regular warriors.

Ceremony and material splendor came to keynote the social existence of the samurai of the Edo Period (1600–1867). During the initial phase of this era of internal peace, however, there were two major military campaigns to exterminate forces that still threatened the new Tokugawa regime—the war which annihilated the remnants of the Toyotomi clan in 1615 and the campaign against rebellious Christians in 1637. As a result, memories of the rustic life in the provinces and of the tragedies of war were memories of a past not far distant, and they influenced considerably the molding of the cultural life of the new era. The kōwaka, which recounted the heroics and tragedies of the samurai of bygone eras, appealed strongly to the mood of the times. At the court of the Tokugawa Shogun, the ceremonies for the fourth month of the year always included a performance by the kōwaka masters. The master performers were direct vassals of the Shogunate and enjoyed an official status and prestige far surpassing those accorded the master performers of the nō. Yet by the Genroku Era, a cultural period extending roughly from the 1680's to the 1730's, people could only hazily recall that kōwaka was the name of an obscure dance form of the past. It ceased even to be mentioned in the chronicles, although the performers are known to have attended the shogun's court annually.

By the time Japan entered her Modern Era in 1868, the kōwaka seemed to be a totally forgotten form. Konakamura Kiyonori

(1821–1895) touched briefly on the kōwaka in his pioneer study
of the history of Japanese music,[3] but the information was buried
in a maze of data on many other archaic forms of art and failed
to attract serious notice. Only as a result of the modern reprinting
of the *Texts for Kōwaka Dances* were students of literature and
drama made aware of the fact that such a form had ever existed.
One of the scholars who took an interest in the kōwaka at that
time was Takano Tatsuyuki (1876–1948), who was later to become
an eminent historian of the Japanese song and drama. During the
summer of 1907, Takano journeyed to Kyushu to see if this art
form had survived in the farming village of Ōe in Fukuoka
Prefecture. The possibility had intrigued him ever since he noted
the following passage in Bakin's *Potpourri of Records* (1811):

Kōwakamaru's skill at intoning phrases and at dancing is described
in the chronicles of war, and traces of his influence may still remain
in the various provinces. Although most people of Edo do not know
it, the dance of kōwaka has been transmitted through the generations
in the farming households of Ōe Village in Yamato County, in the
Province of Chikugo. . . . That which is called the dance of kōwaka
today, I understand, is simply singing to a beat produced by the
slapping of a fan, and it is ridiculous to call this a dance. The people
of Ōe possess *eboshi* headwears and costumes that have been handed
down from days of old. I have heard that they dance in front of a timeworn cloth backdrop to the beat of the *tsuzumi* drum.[4]

Takano did rediscover the existence of the kōwaka. He then
turned to historical sources in order to learn more about its past
and incorporated the results in his many published studies.[5] His
findings, which were gleaned largely from records retained by the
descendants of the master performers of the past, provided ample
evidence to attest the role once played by the kōwaka in the historical culture of Japan.

THE POSITION OF THE KŌWAKA IN THE
HISTORY OF THE PERFORMING ARTS

We know almost nothing about how the kōwaka was performed
during the late sixteenth and early seventeenth centuries, when it
was at the zenith of its popularity. Inasmuch as the performances
were referred to variously as *kōwakamai* ("kōwaka dance"),

kusemai ("kuse dance"), *maimai* ("dance-dance"), or simply *mai* ("dance"), we might surmise that the kōwaka was basically a form of dance. But the name of a performing art did not always bespeak its content. For instance, because the nō drama was created by men who belonged to a troupe of *sarugaku* performers, the nō was known until fairly recent times by the name "sarugaku" (literally, "monkey music"), which referred originally to a popular side show comprising acts of jugglers, puppeteers, acrobats,

1. The samurai's *eboshi,*
worn by a kōwaka performer

mummers, and other performers. Just as the nō continued to be called sarugaku for centuries after it had evolved into an artistic form of a distinctly different order, the kōwaka was long referred to by the name of the form out of which it apparently evolved: kusemai.

The kōwaka and the nō seem to have been equally prized by the samurai of the late sixteenth century. Accounts such as the following, entered in the *Diary of Uno Mondo* in the Fifth Month of 1582, tell us that the two were performed on similar occasions

and before similar audiences, and that they were to some extent
comparable and competitive forms:

> At the monastery of Sōkenji in Azuchi, the Grand Master Kōwaka per-
> formed the kusemai, and after that the Grand Master Umewaka, a
> sarugaku performer of Tamba, performed the nō. The *mai* of Kōwaka
> was exceptionally impressive, and ten pieces of gold were awarded to
> the troupe. The nō by the Grand Master Umewaka was poor, and
> [Nobunaga] was displeased; nonetheless, [Umewaka] was also awarded
> ten pieces of gold.[6]

The creators of the nō drama, Kan'ami (1334–1384) and Zeami
(1363–1443), wrote numerous volumes describing the essentials of
nō performance, but no such writings exist to enable us to re-
create the performance of the kōwaka. Old chronicles contain a
number of entries with regard to kōwaka performances, but seldom is anything mentioned besides the names of the players and
the pieces performed. There is no direct evidence that mimicry
was one of the means of portraying the story through performance. Nor is there evidence for determining whether or not
dialogue was one of the elements of performance. If both mimicry
and dialogue were lacking, it would be difficult to qualify the
kōwaka as a form of staged drama.

The performance of both the kōwaka and the nō was characterized by the prominence of the two principal players. In the
kōwaka they were called *tayū* ("grand master") and *waki* ("sup-
porter"), and in the nō, *shite* ("protagonist") and *waki* ("sup-
porter"). The term *tsure* ("companion") was employed in the nō
to designate additional players of minor roles. When a third
player appeared in a kōwaka performance, he was also called a
tsure. This parallel in terms suggests that kōwaka players, like
their counterparts in the nō, may have been assigned specific
character roles; if so, dialogue may have been used. The text itself
provides no clue as to whether or not there was dialogue. Kōwaka
texts were composed in narrative form, and dialogue is not indicated explicitly as in the typical playbook; this technique of
composing drama in narrative form, however, was also employed
as a convention in the writing of *jōruri*, playbooks for the puppet
theater. Tsunoda Ichirō, a specialist in the history of the jōruri,
writes:

The stage technique in which a third-person mode of expression in the text is delivered in the first person in performance evolved in the nō drama, thus enabling the direct dramatization of a text composed in the form of a narrative. The evolvement of the jōruri puppet play into theatrical art simply represents an extension and development of this technique. . . . Thus there came into being the unique classical drama of Japan, in which an epic is, at the same time, drama.[7]

When we look at the kōwaka that is performed today in Ōe Village, we note not only the lack of mimicry and dialogue but also the absence of any choreographic patterns that can be properly termed "dance" in the European sense. The performance is staged by three men who are garbed in the ceremonial attire of the seventeenth-century samurai and recite the kōwaka text in a highly stylized vocal fashion, utilizing various modes of speech and melodic intonation. Neither masks nor costumes are used for portraying characters. The players stand abreast of one another throughout most of the performance, maintaining a rigid, erect posture with arms outstretched. The climactic sections of the story are set to a vigorous, rustic melody. During the reciting of these sections, the principal player—distinguishable by his elongated hat (*tate-eboshi*) and his central position—walks about, tracing an hourglass pattern across the front of the stage, his feet stamping loudly in cadence with the rhythm beat out on the *tsuzumi* drum. The performance is almost dithyrambic in its simplicity.

The kōwaka may well have had greater complexity and sophistication in its early days. A kōwaka piece today takes an average of about two hours to perform, and the longer pieces continue for upwards of three hours. During the Medieval Era, specialists in Japanese dramatic history say, nō dramas were performed in approximately half the time that they now require. In contrast to the nō, which today contains many largo passages, as well as extended rhythmic interludes during which recitation of the text ceases entirely, the kōwaka performance is a continuous recitation of the text. The tempo remains moderate throughout, even during the singing of intoned passages. It is hardly conceivable that kōwaka were performed at much faster tempos. Viewers today feel that the kōwaka must have been more intricate and colorful in performance. It must have been visually entrancing, they reason, to have held an audience attentive during such long performances. How great the tedium would have been, had it been otherwise, for a program ordinarily consisted of several pieces! Although medieval chronicles contain remarks in praise of the elegance of the dancing in the kōwaka, the only rhythmic physical movement seen in the performance today is the foot-stamping—a vestige perhaps of more complex choreographic patterns of the past. As for the musical elements, it can be shown empirically—for the old texts carry neumes which indicate intonational patterns—that some of the motifs have been lost, and that many of those which have survived have been simplified. Losses would conceivably be even greater in the visual aspect of performance, since the performers did not have the guidance of a system of mnemonics.

Today there is no true dialogue, but the passages that are marked *kotoba*, or "speech," in the text are recited by individual players. These spoken passages are apportioned among the performers so that the reciter changes when the emphasis of the narrative shifts from one character in the story to another. There is no dialogue, for the performer does not speak in the person of the character. In both the nō and the kabuki theater—in the case of the latter, only when dramas adapted from the puppet theater are presented—dialogue is delivered by the players, whereas narrative passages are usually recited by the chorus. The kabuki chorus in this instance usually comprises a single jōruri reciter, somewhat in the manner of the "chorus" of Elizabethan drama. A similar actor-narrator division could have been possible in kōwaka performances. The drummer, normally the most competent member of the troupe, could have fulfilled the function of the narrator-chorus. The texts were partially suited for such purposes, as is attested by the fact that they were used virtually unaltered as playbooks for the early puppet theater.

The kōwaka in historical time, on the other hand, may have been much the same as it is today, and yet have been esthetically pleasing to its audience. There is the possibility—one which is examined thoroughly in the discussion of "The Kōwaka Today" (Chapter III)—that the kōwaka has been transmitted so faithfully that its original esthetic essentials are still embodied in the performance. What may seem an artless grace to the observer today, for instance, may well have been a studied simplicity calculated to strike an emotional response in an audience of warriors during a bygone era of war. The kōwaka as it was performed during the late Medieval Era cannot be re-created for want of descriptive material, but we do know that it was a performing art preferred above all others by many feudal lords in that era, and that those lords encouraged their vassals to cultivate the kōwaka even by hiring teachers to instruct them.

It is curious that the kōwaka did not continue to flourish in a country where most of the major forms of art have been preserved or have even continued to evolve and develop through the centuries. Its significance in the history of the performing arts has never been adequately evaluated, again for want of descriptive material. Scholars who made studies subsequent to Takano's pioneer study felt that the genealogical records, which Takano had used as his principal source, were not reliable as source material for studying the early history of the kōwaka. For it was a general practice in the early Edo Period to improvise genealogies in order to claim illustrious forebears. Their studies delved mainly into social history and contributed much that is of interest in regard to the probable origin of the performers of the kōwaka, but they failed to shed further light on the topic itself.[8] Some of them chose to regard kōwaka not as the name of a form that is generically related to the kusemai, but as another name for it. Others decided that kōwaka simply referred to a particular troupe of performers of the kusemai, which, during the period under discussion, was usually performed by women and boys for audiences which were attracted primarily by the sensual charms of the performers. In effect, they lumped together under a single generic label forms which catered to widely diverse levels of audience and which aimed at quite different ends in esthetic expression.[9] By equating the kōwaka with artistic forms that seemed rather unimportant to students interested in this cultural period—although these forms may actually have been either antecedent or kindred to it—these studies reduced the ostensible importance of the kōwaka as a research subject requiring further illumination and, consequently, discouraged fresh inquiries. The studies did, on the other hand, inquire into areas that had not been investigated previously. They broadened the scope of inquiry by illuminating the fringe areas, and their discoveries have borne fruit in enabling subsequent students to begin their researches with a clearer perspective of the subject.

Many of the specialists today in literature of the Medieval Era feel that the traditional accounts, which their learned predecessors tended to discredit, contain much that can be interpreted as historical information that will shed light on the history of the kōwaka. Studies of the kōwaka that again focus on the content of the subject have appeared in recent years,[10] but they have been few and far between. Apart from the comments of narrow specialists, the authoritative voice still remains that of those eminent scholars of the previous generation who were skeptical of traditional accounts and propounded the view that the kōwaka was unique only in its name. And, unfortunately, this view underlies the description of the kōwaka in Kawatake's *A Comprehensive History of the Japanese Theater* (1959),[11] which will probably be looked upon for years to come as the authoritative textbook for the history of the theater.

Literary historians have felt that the study of the kōwaka as a performing art should be undertaken by scholars in the discipline which is termed *engeki-shi,* or "history of the theater"; but no original research on the kōwaka has come out of that area since Takano's. The kōwaka, as a theme for research, does not fall clearly within the purview of what is termed *engeki,* or "theater," * and this may have discouraged some students. The problem of genre has long confounded Japanese students of the arts, principally because the generic labels which were borrowed from the West often do not match the contents of the Japanese art forms to which they have been applied. The kōwaka serves as a case in point, for, although its importance as a historical art is undeniable, its component elements of performance are not basically equivalent to those of drama, opera, or ballet. Because of its lack of mimetic dancing—something it may well have had in historical times—the kōwaka is relegated to the broader classification of *geinō,* which, because it encompasses all forms of arts

---

* *Engeki* is, literally, "to perform plays." In its definition, specialists in the field usually cite four requisites: a physical theater, players, audience, and drama (play). In practice, however, all performing arts which are deemed historically important are brought in for discussion under this category.

performed before an audience, might be rendered in English as "performing art."

The histories of the many performing arts still extant in Japan are being compiled today by specialists in folklore. Since music is a major component of almost all these arts, musicological analysis will undoubtedly come into favor as a valuable method for determining generic affiliations among these forms. These specialists have been directing their efforts toward the comprehensive survey of all extant forms, for folk art was known to be declining rapidly in the postwar period. Now that this general survey is in the process of completion, perhaps we can look forward to detailed analytical studies of those performing arts which have until now remained outside the mainstream of scholarly inquiry.

THE POSITION OF KŌWAKA TEXTS IN THE HISTORY OF JAPANESE LITERATURE

There are extant today texts for fifty kōwaka, and of these, forty are tales which treat dramatic highlights from the twelfth-century saga of the Genji and the Heike or from the romance of the celebrated vendetta of the Soga Brothers which took place in 1193. They are lively tales which extol the virtuous warrior, exalt valorous and honorable death, and find pleasurable charm in the pathos of tragedy. Loyalty, filial piety, faithfulness, courage, and chivalry are glorified. Kōwaka were often performed in military encampments. The tales were calculated to draw the audience into sympathy with the tragic heroes, to involve the viewers vicariously in situations of tragedy which were familiar to them as a result of their own experiences in war. That the tales were intended to evoke pathos is suggested by a conventional concluding passage, "The eminent and the humble, the gentle and the lowborn, alike felt compassion for the torment that was in the heart of this warrior." The conspicuous absence of comedy and romantic love as thematic material suggests that frivolity in any form was eschewed.

The fifty pieces extant represent most of the kōwaka which are known to have been performed in historical times. Sixty-two additional titles are mentioned in various historical sources, but, according to an analysis made by Sasano Ken, fifty-one of these are simply variant titles for pieces which are extant. This leaves only eleven which are titles of kōwaka that have presumably been lost.[12] Favorite passages from kōwaka were often compiled into collections of kōwaka "songs" (*kayō*), and fragments of several of the lost pieces have survived in such collections.

The literary styles of the kōwaka texts and most other types of prose literature written in the Muromachi Period, or between roughly the fourteenth and sixteenth centuries, may be subsumed under the broad classification of "classical" Japanese prose. The stylistic difference among them is largely one of degree. The prose of the *Chronicle of the Grand Pacification* is frequently studded with high-flown Chinese loanwords and tends toward the stilted and angular, whereas the shorter fables which abounded in this period are generally composed in a style which flows easily, which is less pretentious. Approximately intermediate between the two is the style of the kōwaka texts and of the two historical romances written in the fourteenth century, the *Tale of the Soga Brothers* (*Soga monogatari*) and the *Annals of Yoshitsune* (*Gikeiki*).

We do not know precisely when and by whom the kōwaka texts were written except for two composed in the late sixteenth century. They probably represent modifications of tales which date back at least to the fourteenth century—historical and legendary tales of the sort that were compiled into the *Annals of Yoshitsune* and the *Tale of the Soga Brothers*. Although the kōwaka and the historical romances share many themes, very little can be said with regard to the relationship between the two types of literature. There is virtually no information concerning the authorship of medieval prose fiction in general, and there is little likelihood that more light will be shed on this question through further research. Suffice it to say that the material for both the kōwaka texts and the historical romances was drawn from similar sources—earlier romantic war chronicles, such as the *Tale of the Heike* (*Heike monogatari*) and the *Rise and Fall of Gempei* (*Gempei seisui ki*),* and traditional and legendary ac-

---

* *Gempei* is an abbreviation of "Genji and Heike." The period of the epic struggle between these two warrior clans is often called the Gempei Era.

counts that were either transmitted orally or set down as written tales during the thirteenth and fourteenth centuries.

The problem of assessing the position of the kōwaka texts in Japanese literature is, at first glance, a perplexing one. In literary history, the kōwaka texts are referred to as *bukyoku* ("dance pieces") or, more commonly, as *kōwaka-bukyoku*.[13] And they are treated more or less as an independent literary genre. Yet, on the one hand, the text for the kōwaka *Beach-Outing* (*Hamaide*) is included in the *Book of Fables* (*Otogi-zōshi*), a collection of twenty-three Muromachi Period tales which was first printed in the seventeenth century; [14] and these tales are assigned to the literary category of "book of fables" (*otogi-zōshi*), the title of the later-day anthology having been adopted as an inclusive label for all short tales of the Muromachi Period.[15] On the other hand, several kōwaka can be found in anthologies of texts of puppet dramas, for kōwaka texts were frequently used as playbooks in the early seventeenth century when the puppet theater was in its embryonic stage.[16] Thus we find several kōwaka classified as *ko-jōruri*, or "old-jōruri." [17] To confuse the picture further, we can find kōwaka texts included in collections of *kana* books (*kana-zōshi*), or "books in the vulgar script"—a form of Edo Period fiction that was to culminate in the well-known books about the gay and buoyant "floating world," the *ukiyo-zōshi* of the novelists Ihara Saikaku (1642–1693) and Ejima Kiseki (1667–1736).

The problem of genre is one which confounds students inquiring into the prose literature of the Edo Period, for the genre titles may reflect, not the literary style or the content, but the color of the jacket, the size of the book, the ratio of illustrations to worded text, a historical period, or a style of calligraphy. In modern movable-type editions, which the students today read, the various forms of prose literature are reproduced in an identical format, and usually without illustrations. As a result, the student must learn to tell the various genres apart on the basis of the literary style and content alone; but this is difficult to do in many instances, impossible in some. The picture of the genres might be compared to a chart of various undefined colors which blend imperceptibly one into another. It would be a great convenience, particularly from the standpoint of the Western student of Japanese literature, if the colors could be defined, and if the blended areas could be analyzed into primary colors so that some kind of discernible boundary might emerge.

Inasmuch as kōwaka texts could be accommodated within collections of books of fables, *kana* books, and old-jōruri, we might conclude that these do not represent literary categories which are mutually exclusive, but that they represent categories which are hazily defined or which overlap into one another. One thing which these four species share to some extent is an over-all literary style. They are written in prose, predominantly in the *kana* syllabary; they are, basically, narratives in the third person,[18] composed in a language bordering on the classical literary style and generally devoid of vulgarisms in the colloquial idiom.

Whereas fiction in the Edo Period was written largely for the *chōnin,* the "plebeian townsman," and distributed widely as a result of the development of printing, there was little in the way of written literature available to the commoner of Muromachi Period society. The medieval books of fables were ostensibly intended for the unsophisticated reader; but they were available only in manuscript copies or as exquisitely colored picture books, and commoners could seldom acquire them. The tales are believed to have been written for diversion by court nobles, Buddhist monks, and upper-class samurai; they were not looked upon as serious literary work. Consequently, an author seldom inscribed his signature on his work, and today there is only one instance where the authorship of a medieval fable has been substantiated.[19] These tales are legendary fables, or they are historical tales involving characters drawn from all levels of society, or, frequently, they are love stories of considerable charm. The tales have a variety of tones; they may be tragic or comical, ennobling or ludicrous, didactic, satirical, or something else. They are generally composed in a simple and unadorned style, and there is little pretense at literary elegance. Some were, perhaps, no more than the sum of a series of lengthy captions in picture books; and the writing in these tales is kept at a functional level of merely explaining the story, with little regard given to achieving an artistic mode of telling the story.

Although prose fiction of diverse types was produced during the span of more than two centuries which make up the Muromachi Period, Japanese literary historians have found it feasible to recognize "books of fables" as a broad category embracing all prose fiction produced during this period, with the exception of those of epic length, such as the *Annals of Yoshitsune* and the *Tale of the Soga Brothers*. They then classify these tales into sub-orders according to general themes, general types, or both.[20] Because the book of fables is such a broadly inclusive category of Muromachi Period prose fiction, the kōwaka texts will of necessity come within its purview. Although the texts were used as librettos by kōwaka performers, they were also circulated as tales to be enjoyed in reading. The kōwaka texts did not acquire a poetic structure of the sort which one associates with the European recitative, even though they were designed to be recited aloud, and parts to be sung. Denuded of intonational symbols, they are, for all practical purposes, prose fiction.

The *kana* book was, in its early stages, an extension of the book of fables into the Edo Period. The initial enthusiasm for the printing press produced a rash of publications during the first three decades of the seventeenth century, and many of the Muromachi Period tales appeared in booklet form during this period. The term *kana* book has been applied loosely to include all printed booklets written predominantly in the *kana* script, generally large-leafed and profusely illustrated,[21] which appeared in the Osaka-Kyoto area between roughly 1600 and 1680. As a result, not only medieval fables but even kōwaka texts are found in collections of *kana* books.[22] The term *kana* book, however, is used nowadays in a more restricted sense to designate a genus of Edo Period fiction comprising tales, usually of didactic significance, written largely by samurai scholars, who found their subject matter in Edo Period society. Such *kana* books are significant collectively as the forerunner of the real *chōnin* fiction of the Genroku and later eras. The criteria for the category *kana* book remain, nonetheless, chiefly those of format and of historical period and geographical area; as a result, the category embraces tales which could, on the basis of literary content, represent a variety of literary species.

In old-jōruri texts, we can note a stylistic consistency that can be traced through from the earliest—among them, kōwaka texts— to the latest pieces, which include compositions of the great playwright Chikamatsu Monzaemon (1653–1725). His *Imagawa*

Ryōshun (published in 1693),[23] for example, is embellished with passages of notable poetic elegance but, at the same time, incorporates archaic phrases and stereotyped plot elements which were used as conventions in the kōwaka. During the infancy of the popular theater, jōruri reciters were of necessity eclectic in their selection of texts since the professional playwright had not yet arrived on the theatrical scene. Texts for the early puppet theater treated not only themes from the Gempei Era, with which the kōwaka dealt almost exclusively, but also themes taken from medieval fables, from legends of Buddhist miracles, from historical events of the more recent past, and, eventually, from contemporary *chōnin* society.[24] A distinct feature of old-jōruri is the division of texts into *dan,* or "acts." A comparison of the kōwaka *Takadachi* with the old-jōruri *Takadachi in Five Acts (Takadachi godan)* [25] reveals that, although there is hardly enough textual difference to warrant labeling the latter an adaptation, there are slight revisions at the points of textual division to make it a workable text for a five-act play. A comparison of old-jōruri texts which are adaptations of medieval fables with their original models also reveals a deliberate effort on the part of the jōruri authors to reshape these tales into works that are intended primarily as texts for multi-act puppet dramas.

Terms such as book of fables, *kana* book, and old-jōruri have, thus, been used freely as designations for literary categories, but the specialists in literature themselves have yet to agree on definitions based on precise criteria. As a result, the student has no standard by which to judge whether a particular literary work typifies the generic label it bears, whether it is a work that is transitional, or whether it is listed under that generic label as a matter of convenience in classification. As far as the kōwaka texts are concerned, we can say that there is a consistency in the types of themes treated, and that most of the fifty extant pieces exhibit a homogeneous literary style. The stylistic cleavage between the kōwaka texts and the bulk of Muromachi Period prose literature is probably not so pronounced as to warrant a separate generic status for kōwaka texts as literature. But the texts do exhibit sufficient uniformity both stylistically and thematically so that they might be regarded collectively as a distinct species of Muromachi Period prose literature.

II: THE HISTORY OF
THE KŌWAKA

MOMONOI NAOAKI, THE
ALLEGED FOUNDER OF THE KŌWAKA

T H E evidence for the alleged invention of the kōwaka by one
Momonoi Naoaki, known as Kōwakamaru during his youth,
is furnished by the genealogical records of a family that claims
descent from the founder of the art. The family has been known
by the surname of Kōwaka.[1] In the absence of other corroborative
evidence, this allegation can be turned into fact only if these
documents are proven reliable.

The Kōwaka family has been domiciled since the days of its
founder in Nishi-Tanaka Village, Niu County, Echizen Province
—an area approximately five miles southwest of present-day Fukui
City. Members of this family served the court of the Tokugawa
shogun as hereditary performers of the kōwaka. They were the
official custodians of an art which they themselves guarded
jealously from the prying eyes of the villagers. Residents of Nishi-
Tanaka Village even today recall the tradition that commoners
were forbidden on pain of death from listening to the rehearsals
which took place within the Kōwaka family mansions. These
genealogical records trace the Kōwaka ancestry back through the
Momonoi branch of the Ashikaga family to the Genji clan and
ultimately to Emperor Seiwa (850–880; reigned 858–876). Momonoi Naoaki is regarded as the founder of the Kōwaka lineage. But
an examination of the family documents reveals a vagueness
shrouding the lineal connection between their founder, Momonoi
Naoaki, and the person who was alleged to be his grandfather:
Momonoi Naotsune, the last known patriarch of the renowned
House of Momonoi of the early Muromachi Period.

Momonoi Harima-no-kami Naotsune was one of the prominent

political figures of the *Nambokuchō,* or the Period of the
Northern and Southern Dynasties (1336–1392). This was the era
of schism within the imperial family, begun when Emperor Go-
Daigo (1288–1339) refused to relinquish the imperial regalia to
a puppet emperor instituted by Ashikaga Takauji (1305–1358)
and founded the Southern Imperial Court in the mountains of
Yoshino. It was an era of turbulence in the capital, which was
frequently torn asunder by warfare, and in the provinces, where
local feudal barons transferred their allegiance back and forth
between the feuding courts with each shift in the balance of political power. The House of Momonoi was a branch of the
Ashikaga family that had settled in the province of Shimotsuke
during the Kamakura Period. Momonoi Naotsune at first fought
on the side of his kinsman, Ashikaga Takauji, who had become
shogun in 1338. When a schism developed in the Shogun's house,
and Ashikaga Tadayoshi (1306–1352), the Shogun's younger
brother, defected to the Southern Court in 1350, Momonoi
Naotsune took the side of Tadayoshi. He was thenceforth to fight
in behalf of the Southern Court—even though Tadayoshi defected from the Southern Court and rejoined his brother in
Kyoto only a few months thereafter. Momonoi Naotsune's army
occupied the capital briefly in 1351, putting the Ashikaga Shogun
to flight, and again in 1355 during a temporary upsurge in the
fortunes of the Southern Court. Having lost his hold on his own
domain of Echigo during the years of campaigning away from
the province, he wrested Etchū Province from the Shogunate and
held sway there until 1366. Naotsune's bid for a reconciliation
was refused by the Northern Court, and in 1369 he again organized an army of resistance in Etchū Province. But in the
following year he suffered a major defeat at the hands of a Shogunate army under the command of Shiba Yoshimasa (1350–
1410); his stronghold, the Matsukura Fortress, fell, and his son
and lieutenant, Naokazu, was killed. He continued to resist the
Shogunate for another year before his army was finally dispersed.
With this, the Momonoi disappear from the pages of history.[2]

Where the story of the Momonoi fades out of the standard
histories it is resumed in the Kōwaka family records. There are
more than a dozen versions of the genealogy, dated variously
between the early Edo Period and 1861. The history of Kōwa-

kamaru, or Momonoi Naoaki, as related in the older documents contains a number of conflicting details. But the discrepancies are gradually eliminated in succeeding revisions, and the genealogical documents written in the late Edo Period are quite consistent with known history.

The genealogical document which is regarded as the oldest, drawn up some time in the early Edo Period, states that Momonoi Naoaki lived from 1405–1470, and that he was ten when his father, Naokazu, died.[3] Thus, we have Momonoi Naokazu living until 1414, or forty-four years beyond the date on which history records his death. Another document, believed to be of somewhat later date, states that the father, Naokazu, was killed during the siege of 1370, but that Naoaki himself escaped from the fortress under cover of darkness; it then gives 1480 as the year of Naoaki's demise, giving him a life span of over 110 years.[4] The document with the earliest known date of recording, 1672, states that Naoaki died in 1480 at the age of seventy-nine, thus making his dates 1402–1480; * it provides no data concerning his father, however.[5] Later versions of the genealogy give Naoaki's dates variously as 1393–1470 and 1418–1480.

The foregoing suggests that there was a fifteenth-century personage who was called Momonoi Naoaki by the Kōwaka family of later times and who was regarded as the founder of this family. The Kōwaka claimed that their founder was a grandson of the historically renowned Momonoi Naotsune. The difficulty in this allegation lay in the fact that their founder, Naoaki, could not be linked with Momonoi Naotsune in a plausible fashion. Naotsune's known son, Naokazu, had perished in 1370; yet, according to the earlier versions of the Kōwaka genealogy, he had sired their founder, Naoaki, whose lifetime apparently spanned the greater part of the fifteenth century.

Perhaps this glaring discrepancy with recorded history was a source of embarrassment to the Kōwaka family, for a scrutiny of the later versions of the genealogy reveals what appears to have been a concerted scheme to revise gradually the details surround-

---

* By Western reckoning, the age would probably be seventy-eight. According to traditional calculation, a Japanese baby is at the age of one when he is born and becomes two on New Year's Day, even though he may be only a few days old. Persons' ages are by Japanese reckoning throughout.

ing Momonoi Naoaki's parentage. Two genealogical documents, drawn up in 1677 and 1678 respectively and submitted to the Tokugawa Shogunate as official records,[6] list the Naotsune-Naokazu-Naoaki order of descent without giving any particulars of chronology. In a document dated 1696, a new name, Naotomo, appears on the family tree in the place of Naokazu, and a Naotsune-Naotomo-Naoaki lineal order is indicated.[7] A document drawn up subsequently, in 1698, identifies this Naotomo as a younger brother of Naokazu.[8] Finally, a genealogical document of the early 1700's furnishes details on Naotomo: he was born in 1350; he was campaigning in Echigo Province when the Momonoi stronghold in Etchū fell; he went into hiding in the area of Niu County in Echizen Province, awaiting the opportunity to resurrect the Momonoi name, but all hopes vanished when the schism in the imperial dynasty was resolved in 1392; he died in obscurity in 1412; his son Naoaki, who was born in 1393, was taken to Kyoto and entrusted to an uncle, Senshin, who had taken the tonsure after the downfall of the Momonoi and was serving as superintendent priest of the Kōrin Cloister on Mount Hiei.[9]

It is of interest to note that the documents in which the historically known name of Naokazu is replaced by the anonymous Naotomo were all drawn up by one particular branch of the Kōwaka family—the senior branch, known as the Hachirokurō branch. Since the earlier-dated records of the Hachirokurō branch, as well as the records of the other two branches, all list Naokazu as the father of the founder, it is probable that the name Naotomo was invented in order to give greater coherence to the story that the Kōwaka founder was sired by a descendant of the illustrious Momonoi Naotsune.

Only the very earliest among these numerous documents would be of value as historical evidence, for the later versions were apparently revised to some extent in order to explain previously hazy areas in the family history in a more convincing way. However, the earliest document contains such a gross historical misstatement that one must guess whether this was due to faulty legend—the record having been written some two centuries after the actual events—or whether the entire document was a fabrication with the intent to claim an illustrious historical personage as a progenitor. Even the least skeptical of historians would

probably select the latter alternative, for it was a prevalent practice around the beginning of the Edo Period for samurai to
provide themselves with estimable genealogies, especially such as
would trace their ancestry back to the Genji of the Heike or to
the Fujiwara and other courtly families. Branches of both the
Minamoto and Taira clans were scattered widely throughout
Japan during the Heian Period. Members of the court nobility,
on the other hand, had always been loath to relinquish the social
and cultural life of the capital; but after the Ōnin War (1467–
1477), which devastated almost the entire city of Kyoto, many of
them were forced by economic necessity to resettle in the provinces. Many of the samurai of provincial stock who were later to
claim descent from these families were undoubtedly justified in
their assertions. But since the members of the new samurai aristocracy of the sixteenth and seventeenth centuries fabricated
freely in order to tidy up their family trees, the historian today
is justified in his skepticism of such claims. Those who insist on
coherence in data will reject this early document as historical
evidence.

Actually, however, the only point of serious doubt in the
genealogy is the link between the Kōwaka family founder and
Momonoi Naotsune. The document probably represents a fairly
accurate record of the Kōwaka family back to that point; there
are correspondences between data provided in this document and
data included in chronicles of unquestioned reliability. Thus, it
might be thought that the founder of the Kōwaka family, whose
dates are ca. 1393 to ca. 1470, was listed in the Kōwaka family
genealogy with the surname of Momonoi so that he could be
described as a scion of the famed Momonoi.

There are, on the other hand, historical circumstances that
tend to confirm that such a person as Momonoi Naoaki did exist.
Foremost of these is a full-length portrait of Momonoi Naoaki
which is credited to the painter Tosa Mitsunobu (1434?–1525?) [10]
and which, according to Kōwaka family records, was commissioned after Naoaki's death by his son. It is not likely that a prac-
titioner of a performing art would have borne the surname of
Momonoi—one which denoted kinship to the family of the
Ashikaga shogun—without a fairly substantial claim. A similar
situation existed under the Tokugawa Shogunate, for the Toku-

gawa and the Momonoi both traced their ancestry back to the Genji. It seems more likely than not that the Kōwaka family had legitimate grounds for their claim to be descendants of the Momonoi. Throughout the Edo Period the surname of Momonoi was inscribed on the tombstones of their deceased. Moreover, the posthumous titles were of the style reserved for persons of noble breeding, and the improper use of such titles would have been considered a serious transgression of convention during the Edo Period, when the stratification of society into occupational classes was rigidly upheld through minutiae of codes and regulations. The Kōwaka people, it seems, would have been particularly discreet in such matters because, although they were of samurai status, they were practitioners of a performing art. In view of the social stigma attached to the entertainment profession, the social background of the Kōwaka family was bound to receive public and official scrutiny aimed at uncovering traces of a base origin. The strength of its tradition as an art form of the military aristocracy would tend to signify that the originator of the kōwaka had some contact with the aristocracy. The fact that the contents of the kōwaka deal exclusively with warriors and martial exploits suggests that the person who first devised the repertoire was intimately associated with the military aristocracy.

The exact lineal connection between the Kōwaka family founder and Momonoi Naotsune may never be clarified, but the following remark in a 1706 commentary on the Kōwaka family genealogical records provides a clue that merits some consideration: "It would be chronologically inconsistent to list Kōwaka-maru as a son of Naokazu since his birth occurred thirty-three years after Naokazu's death in battle, but it would be appropriate to list him as the latter's grandson." [11] One of the earlier Kōwaka family records states that Kōwakamaru, the son of Naokazu, escaped from the Momonoi stronghold during the siege, and it is possible that this surviving son of Naokazu may have been the father of Kōwakamaru. It was not uncommon among craftsmen or artists for the mastership to be passed on directly from grandfather to grandson, the father becoming a genealogical nonentity.[12] Perhaps the most that can be said in view of the nature of the evidence available is that it is possible for such a person as Momonoi Naoaki to have existed historically, but that the evidence is far from sufficient to warrant the conclusion that the founder of the Kōwaka family, referred to by his descendants as Momonoi Naoaki, was a direct lineal descendant of the renowned Momonoi Naotsune.

Takano Tatsuyuki, who was the first to investigate the history of the kōwaka, did not collate the Kōwaka family records in order to assess their reliability as historical material. He wrote his description of Momonoi Naoaki by piecing together fragments of information from several of the later revised family records. He acknowledged that genealogical records are frequently unreliable; then he proceeded on the principle that ". . . in the absence of reliable written records, [the history of the Kōwaka family] should be based on the family's genealogical records."[13] He did not seem particularly disturbed over such inconsistencies in his description as giving Momonoi Naoaki's dates as 1393–1480 and then stating that he died at the age of seventy-eight. Literary historians have attempted to resolve the inconsistencies in the Kōwaka family records by varying their interpretations of the data; but they accepted Momonoi Naoaki and his relationship to Momonoi Naotsune as historical fact and then attempted to explain away the inconsistencies.

The description of Momonoi Naoaki based on the most coherent but apparently fabricated versions of the Kōwaka family records seems to have become standard historical information. The entry in a volume of the *Great Encyclopedia of Japanese History* (*Nihon rekishi daijiten*) published in 1959 reads as follows:

Momonoi Naoaki (1403–1480): Childhood name, Kōwakamaru. He held the court rank of lower junior-fifth grade and the position of lesser assistant of the inner palace (*kunai shōyū*). When his father, Naotomo, who had fled the Matsukura Fortress, died in 1412, Kōwakamaru was ten years of age. He went to live with Senshin, a relative who had taken the tonsure and was residing in the Kōrin Cloister on Mount Hiei. He is said to have worshipped Avalokiteśvara and to have been fond of books both Japanese and Chinese. He studied vocal music in particular and once recited the booklet *Battle of Yashima* (*Yashima no ikusa*), providing it with a melody, and for this was acclaimed by the learned monks. The retired Emperor Go-Komatsu [1377–1443; reigned 1382–1412] summoned Naoaki for an audience and bade him collect other pieces. This was the beginning of the kōwaka. The melodies of Buddhist liturgical music were incorporated as in the singing of the *Tale of the Heike* and the reciting of the *Chronicle of the Grand Pacification*. There was some choreography inasmuch as the chronicles, *Kakitsu ki* and *Ōnin ki*, mention the "kōwaka dance." According to tradition he was awarded the title of *taifu* through a decree of Emperor Go-Hanazono [1419–1470; reigned 1428–1464], and he styled himself Kōwaka Udayū Yasuzane. He incurred the displeasure of the Shogun Yoshimasa [1436–1490], but he was pardoned in 1465 and served Yoshimasa's son [sic] Yoshimi [1439–1491]. He received his stipend from Hosokawa Katsumoto 1430–1473]. He later returned to Echizen Province and received the patronage of the Asakura family. He is said to have secluded himself at Hakuzan [Shrine] and composed new pieces, thirty-six in all. He was interred in the Old Buddhist grounds at Ichijōgatani. [His posthumous title is] Shō-ō-zen-kitsu-kyoji. There is extant a portrait which his son Yasuyoshi commissioned from the painter Tosa Mitsunobu.[14]

THE ANTECEDENTS OF MEDIEVAL PERFORMING ARTS

The story of the creation of the kōwaka by Momonoi Naoaki, as set forth in the Kōwaka family records, is impressive, as any story of genesis should be. It has its mythical elements. We are told how the mystic cry of a pheasant suggested new melodies and how a miracle of divine intervention produced the creative inspiration for writing new texts. The traditional accounts of Kōwakamaru contain some items of information which can be interpreted so as to shed light on the question of the origin of the kōwaka. For the most part, however, its beginning must be sought somewhere in the broad spectrum of the numerous forms of entertainment arts that evolved and developed, one influencing the other, within the plebeian stratum of medieval society.

The folk art of Japan encompasses diverse forms of dance and song. Some of them were either innovated or greatly modified during fairly recent times, as is evidenced by their typically Edo Period costumes or the use of the samisen, the three-stringed instrument which has been in popular use only since the seventeenth century. Others, which are of undetermined age and extraction, may have originated in the remote antiquity of Japan or even in foreign lands. Specialists have not even begun, how-

ever, to probe into the problem of the origin of many curious
forms of folk art which are found today in the various localities
of Japan. As a result, in this discussion it will be feasible to treat
only those performing arts which are described in recorded history—those which were generally performed by professionals and
which played to broad segments of society in the area embracing
Kyoto, Osaka, and Nara, which constituted the cultural as well
as population center of Japan before the seventeenth century.

It is beyond the scope of this study to attempt anything more
than a cursory survey of the older forms of the performing arts
and the extent to which they may have influenced the new. Even
this will be difficult, however, for there is little in the way of
specific descriptions which would enable us to assemble accurate
pictures of historical forms. Dance is a major element in almost
all the performing arts which are to be discussed, and here particularly concrete information is almost nonexistent. The musical
structure of the performing arts would provide an important key
to the analysis of origin and influence, but there is no record of
plebeian forms of music in Japan prior to the Edo Period, with
the exception, perhaps, of the music of the nō drama. The nō,
it should be remembered, evolved from a purely plebeian form
of entertainment and continued to be performed by commoners
but gradually acquired respectability, so that by the Edo Period
it had ceased to be classed as a vulgar form of art. Much is
known, however, about certain aristocratic forms of music which
flourished in the Ancient Era, and these should be investigated
for the light they may possibly shed on the music of performing
arts which developed in later history.

THE CLASSICAL MUSIC: THE MUSIC OF *Gagaku**

One observable parallel in the evolution of music in Japan and
in Western Europe is that the forms of music which were regarded as sacred—in Japan the *gagaku,* or "correct music" of the

* Gagaku encompasses two broad subdivisions: orchestral music and *bugaku.*
The latter is dance with orchestral accompaniment. Only as a convenience of
discussion shall I use the term "gagaku" in referring to the music, and
"bugaku" in referring to the dance.

ancient court nobility, and in Western Europe, the music of the
Christian Church—have been described on the basis of carefully
formulated theories of music, so that we know something about
the modes and scales that were used, as well as melodic patterns.
The greater part of gagaku was originally imported into Japan
from China. The word itself was borrowed from China, where
it is pronounced *ya-yüeh* and denoted "correct," or "orthodox,"
music. In China, only music classified as *ya-yüeh* was considered
suitable for performance in Confucian rites and ceremonies.
Other forms of music—among them, "informal music" (*yen-yüeh*),
which was also called "vulgar music" (*su-yüeh*), and "barbarian
music" (*hu-yüeh*)—were regarded as "perverse" in varying degrees. This excerpt from the "Essay on Rites and Music" in the
History of the Former Han Dynasty (A.D. 76) gives us an idea of
the strength and depth of the tradition of orthodoxy which regulated music in China of the Early Han Period (202 B.C.–A.D. 9):

> Since music is that in which the paragons find pleasure, it can be
> used for refining the Heart and Mind of the people. Because it touches
> people deeply and readily causes morals to shift and customs to change,
> the Former Kings [Yü of Hsia, T'ang of Yin, and others] clarified their
> teachings through it. To explain this further, the people possess the
> natural attributes of vital fluid, vital air, passion, and rationality,
> whereas they lack constancy in compassion, pleasure, joy, and righteous-
> ness. They function in response to the stimuli [of music] which fashion
> the mode of their Heart and Mind. Therefore, when tones are produced
> which are delicate, faint, waning, and expiring, the people are pensive
> and disquieted. When tones are produced which are perspicuous, con-
> sonant, adagio, and unstrained, the people are euphoric and happy.
> When tones are produced which are coarse, harsh, fierce, and rousing,
> the people are unyielding and resolute. . . . When tones are produced
> which are unfixed, specious, distorted, and arbitrary, the people are
> wanton and disorderly. The Former Kings were embarrassed by [the
> people's] disorderliness and, therefore, regulated the tones of the canons
> and lauds. They based them on the [people's] passional and natural
> attributes, investigated them in terms of degree and number [that is,
> they determined pitch and scale], and regulated them for rites and
> ceremonials.[15]

We can easily find parallels in the ancient world of the West.
To the Greek modal scales were ascribed such values as "master-
ful and military" (Dorian), "effeminate and gossiping" (Lydian),

and "slack" (Phrygian).* That the importance of "correct music" was recognized in Egypt is attested by a remark, recorded by Plato, with respect to Egyptian music: "What they ordained about music is right; it deserves consideration that they were able to make laws about things of this kind, firmly establishing such melody as was fitted to rectify the perverseness of nature." [16] The Japanese do not appear to have been so deeply concerned about the ethical meanings of the musical material and terminology which they borrowed from China during the Sui (589–618) and early T'ang (618–906) periods. The repertory of gagaku contained much that would have been adjudged "perverse" on the basis of traditional Chinese criteria, for its "Chinese" pieces were almost exclusively of the "informal" or "barbarian" categories. Furthermore, the repertory contained music from Korea, the former state of Bokkai (Chinese: Po-hai) in southeastern Manchuria, and, purportedly, India; also included were archaic Japanese melodies as well as pieces composed by the Japanese in imitation of the styles of the imported music. The word *gagaku* can also mean "elegant music," and it was probably more in this sense than as "correct music" that the Japanese court aristocrats regarded the music of her culturally advanced neighbors.

The theory which regulates the tonal pitches of gagaku was essentially a replica of that of ancient China.[17] Here may it be understood that the ensuing discussion of musical modes and scales touches upon the theoretically known, and has little to do with music as it may actually have been practiced. The two principal heptatonic scale types used in gagaku—the *ritsu* and the *ryo*—were different in their structure from the classical heptatonic scale of China. The heptatonic scale was obtained by adding two auxiliary alternants to the five tones of the pentatonic scale. The *ritsu* scale type is structurally similar to the Phrygian modal scale of ancient Greece; and because the interval between the first, or ground, tone and the third tone is approximately equivalent to a minor third, it has been compared to the Western

---

* For a convenient table of such ethical values abstracted from Plato's *The Republic* and Aristotle's *Politics*, see Theodore M. Finney, *A History of Music* (rev. ed.; New York, 1949), p. 19. Such terms as Phrygian and Dorian are not to be confused with the identical set of labels later employed by Boethius for his ecclesiastical scales.

"minor" scale.* It has been dubbed the "Japanese" scale, and is used rather extensively in present-day gagaku. The *ryo* scale is structurally similar to the Hypophrygian modal scale † and is somewhat reminiscent of the Western "major" scale, inasmuch

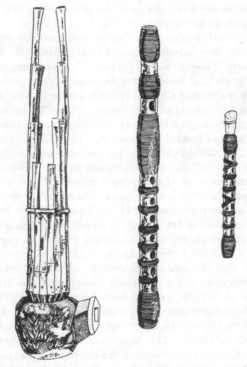

2. The wind instruments of gagaku: (*from left*) *shō*, transverse "Chinese" flute, and *hichiriki*

* The modal impression of melodies using this scale is quite different, how-ever; for the third tone is not one of the five basic tones of the *ryo* scale type, but simply an auxiliary alternant. The interval of a minor third, therefore, is not nearly as important as the fourth between the ground tone and the fourth tone or the fifth between the ground and fifth tones. If the ground tone were "D," the seven tones would constitute a scale of D-E-F-G-A-B-C-D. (The correspondence is only an approximate one acoustically.)

† With "D" as the ground tone, the notes would constitute a scale of D-E-F♯-G-A-B-C-D.

as the interval between its first and third tones is approximately equivalent to a major third; it has been given the label of "Chinese" and is less often used today. The classical scale of China is structurally similar to the Hypolydian modal scale.*

The gagaku *ryo* scale type and the Chinese classical scale are usually described as structurally identical, but the musicologist Tanabe Hisao states, "In the past, scholars have always attempted to apply the tonal theory of China *in toto* in their analysis of gagaku scales, and as a result they described the *ryo* scale of our gagaku as if it were the same as the Chinese heptatonic scale; none of the gagaku pieces of our country is based on the Chinese heptatonic scale." [18] Both the *ryo* and the Chinese heptatonic scales may have been derived from the same pentatonic scale. The difference, according to Tanabe, is in the alternants; the two added notes in the *ryo* scale are raised, or sharpened, alternants of the third and sixth degrees, but the two added notes in the Chinese heptatonic scale are lowered, or flatted, alternants of the fifth degree and the octave.[19] The difference between the two scales would be comparable to that between the Hypophrygian and Hypolydian modal scales. (Here two notes of caution must be sounded. First, the textbook description of Greek modal scales has been introduced into the discussion merely as an aid in describing the more exotic modal scales of the Orient; there are differences in the principles regulating pitch and melodic organization, and these differences will be reflected in stylistic dissimilarities in melodies based on either musical system. Second, although the alternants in gagaku may theoretically be half-tone alternations, in practice today they are often microtones of unspecified interval.) The fact that the *ritsu* and *ryo* scale types differ from the classical scale of China does not mean, however, that they could not have come from China, for the diverse forms of music practiced in T'ang China represented the musical systems of various regions of Asia and the Near East. In addition to comparing scale types, we must be able to compare the modes that were used in gagaku † with those of ancient China if we are

---

* With "D" as the ground tone, the notes would constitute a scale of D-E-F♯-G♯-A-B-C♯-D.

† Six modes are employed in gagaku today. Three are of the *ryo* scale type and have ground tones of D, E, and G. The other three are of the *ritsu* scale type and have ground tones of E, A, and B.

to make precise statements with regard to borrowing. Here the problems are manifold, because a mode in gagaku, as distinguished from a scale type, implies a series of tones at fixed pitches. We would have to know how the music was performed in ancient times in both Japan and China.

There is much about gagaku that remains unknown to us. We do not know, for instance, if the music was performed exactly as it is described in theory or what influence the imported forms and native Japanese forms of music may have exerted on one another. The imported music was instrumental, and the melody was carried principally by wind instruments—the oboe-like *hichiriki,* the *shō* mouth organ, and the transverse flute—which are fixed-pitch instruments. The tones which can be produced on these instruments—and, therefore, the musical modes in which they can be played—are determined by the construction of the instrument. To what extent they are determined depends, of course, on the rigidity of pitch of the instrument. Tones produced on the *hichiriki* are very flexible, whereas the fifteen notes produced by the bamboo tubes of the *shō* are as rigid as the notes of the organ. The transverse flute is intermediate between the two. Of interest in this connection is the thesis of Yamanoi Motokiyo, a musicologist and instrumentalist, in which it is argued that archaic Japanese melodies, as well as "Chinese" and "Korean" pieces created by Japanese musicians, were composed on the flute, and that the reconstruction of ancient music of Japan must, therefore, be based on the natural-blown scale of the flute rather than the theoretical *ryo* and *ritsu* modes.[20] Yamanoi contends also that melodies of gagaku were forced into the confining molds of the *ryo* and *ritsu* modes by musical theorists of the Heian Period.[21]

In Japan music has been taught orally and through imitation. Native Japanese music was primarily vocal. It may be that native Japanese melodies were eventually attuned to musical modes which could be played on imported instruments, for the voice is more mercurial in its flexibility. Yet even in gagaku today we hear melodies sung in modes that are not altogether playable on instruments of accompaniment. To cite an example which is available in recording,[22] when the gagaku troupe performs a rōei song that is notated in the *ritsu* mode of E (the principal tones in ascending order are E, F♯, A, B, and C♯), the singers intone a

C-natural rather than the C♯ when the melodic line descends, whereas the *shō,* playing in unison with the singers, produces a C♯. The *shō,* incidentally, cannot produce a C-natural in its lower range. The singers may be discomfited by the resultant clash of a semitone, but they do not attune their singing to the fixed pitch of the *shō.* Motifs in which the C-natural occurs may remind us of those we hear in melodies in our minor mode. To the Japanese they may be reminiscent of motifs heard either in the popular music that was developed by plebeian entertainers of the Edo Period or in archaic Japanese melodies—for example, the *Yamato-uta, Azuma-asobi,* and such Shinto songs (*kagura*) as *Niwabi* and *Haya-uta*—which are sung by musicians of the Imperial Court. The modes used in these divergent forms of music are by no means identical, but there are some resemblances in the arrangement of the tone material, so that similar motifs emerge. Though it might be argued that an original C♯ in the melody became a C-natural during the Edo Period, when court singers may have been influenced by the new plebeian music, it is unlikely that traditional melodies would have been modified to such an extent that even the modal feel is altered. It is more reasonable to assume that archaic motifs have endured because of the effectiveness of the traditional oral method of teaching, or because of the relative rigidity of musical modes. The Japanese have generally used music notation as a memory aid rather than for precision in transcribing music. The subtle rhythmic and microtonal shadings which characterize traditional Japanese music are far too elusive to be captured in Western notation. It is quite likely, therefore, that *rōei* songs were transcribed in the theoretical *ryo* and *ritsu* molds but were never sung exactly as indicated by the neumes in the notations. The *rōei* songs, to be sure, have been a part of the gagaku repertoire only since the early Meiji Period. The above argument may be strengthened, however, by the fact that similar tonal discrepancies occur throughout the instrumental repertoire of gagaku.

Gagaku is often described as music that has been transmitted in its pristine form down through the ages. There may have been innovations and modifications made during the Nara Period and in the efflorescence of the Heian Period when gagaku was a creative art. But we can be rather certain that it has changed little in the nine centuries since then, for gagaku became an

ossified art, to be preserved by the crestfallen court nobility as
a tradition of a bygone era of splendor. The descendants of
musicians who immigrated from Korea and China have served
as the custodians of gagaku throughout the ages. Their aim has
been to perpetuate the music of a past era of cultural greatness,
and innovation has not been a part of the tradition of musical
transmission. This is as much as we are told. Although we might
say that changes in gagaku have therefore resulted chiefly from
loss, there may very well have been changes due also to influences
received from newer forms of music. Performers of gagaku since
the Meiji Period (1868–1912) have unwittingly allowed Western
influences to filter into their music,[23] but their intent at least
has been to maintain the age-old tradition that gagaku is not
to be profaned by any willful modification, except for those
needed in order to unify the various styles of performance so
that members of different schools of gagaku could perform together; for the music, they believed, had been transmitted through
many long centuries precisely as it was performed during the
classical past.

Musical modes and scales are generally considered to be resist-
ant to changes in their internal structure. A complete correspondence between the tone material of gagaku and those of other
performing arts would probably indicate a direct borrowing
from gagaku rather than a coincidental development. Since much
is known about both the content and history of the gagaku, a
study of the time and the manner in which it influenced the
music of other performing arts may serve to shed light on the
interrelationship among those performing arts. At this point,
however, it will be of interest to survey briefly the principal performing arts of the Nara and Heian periods in order to note
the possibility of their having influenced the plebeian forms of
entertainment which were to flourish in the Kamakura and
Muromachi periods. It will then be feasible to discuss the relationship of the kōwaka to the nō and other performing arts
that developed during the Medieval Era in Japanese history.

THE ARISTOCRATIC ARTS: *Gigaku* AND *Bugaku*

The oldest of all performing arts in Japan is, presumably, the
kaguri, or "Kami music," which tradition traces back to the sing-

ing and dancing that enticed the Sun Kami out of the celestial cave in which she had secluded herself. The kagura originally seems to have comprised ritualistic dances and mimes performed by shrine maidens in a state of Kami possession or by bearers of a twig, a tuft of grass, or some other object that symbolized the spirit of Kami. Kagura is mentioned in written records for the first time in the early Heian Period, but by that time it had probably already evolved into performances which were offered to the Shinto deities as entertainment.

What is regarded as an especially pure strain of kagura—one which today is called *mi-kagura,* with a prefixed honorific, so that it may be distinguished from the more popular varieties— has been perpetuated in the Imperial Court. The mi-kagura has a fixed repertoire of twelve numbers which are performed in accordance with rigid rules. They are primarily songs that are sung to the accompaniment of the flute, *hichiriki, wagon,* and drums. The six-holed transverse flute, called either the "kagura flute" (*kagura-bue*) or "Japanese flute" (*Yamato-bue*), is supposedly a native Japanese instrument and is constructed differently from the smaller flutes that are used in gagaku. The *wagon,* or "Japanese cithern," is a small six-stringed *koto* which also is considered an indigenous instrument. There is some dancing by the director of the troupe during several of the numbers. The mi-kagura is regarded as always having served a purely ritual function, and as having remained outside the stream of development of entertainment forms. There are many other varieties of kagura extant. Some are presented by traveling troupes which go from village to village, performing the "Lion Dance" and other rituals of exorcism. Those kagura which are formally staged performances may, for convenience, be subsumed under the broad category of "common kagura." The common kagura is still performed at Shinto shrines in all parts of Japan. Its function is to add to the festivity of religious occasions, and the repertoire accordingly comprises entertaining dances and pantomimic dramas out of mythology set to the lively music of a flute and a variety of percussive instruments. In evolving from a purely religious ritual to a performance intended primarily for entertainment, the kagura was influenced to a great extent by various forms of folk art and by the nō drama; it appears to have imparted little in return to the other performing arts.

The important entertainment arts during the early period of Japanese history were those which were brought to Japan from continental Asia: *gigaku, bugaku,* and *sangaku.* Gigaku was imported into Japan from Korea, but most of the dances and pantomimic pieces in its repertoire had probably been brought to Korea from China and regions farther west. The dances of bugaku comprised those imported from China and other regions of Asia between the sixth and eighth centuries. Many of the Chinese pieces were presumably brought eastward from Kucha in the Tarim Basin, and as such they probably had their origin in regions centering about ancient Tokhara and Gandhara. Sangaku, which consisted mainly of acrobatics, juggling, and magical tricks, was the *san-yüeh* (literally, "scattered music") of China that had enjoyed great popularity among nobles and commoners alike, particularly in the Sui and early T'ang periods.

The arrival in Japan of gigaku is recorded as follows in the *Chronicles of Japan (Nihon shoki)* of 720 as an occurrence during the Second Month of the year 612: "Mimashi, a person of Kudara [in Korea], arrived as an immigrant. He is said to have studied in Wu [China] and learned gigaku. He was given permanent residence in Sakurai, where he gathered youths and taught them gigaku. Mano Obitodeshi and a Chinese named Sai Mon (or Samo), who arrived recently, learned and transmitted these dances." [24] Gigaku was known in Japan also by the name "song-dance of China" (*Kure no uta-mai*).[25] It comprised dances and pantomimes by performers wearing large skull masks to the accompaniment of music provided by a transverse flue, hip drums, and brass cymbals.[26] More than two hundred of these masks, made of either wood or dry lacquer, are preserved in the Shōsōin,* the Tōdaiji monastery, and the National Museum in Tokyo. Their grotesque, non-Oriental features bespeak their distant origin; in fact, one need only to look at a few of them and he will notice striking typological similarities between characters in gigaku and in early Greek drama.

Gigaku will be described in some detail, because its role in the history of the Japanese theater has been the subject of many specu-

---

* A repository, located in Nara, of the personal belongings of the Emperor Shōmu (701–756).

lations. Gigaku reached its height of popularity during the first
half of the eighth century, after which it declined steadily, to appear no more after the beginning of the Edo Period. Fortunately
we find a fairly detailed account of a program of gigaku in a book
titled *Kyōkunshō (Selections for Instruction and Admonition)*,
written in 1223.[27] According to this book, gigaku was presented as
a spectacle at the Tōdaiji and Kōfukuji monasteries in Nara during
Buddhist festivities. The *netori*, or formal tuning of the orchestra, signaled the start of the performance. Following the orchestral
prelude, performed by a flutist, two drummers, and two cymbalists,

3. Mask of the lion
in gigaku

the costumed players entered the central grounds in stately procession. The program opened with the "Lion Dance" (*Shishi-mai*),
and there followed solo dances by performers costumed as the
Chinese "Duke of Wu" (*Go-kō*), the virile Buddhist deity "Vajrayakṣa" (*Kongō*),[28] the mythical Indian Garuḍa bird (*Karora*), and
a priestly Indian figure called "Brāhmaṇa" (*Baramon*).

Then came the pantomimic numbers, to which dramatic historians have given considerable importance as the first dramas to
be performed on Japanese soil. The first two of these, "Konron"*
and "Strong Man" (*Rikishi*), were combined into a two-part play;
they are the most significant in terms of mimicry in the portrayal
of action and are described as follows in the *Kyōkunshō:*

---

* Konron (Chinese: K'un-lun) is an ithyphallic being who presumably represents the dark-skinned native of South Asia known by the name K'un-lun in
Chinese history and fiction.

Next, "Konron": [The accompaniment is in] rhythm "ten"; it should be played three times; play it in the *ichikotsu* key.[29] To begin, five women are standing in front of a lantern; two of them are holding percussive rings, and two others are carrying bags. Then two dancers [the Konron] make their appearance and dance. Finally, manipulating their fans and casting suggestive glances, they simulate making love to two of the five women. Next, "Strong Man" (he appears, clapping his hands; Vajrayakṣa opens the gate): Attune to the *ichikotsu* key (play this very fast; it should be played three times). This is called the phallus-swinging dance. There is a representation of the five women being made love to, and of the infidel Konron being subjugated. They are pulled about by ropes tied to their phalli. [Strong Man] tears off the phalli and swings them about as he dances.[30]

4. A gigaku drama: (*from left*) the lascivious Konron, the harassed Chinese maiden, and "Strong Man," the champion

Following this were two farcical pantomimic pieces—"The Great Ku" (*Taiko*), a humorous portrayal of an old woman toddling on atrophied legs and being pushed along by two children as she makes her way to a Buddhist temple, and the "Drunken Hu Barbarian" (*Suiko*), a parody on drunkenness. The mask of "The Great Ku" preserved since the eighth century in the Shōsōin is, curiously, that of an elderly male—a fact certainly suggesting that the content of this particular piece had changed by the thirteenth century. These pantomimic pieces were undoubtedly didactic in intent, and there are, of course, parallels to be found in the history of European drama. The pantomimes were followed by a concluding orchestral number titled "Martial-Virtue Music" (*Butokuraku*), after which the entire troupe departed from the grounds, again in majestic procession. The various gigaku pieces were thus coördinated into a pageantry that is structurally reminiscent of the Old Comedy of Ancient Greece.[31]

From its description in the *Kyōkunshō*, we know that gigaku contained elements which were farcical and some which we today might consider obscene. This fact prompted Takano Tatsuyuki to speculate that what was imported in the year 612 from Korea as *gigaku* was actually the same thing as *sangaku*. For sangaku, as will be noted below, comprised a variety of amusing acts: there were choreographic numbers, as well as mimetic pieces which were farcical and, occasionally, obscene. Actually, gigaku and sangaku seem to have been contemporary forms during the Nara Period, and distinctly differentiated from each other. This is clearly attested by the fact that they were listed separately in programs of religious festivities; moreover, under the auspices of the government the performers were organized into separate "music houses" (*gakko*)—the Gigaku House and the Sangaku House—to facilitate the training of performers who would serve at religious ceremonies.

It is generally accepted as fact that sangaku gave rise to sarugaku, which in turn was refined into the nō. Having first suggested the above gigaku-sangaku equation, Takano opined, therefore, that gigaku was the direct antecedent of sarugaku and, hence, of the nō drama.[32] As supporting evidence for his thesis of the gigaku-to-nō sequence of evolution, he pointed out the similarity in the instrumentation of the orchestras which accompanied gigaku and the early nō. Music for the early nō drama was provided by a flute and a hip drum; the instruments used for the accompaniment of gigaku were the flute, hip drum, and cymbal. And on this basis—and having assumed rather precariously that the nō must have evolved from either gigaku or bugaku—he concluded that the nō must have evolved from what has been called gigaku. The problem of the origin of the nō was not, of course, to be settled simply by choosing one of these two alternatives. A fascinating piece of evidence was presented by Takano in the course of his argument. Having noticed that some of the

old nō masks showed clearly that sections above the forehead had
been cut away, he theorized that face masks first used in the early
nō drama were probably gigaku masks that had been made lighter
by the removal of the section which covered the skull. Since
these masks were much too small to be modifications of actual
gigaku masks, Takano postulated that nō masks were made this
way purposely in later times in order to preserve the tradition of
their origin. Although it did seem inexplicable that such finely
carved masks should otherwise be marred by such crudely finished
edges, other scholars have since then called attention to a dictum
on nō aesthetics which Zeami recorded in his *Discourses on the
Principles of Sarugaku* (*Sarugaku dangi*) of 1430 as a more probable reason for these masks to be mutilated in such a fashion:

A face mask should not have a long forehead. There are persons today
who would begrudge trimming it shorter. This is absurd. If one wears
a headpiece—the *eboshi,* for example—[part of it] will be under the
[mask's] forehead, and the [resultant] tilt [in the mask] will bring about
a lack of balance that is undesirable. Though it may not be visible if
a hairpiece is worn, a high forehead is undesirable because it may show
through the scattered strands of hair. The upper part of a long face
mask should be cut away.[33]

Yoshida Tōgo had earlier proposed a similar gigaku-to-sarugaku
sequence of evolution, on the evidence that the hamlet of Moriya,
where the headquarters for gigaku performers had been located,
was precisely the locality in which the sarugaku "troupe" (*za*)
known as Emman'i originated.[34] The Emman'i Troupe (known
later as the Komparu Troupe) seems to have been the oldest and,
until Kan'ami and Zeami raised the Yūsaki Troupe to a position
of preëminence, the foremost among the sarugaku troupes of
Yamato Province. This coincidence of location was, however, the
only evidence which Yoshida was able to offer toward substanti-
ating the gigaku-sarugaku link which he proposed.

The gigaku of the thirteenth century may have differed in
many respects from that which was imported centuries earlier
from Korea. Instead of the six-holed "Korean" flute, which was
presumably used earlier, the seven-holed "dragon-flute" (*ryūteki*),
a later importation from T'ang China was used; and what may
originally have been a copper gong was replaced by paired

cymbals made of brass. The dragon-flute has always been used in the so-called "Chinese" pieces in gagaku, and it is possible that the musical accompaniment for gigaku—as it was played in the thirteenth century, at least—did bear some degree of resemblance to gagaku. We know from the description in the *Kyōkunshō* that the gigaku orchestra played in the keys of *ichikotsu, hyōjō,* and *banshiki,* which are identical, if only in their names, to those used in gagaku. Although transcriptions made in 1294 of flute scores used in the musical accompaniment for gigaku have been thoroughly analyzed, they do not yield the precise musicological information that is needed in order to reconstruct the scales and determine the characteristics of the keys.[35] We still do not know how closely the music of gigaku was related to gagaku.

That gigaku pieces were absorbed into the bugaku repertoire is mentioned frequently in secondary sources, but a survey of all the known pieces reveals only a few parallels in titles. The "Martial-Virtue Music" (*Butokuraku*) in bugaku may have been taken from the gigaku piece of the same title. If indeed a borrowing had taken place, it could just as well have been from

5. Character in *Konron hassen,* a bugaku

bugaku into gigaku. There is no record of the contents of performance of either piece to enable a comparison; only the music of the bugaku has survived. Although "A Hu Drinks Wine" (*Konju*) in bugaku is reminiscent of the "Drunken Hu Barbarian" (*Suiko*) in gigaku, it is actually one of the eight pieces known as *Rin'yū-gaku* ("music of Champa"), thought to be of Indian origin and purportedly brought to Japan in 736 by the Annamese Buddhist priest Futtetsu. Thus it may represent the reimportation

6. Bugaku by firelight at the Kasuga Shrine in Nara

of a similar piece. The "Eight Sylphs of Kunlun" (*Konron hassen*) is often cited as a bugaku version of "Konron," but the two pieces are quite different. The characters in the bugaku piece represent auspicious ornithic creatures, but the Konron of gigaku is an ithyphallic anthropomorphic being.

It may be said, in the final analysis, only that the lion dances which are found in the nō, kabuki, and in folk art throughout Japan may have been derived from the "Lion Dance" in gigaku. As the oldest historical form to manifest elements of drama, gigaku probably exercised considerable influence on the dramatic forms of art which developed later in Japan. Since so little is known about its actual content, however, this is likely to remain an assumption, albeit a very probable one.

Whereas gigaku is an extinct art, bugaku has been perpetuated in a state of artistic isolation in the Imperial Palace, at the Kasuga Shrine and the monastery of Kōfukuji in Nara, and at the monastery of Tennōji in Osaka. Bugaku, which means literally "dance-music," as a term denotes gagaku in which there is dancing. The dances of bugaku were imported into Japan from China, Korea, the former state of Po-hai in southeastern Manchuria, and possibly India. So great was its appeal for the aristocracy of the Nara and Heian periods that performances were considered a necessary adjunct to all formal ceremonies and gala festivities. Nonetheless, with the decline in the power and prestige of the court nobility beginning in the late Heian Period, bugaku gradually lost its importance as an art form. It was reserved largely for the aristocracy, and it shared the fate of the social class which fostered it. Yet many of the elements of bugaku undoubtedly filtered down into the plebeian forms of art. Bugaku was not quite so rigidly restricted to the court aristocracy as some histories would lead us to believe. It frequently shared the same stage with plebeian forms of entertainment at religious festivals. The four sarugaku troupes of Nara were under the protective aegis of the Buddhist monastery of Kōfukuji, and they also regularly served the Shinto Shrine of Kasuga. Both of these religious institutions maintained bugaku troupes, and there were many occasions for contact between the bugaku and sarugaku players.

Within the composite blend that represents the nō drama today, there are at least two elements which appear to have been derived

7. Wind section of the orchestra accompanying the bugaku

from bugaku: the *jo-ha-kyū,* which is a concept of tripartite structuring, and the *gaku,* a special type of dance in the nō.

The orchestral accompaniment for a bugaku piece is normally structured into three major parts—the *jo, ha,* and *kyū,* which we might render as "exposition, development, and climax." These parts are, in turn, made up of one or more "sections" (*jō*). The existence of the special term *ha-sanjō,* or "trisectional development," suggests that the middle "developmental" part of a bugaku piece normally consisted of three sections. Nō plays have assumed the tripartite *jo-ha-kyū* structure since the days of Kan'ami and Zeami in the fourteenth century, and it is of interest to note that the *ha* of the typical nō play itself consisted of three sections so that the whole play is structured into five sections. This concept of *jo-ha-kyū* has also governed the programming of the nō drama, which was traditionally performed in sets of five pieces. To cite Zeami's own words, as stated in the *Canon for Learning the Way* (*Shūdōsho*), which he wrote in 1431:

As for the [tripartite sequence of] *jo-ha-kyū* in the nō, the nō with the divine theme constitutes the *jo.* The second, third, and fourth pieces constitute the *ha,* in which all manners of things are presented. The fifth piece is the *kyū,* with which [the performance] is concluded. The *jo-ha-kyū* having been completed, the program of musical performance is brought to a close.[36]

Gaku is used as an abbreviation for either bugaku or gagaku. In the nō, the *gaku* is a dance which is intended to simulate the dignified, graceful style of bugaku and is usually performed by players representing deities, sylphs, foreigners, or beautiful women. The rhythm, stately yet dynamic, is accentuated frequently by the resounding peal of foot-stamping. China is the geographical setting of many of the nō dramas in which the *gaku* occupies a prominent part—for example, "The Celestial Drum" (*Tenko*), "The T'ang Ship" (*Tōsen*), and "Kantan." The dance is intended to produce an ethereal mood, and for such a purpose a style patterned after bugaku, a form traditionally associated with the court aristocracy, was well suited. The *jo-ha-kyū* and the *gaku* are distinct examples of influences received from bugaku into the nō, and they are the only ones that are obvious. In the process of its transformation from the farcical representation that was sarugaku into a highly artistic and elegant drama, the nō may have been profoundly influenced by the stateliness and majestic grace of bugaku. But the extent to which this influence pervaded the nō cannot be gauged—only felt.

There are reasons to believe, on the other hand, that elements of the music of bugaku filtered down into plebeian forms of music. The music for bugaku dances, we may recall here, is gagaku. Gagaku was performed not only by the hereditary Imperial Court musicians but also by members of the court nobility and, later by priests and samurai as well, for music was regarded as one of the necessary accomplishments for the learned. Playing in amateur ensembles was a widespread pastime, and performing groups were to be found even in the remote provinces. Melodic elements reminiscent of the strains of gagaku could have been instilled in plebeian performing arts as the result of influence through direct musical contact with gagaku, but also because musical instruments from continental Asia—instruments similar to those of gagaku—were used by plebeian performers. Gagaku was, essentially, music imported from the Asian continent; it was performed on instruments which were attuned to the modes and scales of foreign origin. The gagaku repertoire does contain many native Japanese songs that were transmitted from eras prior to the arrival of continental music. But these songs have long been performed on "foreign" instruments so that the original modal tones of the melodies may have been altered in the process. Certain types of melodic instruments, owing to their construction, would have tonal intervals, if not musical scales, built into them—for instance, wind instruments and string instruments with fixed frets, such as the *biwa,* a lute which is believed to have originated in Persia and been transmitted to Japan through China.[37]

The melodic instruments of the gagaku orchestra were seldom used in popular music. The *biwa* was, however, used widely in plebeian entertainment arts during the Medieval Era and may have influenced the tonal color of popular Japanese music to a considerable degree. *Biwa*-playing monks (*biwa-hōshi*) were reciting tales in popular variety shows during the tenth century. In fact blind mendicant priests (*mōsō*) recited sutras and tales to the accompaniment of the *biwa* at even earlier times. But the slender *biwa,* which the blind Buddhists played, initially had five strings and five frets, whereas the *biwa* used in gagaku has always had four strings and four frets. The music of the monks, and perhaps the construction of their instrument, reflected a different tradition in music—that of Buddhist liturgical music.

BUDDHIST LITURGICAL MUSIC: *Shōmyō*

At this point it is necessary to touch briefly upon the *shōmyō,* or Buddhist liturgical music, of Japan, for the period of its diffusion in Japan coincided in part with the period in which gagaku flourished. Because it was diffused widely throughout all levels of Japanese society as a result of the spread of Buddhism, shōmyō is thought to have provided the roots for much of Japan's popular music. What may have been an Indian strain of shōmyō was used in Buddhist ceremonies during the Nara Period, but there are no records by means of which its musical contents can be surmised.

Kūkai (774–835), who returned from China in 806 to found the Shingon Sect of Buddhism in Japan, and Ennin (794–864), the Tendai Sect priest who is noted for his extensive travels in T'ang China, are credited with introducing the two styles of shōmyō that have been transmitted to the present age. Two of the important scales which, in theory, provided the basis for shōmyō melodies are named *ryo* and *ritsu,* and they are usually described as structurally identical with the *ryo* and *ritsu* scales of gagaku.[38] It should then follow that the presence of the *ryo* or *ritsu* scales in other forms of Japanese music could be ascribed to the influence of either gagaku or shōmyō—although more likely to the influence of the latter, which was diffused more widely throughout society in early times. Certain reservations are necessary, however. It seems that the terminology of gagaku was borrowed by Buddhists primarily as a convenience, and the question remains whether the terms in shōmyō denoted the same musical values assigned to them in gagaku. We have no assurance, therefore, that the *ryo* and *ritsu* scales of shōmyō were the same as the *ryo* and *ritsu* scales of gagaku. We can say only that they may have been structurally similar for two reasons. First, both Gyōnen (1240–1321) and Tanchi (1163–1237), whose theoretical writings on shōmyō have been canonized by Buddhists, based their *ritsu* scale on the notes of flutes which were identical with the flutes used by gagaku musicians. Second, both shōmyō and much of gagaku were derived from T'ang China. We have no way of knowing what Buddhist liturgical music was like in ancient China; but we may probably assume that the Buddhist music of China developed independently from that of India, since the music of China and the music of India were based on mutually incompatible musical systems.[39] It is said that the obscurity of the Indian music was, indeed, one of the reasons why Ts'ao Chih (192–232), the princely poet of Wei China, decided to compose Buddhist hymns in the Chinese musical idiom.

For all practical purposes, we know nothing about the actual musical content of Japanese shōmyō in premodern times. Melodic patterns of the past can only be assumed on an a posteriori basis, because we have no records which would permit the accurate reconstruction of melodies. The concern on the part of the Buddhist clergy to transmit the melodies faithfully should have been at least as great as in the case of gagaku music. Shōmyō melodies have been recorded through the use of a system of *hakase,* or "neumes," which indicate the general direction of the melodic line, trills and other embellishments, and the relative duration of notes. Yet the change has been such that melodies today frequently run counter to the directions indicated by the neumes. Buddhists traditionally eschewed the use of melodic instruments, so that teachers did not have the aid of instrumental techniques to assist their fallible musical memory. Specialists in shōmyō today admit that melodies have changed perceptibly even within the brief span of their own generation.

The similarity between many of the present-day forms of music and shōmyō is, nonetheless, one which can be perceived, and there are circumstances in history that may account for it. Buddhistic incantation was a service provided by the blind *biwa*-playing monks who became the bards of medieval Japan, and it would be difficult to imagine their melodic recitations not having been influenced and modified by shōmyō. The *Tale of the Heike* was so widely acclaimed as a ballad in medieval Japan that many of these monks began to specialize in its recitation. The music to which it was sung came to be known as *heikyoku,* or "Heike

8. The *biwa: (from left)* the *biwa* used in gagaku, the *mōsō-biwa* of
blind mendicant Buddhists, and the *Heike-biwa* of medieval *bards*

melody." Nakayama Yukinaga (1159?–ca. 1221) is believed to
have written the *Tale of the Heike* as an epic-ballad to be recited
melodically to the accompaniment of the *biwa;* he apparently
based the music not on the traditional incantations of the blind
mendicant monks, who had been plying their trade in southern
Japan perhaps as early as the eighth century, but on the melody
of a shōmyō titled *Rokudō kōshiki,* composed by the Buddhist
priest Genshin (924–1017).[40] In time the bards who specialized
in reciting the *Tale of the Heike* began to use a new four-stringed
instrument that was probably developed in order to facilitate the
playing of this new music.[41] Known as the *Heike-biwa,* it resembles the instrument used in gagaku except that it is smaller
and has a fifth fret. Other blind mendicant Buddhists continued
to play the slender *mōsō-biwa*—which, however, had been modified by the loss of the fifth string—and to recite sutras and tales in
return for alms. Because these monks performed widely before
every segment of the population, it would be rather surprising
if the other performing arts—the folk arts in particular—were not

infused with its influence. The presence of influences from shōmyō in folk music is often emphasized by the learned specialist on folk art, Honda Yasuji,[42] and others, and it may some day be substantiated through comparisons based on detailed musicological analyses.

Empirical studies are, of course, indispensable when historical information is lacking. This is certainly true in the history of performing arts, where often we can do no more than formulate assumptions with the scanty historical evidence that we have. Here, particularly, empirical findings may prove invaluable as corroborative evidence. The foremost specialist on Tendai Sect shōmyō, Yoshida Tsunezō, has indicated that a scale named *chūkyoku*, one which is unique to Japanese shōmyō, contains tonal intervals that are equivalent to one and a half semitones.[43] The regular use of this exotic interval is a conspicuous characteristic of present-day jōruri. But a peculiar tonal interval is merely one of many elements in music, aside from modes and scales, which can be analyzed empirically for purposes of comparison. The rhythmic patterns, vocal timbre, or the style of melodic embellishments would be equally valuable in such analyses. None would be a determinant by itself, however. Just as a sufficient number of overlapping isoglosses may reveal a relationship between two languages, if it can be shown empirically that shōmyō and jōruri share a large number of such musical elements, the fact would strongly confirm the assumption of their relationship. This method may conceivably be applied to an investigation of shōmyō influences in the music of the nō, the kōwaka, and folk art as well. Such studies should yield data that would enable us to make precise statements, rather than assumptions, regarding the presence of such influences.

THE VULGAR ARTS: *Sangaku* AND *Sarugaku*

Sangaku (in Chinese, *san-yüeh*) was essentially a side show comprising a variety of entertaining acts that had been brought into China from the different regions of Asia. It was known in Japan by at least the beginning of the Nara Period. In ancient China this type of entertainment was generally referred to as *po-hsi* ("the hundred amusements"), but according to the *T'ung-tien*, an encyclopedia compiled during the T'ang Period, *san-yüeh* had apparently become the accepted name by the seventh century.[44] In the *T'ung-tien* we find this summary of acts which typified the *san-yüeh*:

In the Han Period there was the "pole-top trick." There was also the "tray[-spinning] dance"; a cup was added to it in the Chin Period, and it came to be known as the "cup-and-tray dance." In the Liang Period, there were the "long-striding [on stilts] trick," "leaping-bell trick," "bounding-and-tumbling trick," and the "leaping-knives trick." All these are extant. There was, also, a "dance-ring trick," which is the present "caper on wheels." The [former] "high-braid trick" is the present "caper on ropes." In the Liang Period, there was the "monkey-flag [pole] trick"; today we have the "pole-climbing trick."[45]

Given these descriptive names, we can readily imagine what the acts were like. Puppetry and something called *ko-wu-hsi*, or "song-dance play," were also mentioned as part of the repertoire of acts. That the latter was a rudimentary drama is suggested by the description of a piece titled "The Stomping-Swaying Maiden" (*T'a-yao-niang*):

The stomping-swaying maiden was born at the end of the Sui Period. In the County of Honei there lived a man who was ugly in appearance and fond of wine. He always styled himself a Servitors' Midst. Whenever he returned home drunk, he beat his wife. . . . [This piece] depicts his wife's deportment. She would sway her body whenever she grieved and pleaded with him, and thus she was styled "stomping-swaying." [46]

The fact that 1,282 performers of *san-yüeh* were attached to the Grand Music Bureau (*T'ai-yüeh-shu*) of the T'ang Administration [47] is a good indication of the extent of its popularity in China at that time.

The court aristocracy of ancient Japan seems to have been fascinated by sangaku because of its exotic appeal and novelty. The repertoire, generally similar to that of the *san-yüeh* of China, comprised jugglery and acrobatics, magical tricks, songs and dances, puppetry, and acts of burlesque. Cultural forms imported from Sui and T'ang China were usually patronized by the government, and sangaku was not an exception. The performers were organized into the Sangaku House, and they took part regularly in courtly and religious festivities. But in 782 the Sangaku House was abolished.[48] Presumably sangaku ceased to be regarded as an art worthy of government sponsorship once the novelty had disappeared, but there may have been other reasons.[49] After that time, sangaku descended into the milieu of popular entertainment, where it was to contribute to the formation of plebeian entertainments that were to gain importance in later eras.

After the mid-Heian Period, popular variety shows were called either "sangaku" or "sarugaku." The word "sarugaku" first appears in historical records in the middle of the tenth century.[50] After that time it was used interchangeably with "sangaku," and later replaced it entirely. Most scholars believe that "sarugaku" represents a phonetic corruption of "sangaku," but they also submit that the word may have been coined because of the droll connotations of *saru* (literally, "monkey"). There are instances, however, in which sangaku and sarugaku appear clearly to refer to two different things. During sumō-wrestling festivals, which were among the regular ceremonies of the Imperial Court, sangaku was performed as an interlude between matches, whereas an item called "sarugaku" was performed as one of the numbers in the program of bugaku which normally followed the matches.[51] Sangaku may have been distinguishable from sarugaku at one time; or, perhaps, the two developed from different artistic traditions. This question, which is discussed in greater detail in the Appendix, cannot be answered fully on the basis of evidence available today. At the plebeian level, at any rate, the two terms were used synonymously. It may be best, therefore, to reserve "sangaku" for the collection of acts that were imported from China perhaps as early as the seventh century, and to use "sarugaku" as the designation for popular variety shows that prevailed in Japan from about the tenth century.

The best source of information on sangaku is a collection of ink sketches known as *Shinzei's Illustrations of Ancient Performing Arts* (*Shinzei kogaku zu*), a work which is assigned to the twelfth century.[52] The sketches of the older arts—these include depictions of more than a dozen different sangaku acts—are possibly copies of drawings made originally in the Nara Period. Commentaries from Chinese sources are inscribed alongside some of the drawings to show that the acts depicted were imported from China.

9. Performance of sangaku, depicted in *Shinzei's Illustrations*

These sketches show players squeezing in and out of pots, juggling balls and swords, swallowing daggers, eating fire, wearing elevated wooden clogs (*geta*) and treading on tightropes, balancing themselves at the waist on sword tips, and performing a variety of balancing acts; also depicted are a trick in which a monkey leaps through a metal hoop and a magical act in which a player is being swallowed by a horse.

In *A Record of the New Sarugaku (Shin sarugaku ki)* written by Fujiwara Akihira (991–1066), the theme of a family outing to see a sarugaku performance is employed as a literary device by means of which the author describes the economic and social life of Heian Period society. In it we find a comprehensive list of the acts performed; the list itself provides the most concrete description we have today of sarugaku:

The sarugaku which we saw tonight was of excellence unmatched in any age. Especially [amusing] were the imprecators, the midget dance, the puppeteers, the T'ang tricks, the juggling of balls, the revolving-drum [act], the eight-ball [act], the one-man wrestling, the one-man dice play, the [act of] stretching and moving without bones and with bones, [the portrayal of] a superintendent priest grabbing his skirt [as he treads] on ice, the [flirtatious] gesturing with a fan by the matron of Yamase, the tales recited by the *biwa*-playing monks, the [number for] celebrating wine making by the *senzu-manzai* performers, [the resounding of] the breastbone in the rib-drum [act], [the movement of] the head and sinews in the praying-mantis dance, [the portrayal of] the Sage of Expansive Fortune searching for his priestly vestment and of the Wondrous-Exalted Bhikṣuṇi begging for swaddling clothes, the facial expression of the mimicker of an affairs director, the [indiscreet] whistling by the functionary [who arrived on the job] early, the image of the venerable elder in the dance of the auxiliary official, the love-struck look on the shrine maiden, the "after you, sir" manners of the youths of the capital, [the portrayal] of an Easterner on his first visit to the capital, and, of course, the various emotive expressions of the rhythm men and the appearance and deportment of the "[monks of] great virtue." All these are forms of the sarugaku. And there was the ludicrous speech. There was not one who did not crease his innards and unlock his jaw [in laughter].[53]

We can only guess what some of these acts were like—for instance, the "stretching and moving without bones and with bones," possibly a contortionist's trick. The repertoire was not without acts of Chinese origin. The "midget dance" was, in its title at least, the same as the Chu-ju [54] dance of medieval China, and the "T'ang tricks" probably included Chinese acts of the sort depicted in *Shinzei's Illustrations*. The above description suggests that mimetic acts of burlesque had come to form an important part of the sarugaku repertoire. Fujiwara Akihira's description of a sarugaku performance on another occasion reveals, however, that mimetic portrayals were at times of a rather coarse order:

[A couple] pretended to be man and wife. One who had learned the [deportment of a] wasted old man played the husband, and one who feigned a lovely young woman played the wife. At first they spoke erotic words and later went as far as to engage in sexual intercourse. Among the men and women of the capital who watched the perform-ance there was not one who did not crease his innards and unlock his jaw [in laughter]. It was the height of frivolity.[55]

Usually, however, the mimetic acts were witty parodies and satires. They were rudimentary dramas from which the sarugaku-nō is believed to have developed. *Kyōgen,* the farcical plays which are still performed as interludes in nō programs today, are said to be vestiges of those early sarugaku acts.

SUMMARY

We have, thus far, noted how the gigaku, which was the earliest historical form to manifest elements of drama, may have exercised considerable influence on dramatic arts which developed in Japan, and we have seen how the bugaku may have influenced the nō in its formative stage. We have noted, also, that influences of gagaku music and shōmyō may have entered into the music of most forms of art which flourished during the Medieval Era.

Of the performing arts of the Muromachi Period, the nō drama was the most important, and, fortunately, its history is well documented in the writings of Zeami. The nō represented a synthetic blend into which were drawn elements of most of the performing arts of the Muromachi Period, and it is largely in conjunction with the study of the early nō drama that historians have uncovered much of the information on the more obscure performing arts of that period, such as *imayō, enkyoku,* and *shirabyōshi.*

Alongside the main stream of artistic development which culminated in the nō there coursed another current of development, the end product of which was the kōwaka. Zeami's writings also enable us to analyze to some extent the nature of the latter current.

THE MEDIEVAL ERA: THE EARLY ARTS

THE DEVELOPMENT OF THE *Nō*

In a discussion of the early nō drama, we must necessarily use the restrictive term "sarugaku-nō" in referring to the nō performed by sarugaku players, for the nō was performed also by players of *dengaku* (literally, "field music") and by monks participating in the *ennen,* the extravagant program of entertainment which normally followed important Buddhist ceremonies. The latter were called dengaku-nō and ennen-nō in contradistinction to sarugaku-nō.

Dengaku probably began, as its name implies, with folk dances in agricultural communities; but by the latter part of the Heian Period it was a variety show to which jugglery and acrobatics had been added. The performers were professional entertainers called "dengaku monks" (*dengaku hōshi*) and were, in the early stages at least, nominally associated with the Buddhist clergy. The dengaku continued to be performed after the development of the dengaku-nō and survives in many parts of Japan today.

The rise of the sarugaku-nō to preëminence was due un-

10. Caricature of dengaku monks, from a medieval picture scroll

doubtedly to the creativeness of Kan'ami and Zeami. But much of their genius lay in their ability to absorb into the nō the artistic essentials of other contemporary forms of art. The fact that Itchū (dates unknown), a master of the dengaku-nō, had been a major influence in the forming of the sarugaku-nō style of Kan'ami is acknowledged in the writings of Zeami.[56] There are no records which specifically assert influences from the ennen-nō. However, since the ennen-nō was produced by the scholarly Buddhist clergy, it undoubtedly embodied literary refinements which were applied profitably to elevate the quality of the sarugaku-nō.

Enkyoku (literally, "party music") originated among Buddhist monks in the thirteenth century and was widespread among the upper classes during the early part of the Muromachi Period. It is a form of song which may have exercised considerable influence on the nō. The texts of enkyoku[57] are extended compositions in rhythmic prose, and usually on Buddhist themes. Most of the extant pieces were written by Meikū (ca. 1240–1306), a monk about whom we know little except that he composed and edited enkyoku texts. The songs contain such a profusion of literary and historical allusions and are so often without a coherent theme that literary historians tend to regard them as worthless potpourris of pedantic phrases and worn poetic expressions. The *michiyuki*, a lyrical description of travel in which names of sites and places are used with poetic effect, is a technique used to produce some compositions of artistic merit. But on the whole, the contents of enkyoku are stylized to excess and lack freshness. As for the music of enkyoku, here again we face an almost total lack of information. Enkyoku were known also as "fast songs" (*sōga*); this, coupled with the fact that they were compositions of considerable length, indicates that they may have been sung at a much faster tempo than the older songs. Inasmuch as they were composed by Buddhist monks, the melodies were probably based on those of shōmyō.

The *michiyuki* is a favored technique not only in the nō, but in the kōwaka, jōruri, and kabuki as well. Texts of nō dramas, furthermore, abound in allusions to Buddhism and to the history and literatures of both Japan and China, and they are slighted by many literary historians because of this. Thus they resemble enkyoku texts more than they do any other previous form of literature. Musically, there are parallels in terminology between the music of the nō and the shōmyō which indicate that the nō was not entirely without influences from the same Buddhist music which influenced the composers of enkyoku.[58] Since enkyoku were artistic products of the most learned class of the time, we may reasonably assume that they served as models for the creators of nō texts, most of whom lived and worked under the aegis of Buddhist temples.

The greatest single contribution to the style of the sarugaku-nō came from the kusemai, a form of dance which was extremely popular in cities during the early Muromachi Period. Kan'ami took the music of the kusemai, modified the melodies into the general style of the popular songs of the day, and incorporated it into the sarugaku-nō. The section of the performance which features kusemai-influenced melodies is called the *kuse*. The vast majority of nō dramas contain a *kuse* section, which occurs at the structural high point of the piece—at the end of the development part. This innovation of Kan'ami is considered the *coup de maître* which raised the sarugaku-nō to a level of artistry unrivaled by the other forms of nō.

The supremacy of the sarugaku-nō was threatened briefly during the early years of the fifteenth century, when the fourth Ashikaga shogun, Yoshimochi (1386–1428), chose to disdain Zeami and to favor the dengaku-nō performer Zōami (fl. 1394–1427). Artistry does not seem to have been the major concern in this matter. In his early life Yoshimochi was shunned by those who made up the intimate sphere of the court of his father, Yoshimitsu (1358–1408); for Yoshimitsu's coolness toward him—although he was the eldest son and heir apparent—had made it appear as though he would be passed over in the selection of the next shogun. When Yoshimochi became shogun, he had little reason to favor those who had been closely associated with his father. There is no question, however, of Zōami's excellence as an artist, for even Zeami praises him unstintingly:

As for Zōami today, his nō and his music seem to have reached [the state of] the serene-flower style. His nō is a fulfillment of music, his music a fulfillment of nō. During a dance duet at the Tōboku Cloister in the Southern Capital [Nara], he traversed from the east side [of the stage] to the west side and terminated his movement with the merest flicker of the tip of his fan. This was so moving that it almost brought forth tears in my eyes.[59]

Zōami, however, was the last of the great dengaku-nō players, and after his death the decline of the dengaku-nō was sudden and complete. As for the ennen-nō, it was already an outmoded form by Zeami's time. It was confined to temple grounds, and its players, unlike those of dengaku-nō and sarugaku-nō, lacked the professional zeal and enthusiasm to develop their art. In the Muromachi Period, furthermore, temples did not hold extravagant ennen programs as regularly as in their former days of opulence; in fact, they tended to dispense with them entirely and instead to engage sarugaku-nō troupes for the entertainment of the clergy.

Thus, by the middle of the fifteenth century, the sarugaku-nō remained the only actively practiced form of nō. It had borrowed from bugaku and had absorbed the artistic essentials of both the ennen-nō and dengaku-nō, as well as of the kusemai; its aesthetic principles had been codified; it had become a highly

From the *nō* drama *Dōjōji*

The demon is gradually overcome by the power of
Buddhist prayers. (Photograph courtesy of Kanze
Motoaki)

From a *kyōgen* play, *The Sado Fox*

The culpable official decides to take the bribe
money offered by the wily farmer of Sado. Performed by Nomura Mansaku and Mannosuke.
(Photograph courtesy of Nomura Mansaku)

artistic form of musical drama—that for which the term nō is reserved.

THE INTERPLAY OF INFLUENCES: *Nō, Imayō, Shirabyōshi,* AND *Kusemai*

The nō is a musical dance-drama. Its mimetic actions are choreographically ordered, and extensive dancing highlights the numbers. The greater part of the text is either sung melodically or intoned in a style that resembles the recitative. What few spoken passages there are—less than one-third of the text in the average piece—are recited in a highly stylized manner. Utterances in ordinary speech tones occur only when a *kyōgen* player comes on stage between acts of a two-act play to summarize what has happened in the first act.

Even in its early stages in the fourteenth century, nō in its elegance was an extreme contrast to the vulgar sarugaku out of which it had risen. The suddenness and completeness of the transformation from sarugaku to nō is a mystifying phenomenon indeed. The farcical representations in the sarugaku are believed to have provided the two basic elements of drama—dialogue and mimicry—and the nō is believed to have come into existence when music and dance were added to this. Nose Asaji describes the transformation as follows:

The popularity of the *imayō* and the influence of the *shirabyōshi* dance at the end of the Heian Period can be regarded as factors which directly precipitated the development of the nō. It seems that because these songs and dances were exceptionally popular, they were incorporated promptly into the performances of the sarugaku players, who were eager to receive the accolades of the public with performances in which the people delighted.[60]

The *imayō* (literally, "present style") was the popular song of the late Heian Period. The *shirabyōshi* (literally, "white beat") was a dance which became widespread after the middle of the twelfth century among lowly female entertainers; the dancers themselves were also called shirabyōshi. Both were plebeian forms of art, but they were not without influences from the nobility. The shirabyōshi is, moreover, believed to have evolved directly into the kusemai, the form of dance which was the immediate precursor of the kōwaka.

Although the imayō and shirabyōshi are essential topics in the history of the performing arts of the Muromachi Period, we have little information concerning them. The origin of imayō songs is traditionally dated in the sixth century,[61] but the songs actually flourished only after the mid-Heian Period. The diary of Murasaki Shikibu (975?–1016?), the celebrated author of *The Tale of Genji,* is among the earliest sources in which "imayō" is mentioned. Describing a garden party at the Tsuchimikado Mansion, she wrote: "The strains of the *koto* and flutes were frivolous, but the tests of strength among the young men and the singing of imayō were at times amusing." [62] These songs were popularized initially by prostitutes and other lowly entertainers, but the nobility had taken to singing them by the time of Murasaki, or around the year 1000. The imayō may have been considered rather bizarre at first, but in due time it acquired respectability and came to be included among the numbers sung at parties within the Imperial Palace.

The retired Emperor Go-Shirakawa (1127–1192) was an ardent student of songs and studied with such imayō singers as Otomae of Gojō Street and Kane of Kanzaki, who were among the most celebrated courtesans of the capital. There was much mingling between courtesans and the nobility during this era; yet the presence of courtesans in the ménage of imperial personages must have been looked upon with considerable disfavor. Go-Shirakawa was, nonetheless, a true connoisseur of the imayō; he flouted social customs in order to learn the art in its current form, and he left for posterity an anthology of contemporary popular songs, the *Ryōjin hishō (Secret Selection of Songs).*[63] Judging from the fragments which remain today, the complete anthology must have contained thousands of songs, and Go-Shirakawa probably had tens of thousands of songs from which to select. The fact that the output of imayō songs was so prolific suggests that there may have been an element of spontaneity in their composition. The Court nobles composed imayō which befitted their own station of refinement. The following song, which appears in the *Tale of the Heike,* is typical. Composed of eight alternating lines of seven and five morae, it is a poetic expression which, except for a difference in meter, is a replica of the elegant but banal style of *waka* (the traditional form of verse) which was prevalent during the late stages of the Heian Period:

> *I came to view the aged capital:*
> *It lay desolate—a field of shallow reeds;*
> *The brightness of the moon was all-pervading,*
> *There was only the piercing autumn wind.*[64]

In the Kamakura Period, the warriors of the new samurai aristocracy delighted in hearing the delicate strains of the imayō melodies from the capital. By this time, however, the art had lost its spontaneity and become traditionalized into the singing of a small repertoire of songs. In the Muromachi Period its place was taken by the *kouta* (literally, "small song"), the new popular song of the era. The melodies of the imayō are believed to have contributed to the music of other performing arts; but this cannot be substantiated musicologically since virtually nothing is known of the melodic structures of imayō.[65] There are extant copies of a few lyrics with musical neumes similar to those used in the Buddhist shōmyō. This fact may have prompted Tanabe to conclude that Buddhist hymns which proselytizing monks had taught prostitutes to sing were the first imayō.[66] But even with these neumes, we have no more hope of reconstructing imayō melodies than we have of re-creating shōmyō melodies of olden times.

The origin of the term shirabyōshi is still a subject of speculation,[67] but the origin of the dance itself is described in the *Essays in Idleness* (*Tsurezuregusa*) of Yoshida Kenkō (1283–1350):

According to Ōno Hisasuke, the *nyūdō* [Fujiwara] Michinori selected dance steps which were amusing and taught them to a woman named Iso no Zenshi, who danced them. Since she was attired in a white *suikan* [shirt], girded with a short sword, and wore an *eboshi*, it was called a "man's dance." This art was transmitted to a daughter of Zenshi named Shizuka. This was the beginning of the shirabyōshi. It extolled the origins of temples and shrines. Many pieces were later created by Minamoto no Mitsuyuki. There were also creations by the retired Emperor Go-Toba which he is said to have taught to Kamegiku.[68]

The first chapter of the *Tale of the Heike* contains a similar origin tale in which two dancers, Shima no Senzai and Waka-nomae, are credited with the creation of the shirabyōshi dance. Assuming that the "dance" mentioned in the above quotation referred to bugaku, we can conclude that the shirabyōshi dance at first consisted of choreographic patterns out of bugaku which Fujiwara Michinori (Shinzei) and perhaps other nobles taught to professional dancing girls. The new dance was quickly adopted by other women entertainers. The dancers Gijo and her sister Giō, who was loved by Taira no Kiyomori (1118–1181), and the youthful Hotoke, who was to replace Giō as Kiyomori's mistress,

11. A shirabyōshi dancer, depicted
in "Seventy-one Occupations"

were all shirabyōshi dancers. In the *Tale of the Heike,* these dancers are depicted singing imayō songs and intoning *waka* and other forms of poetry. Ogata Kamekichi suggests that the dancers sang imayō in accompaniment to their dancing, and that the dances were eventually modified to express the lyrical contents of the songs.[69] This is purely supposition, however, for aside from the passage quoted above suggesting that the dance of the shira-byōshi was based on bugaku, there are no documentary records that would enable us to visualize the dance or to reconstruct the musical accompaniment of the shirabyōshi.

The assumption that the shirabyōshi gave rise to the kusemai of the Muromachi Period is based, first, on the similarity of the costume. The shirabyōshi dancer depicted in the illustration in the *Matched Poems on the Seventy-one Occupations (Shichi-jūichi-ban shokunin uta-awase)*,[70] a work assigned to the early 1500's, is wearing an upper garment called the *suikan*, which is a long-sleeved shirt with a surplice-closing front, and a regular *hakama* ("skirt-trouser"); she is holding a folded fan and has a *tsuzumi* drum at her side. The female kusemai dancer depicted in this same work is attired similarly but for the *eboshi* she wears; she too holds a folded fan and has a *tsuzumi* at her side. Adult male performers of the kusemai, according to a description in the

12. A kusemai dancer, depicted
in "Seventy-one Occupations"

diary of the priest Manzai (1378–1435), were dressed in a more formal attire—the *hitatare* shirt, which is similar to the *suikan* but more decorative, and the *ōguchi*, or "broad skirt-trouser"—but boy performers were attired in *suikan*, *ōguchi*, and *eboshi*.[71]

Second, rhythm was of primary importance in both the shira-byōshi dance and the kusemai. In *Canon for Melodizing (Kyoku-zuke no sho)*, which he wrote around 1430, Zeami describes rhythm, or beat, as the most prominent characteristic of the kusemai:

Kusemai music is of an order quite apart from what is usual in music. [In order to simulate it], the beat must, first of all, be established as the basis, and the melody should be written so that it progresses lightly, riding on the beat. . . . [The music of] the kusemai has the beat as its basis, because it is a style of music in which the singing is done while dancing.[72]

The importance of the beat in the shirabyōshi dance is evidenced by the fact that the dancers were often described as "counting" (*kazoeru*) or "stepping" (*fumu*), rather than "dancing," the shira-byōshi. When Hotoke performed for Kiyomori, moreover, she "stepped" about in circular patterns,[73] and when Shizuka danced before the first Kamakura shogun, Minamoto no Yoritomo (1147–1199), her final dance was one in which she "stepped" about the stage thrice.[74]

The beat and foot-stamping have been emphasized in most forms of Japanese dancing, and the sharing of this characteristic would not be considered significant of a generic relationship between the shirabyōshi and the kusemai but for evidence from a third source, the present-day kōwaka. The only physical movement which can be termed choreographic in the kōwaka today occurs during the climactic sections of a piece when the principal per-former strides about the stage, his feet stamping loudly in cadence with the beat of the *tsuzumi* drum. The example of this striking parallel, however, cannot be applied toward substantiat-ing the assumption of a shirabyōshi-kusemai relationship unless the present-day kōwaka can somehow be equated with the kuse-mai of the fifteenth century.

Third, the shirabyōshi and the kusemai may have been similar in their structure. Evidence for the structure of the kusemai comes from the writings of Zeami. In the *Sarugaku dangi* he stated: "The dance of the kusemai begins with a *shidai* and is concluded with a *shidai;* it comprises two segments (*dan*), the second of which should be accelerated."[75] The *shidai* in the nō today is a three-line introductory verse with a mora structure of 7, 5; 7, 5; 7, 4. A problem arises in the interpretation of Zeami's statement, however, since he did not specify whether he was describing the original kusemai or the kusemai which had been incorporated into nō plays and possibly modified in the process. In certain nō dramas (*Utaura, Hyakuman,* and *Yamauba*) which are believed originally to have been built around kusemai pieces, the *kuse* section begins with a *shidai,* proceeds through two passages called *kuri* and *sashi,* which are of indeterminate length and only partly in meter, enters the two-segment *kuse* proper, and ends with a partial recapitulation of the introductory *shidai.* This structure, were it not for the presence of the *kuri* and *sashi,* would be equivalent to that prescribed for the "kusemai" by Zeami. P. G. O'Neill has shown on the basis of available evidence that the *kuse* sections of these three pieces probably represent the full form of the original kusemai, and that "when Zeami talked of Kusemai having two *dan* [segments], he meant the same as is indicated by the present-day term *ni-dan* [two-segment] *kuse.*" [76]

Takano Tatsuyuki believes that the shirabyōshi dance was also structured into two parts, the second of which was accelerated; and as evidence he cites the fact that the author of an early Muromachi Period fable, *The Tale of the Bhikṣuṇi Akizuki* (*Akizuki monogatari*), refers to the latter section of a shirabyōshi dance as the *seme.*[77] Even though a two-part structure is not specified, such a deduction is possible inasmuch as the term *seme* denotes a lively tempo in drumming. Zeami's description of the shirabyōshi dance in his *Canon for Nō Composition* (*Nōsakusho*), which is dated 1423, is very concise, but it does not suggest a two-part structure. Zeami says: "Since Shizuka, Giō, and Gijo were themselves shirabyōshi, [dances for their portrayal] should be of the style in which a *waka* is intoned, the *issei* [verse] prolonged, a *sanjū* melody sung in the eight-beat [rhythm], and the dance concluded by stepping the *seme.*" [78]

Nose's proposition that the nō was born of the influences of the imayō and the shirabyōshi dance is based on probability. Because there is no corroborative evidence, we can say only that some elements of these art forms may have been absorbed by the nō during the course of its development. There is some basis, however, for the assumption that influences of the shirabyōshi and the imayō were received into the kusemai. As mentioned above, the imayō is known to have been a favorite song form among shirabyōshi dancers, and the similarity in costume and the observable parallels in the contents of performance of the shirabyōshi and the kusemai suggest strongly that they were related forms. The kusemai was, much like the shirabyōshi, a form in which the song and dance were combined. As a performing art, however, it appears to have changed radically in its content, so that the kusemai of the fifteenth century, which we shall now discuss, and what was called kusemai in the sixteenth century could hardly be regarded as belonging to the same order of art.

The only information which we have on the actual contents of the early kusemai comes from the writings of Zeami. His few comments on the structure of the kusemai, which were cited above, enable us to surmise that the performers sang as they executed dance steps in which a rhythmic beat was emphasized, and that the second half was performed with greater vigor than the first half. There is no concrete information about the choreographic patterns. Unlike the shirabyōshi, in which the song was merely incidental to the dance, the kusemai seems to have been a truly composite form in which the song merged with the dance. And it was the song which exhibited such a degree of artistry that Kan'ami incorporated it into the sarugaku-nō. But the melodies were not retained in their original forms, and the music of the *kuse* section of the nō actually represents melodies composed in accordance with certain musical principles that may have regulated the original kusemai. In his *Discourse on the Principles of Sarugaku* Zeami wrote:

We must realize that there are differences between [songs] of the kusemai and the *kouta*. [The singing in] the sarugaku was wholly in the style of the *kouta* and distinct from [the song of] the kusemai, but both have been sung ever since Kan'ami sang the kusemai titled *Shirahige* in the sarugaku. However, [the kusemai music in the sarugaku emulates] only the melodic structure [of the kusemai]; it is not music in the manner of the true kusemai; it represents a softening [of the melody] of the latter.[79]

Although the *kuse* section of the nō does not yield specific information about the music of the original kusemai, it tells us something about its general structure and the contents. The *kuse* sections of *Utaura, Yamauba,* and *Hyakuman* are believed to represent kusemai which were incorporated without any modification into nō dramas. In "A Tour of Naraka" (*Jigoku-meguri*), the kusemai in *Utaura,* the dancer speaks of the transitory nature of life and grieves over the miserable fate that is dictated by karma, and he gives a vivid description of the agonies of those who have been cast down into Naraka, the Buddhist purgatory. "A Tour of the Mountain" (*Yama-meguri*), the kuse-mai in *Yamauba,* is a scenic depiction of the mysterious mountain region that is the haunt of the dreaded "old woman of the mountain" (*yamauba*), and nature is described metaphorically in Buddhistic terms. And in the kusemai in *Hyakuman*,[80] a mad woman tells how she became crazed with grief over the loss of her child; poetic devices such as the pivot word (*kakekotoba*), verbal association (*engo*), and metaphor are employed frequently, and the passages often fall into regular meter—this is unusual for a kusemai—so that stylistically it resembles passages that are typical of nō texts. These examples suggest that the kusemai texts were quite unlike the songs of the imayō or the *kouta*. They were short narratives rather than brief verses and treated co-herent themes rather than fragmentary lyrical impressions.

We can well imagine how popular the kusemai was during the early Muromachi Period, for the names of the celebrated per-formers were known even within the Imperial Palace. The *Memos* written by Tō Yashū (1401–1494) gives this account of the con-tact between the Emperor Go-Komatsu (1377–1433) and Yohachi, who was possibly a female performer:

The retired Emperor Go-Komatsu [lived in retirement 1412–1433] summoned a kusemai dancer named Yohachi and had her perform in his presence. Having heard her three or four times, he summoned her no more, saying that [her singing] echoed the strains of an age of turbulence. Later, just as he had pronounced, there occurred the Akamatsu Insurrection.[81]

The *Diary* of Nakahara Yasutomi (1399–1457) describes the rage for the kusemai in Kyoto in the year 1423. Performers from various provinces vied with one another in performances which were staged in different parts of the city before audiences drawn from all levels of society; most of the commoners sat on the ground, whereas the well-to-do, including the nobility, watched in relative comfort from viewing stands that cost from thirty to fifty times more to enter.[82] Large public entertainments were usually staged for purposes of "subscription" (*kanjin*), or the soliciting of funds for Buddhist temples and Shinto shrines; but the so-called "subscription" kusemai and "subscription" nō were, at the same time, profitable ventures for the performing troupes. The *Daijōin Chronicle of Miscellaneous Occurrences at Kōfukuji Monastery and Kasuga Shrine* (*Daijōin jisha zōji ki*) tells about a spectacular subscription performance held in Nara in 1471 for which "all ten troupes from five localities [in Yamato Province] were pressed into service along with kusemai troupes from other provinces."[83] A few years before this, in 1466, a kusemai performance played for seven consecutive days to a throng of thousands in the middle of Kyoto. Konoe Masaie (1444–1505), who in his later life was to rise to the post of prime minister, saw the troupe perform and gives this account of it in his diary:

The woman kusemai dancer of whom I spoke danced in the subscription performance which was held at Sembon beginning on the tenth day of the month. . . . That woman is nineteen years old. . . . Her face and form were most exquisite; [in her beauty] she was the peer of all. It was an extraordinary thing. The beat of the dance was marvelous beyond description by words. The spectators numbered four or five thousand. . . . [The performers] were from Mino Province. First of all, a man danced the *tsuyuharai* [dew-remover]; a boy fourteen or fifteen years of age then danced a number, following which a woman danced a number. Then the boy and the woman danced as a pair. The troupe comprised more than ten persons.[84]

The account suggests that audiences were attracted primarily by the physical charm of the women and boys who danced the kusemai. The role of the men may have been restricted mainly to the performance of such routine pieces as the opening ceremonial dance.

A kusemai of an apparently different order seems to have flourished alongside that just described. It seems to have been a performance by men—a performance which appealed to its audience owing apparently to qualities other than sensuality. The performer cited in many instances is an elderly man called Kōwaka-tayū, or Grand Master Kōwaka, of Tanaka Village in Echizen Province—a person who was probably among the early forebears of the Kōwaka family, or possibly even the founder Kōwakamaru. The earliest reference to the performance of the kusemai by Kōwaka-tayū is found in the *Kankenki*, a chronicle of the courtly Saionji family, in entries for the Fifth Month of

1442; but the wording is vague.[85] The *Diary of Nakahara Yasutomi* cites two specific instances, in 1450 and 1451, in which Kōwaka-tayū performed the kusemai in Kyoto: [86]

Eighteenth day of the Second Month, 1450: Clear. Kōwaka-tayū of Tanaka [Village] in Echizen Province attended the Muromachi [Shogunal] Palace and danced the kusemai.

Seventh day of the Third Month, 1451: Clear. Kōwaka-tayū of Eichizen Province danced the kusemai at the Hall of Yama-rāja at Sembon [in Kyoto]. Having been invited to attend—although it was rather unexpected—I went and heard the performance.

The *Daijōin Chronicle* records a kusemai performance by Kōwaka-tayū at the Kōfukuji in Nara during the Seventh Month of 1488,[87] and the *Diary of the Noble Nakamikado Nobutane* (*Nobutane-kyō ki*) mentions a subscription performance by Kōwaka-tayū of Echizen Province held in the Sembon District of Kyoto in 1489.[88]

The Kōwaka performers of Echizen Province thus played before all levels of society during the fifteenth century. The Kōwaka family records state that Momonoi Naoaki created the kōwaka and composed the texts during the fifteenth century, but the chronicles of this era tell us nothing about the performance except that there was music and dancing. Since there are no mentions of titles of kōwaka pieces in historical documents before the middle of the sixteenth century, it seems reasonable to assume that kōwaka texts were not yet being used in this early period. The kusemai of Kōwaka-tayū may have been a transitional form that was eventually to evolve into the kōwaka, but this is only conjecture. However, a performance of a "kōwakamai" in Kyoto in 1459 is noted in the *Chronicle of the Kakitsu Era* (*Kakitsu ki*).[89] This is an isolated occurrence, but the fact that the name kōwakamai was used suggests that there may already have been at that time a style of dance which was discernibly different from the kusemai.

The kusemai was already a flourishing art in Kan'ami's time in the fourteenth century. It seems to have evolved from the dances of the shirabyōshi. Kusemai performers were, like the shirabyōshi dancers, professional entertainers in the true sense of the word.

They were not dependent upon the patronage of temples or shrines but, instead, toured extensively and played to audiences of all levels. Many of the early kusemai performers were women, and it is likely that they learned much from the shirabyōshi dancers.

Many specialists believe that men of the occupational group called *shōmonji* became the kusemai dancers of the Muromachi Period. The *shōmonji* were entertainers of low social status in medieval Japan. They are regarded as descendants of the ancient *"yin-yang* masters" (*on'yōshi*), the official diviners who were attached to the Ministry of Central Affairs (*Nakatsukasa*). The *shōmonji* performed divinations and rituals of exorcism; they recited Buddhist sutras, and they also danced the kusemai. They were entertainers who in their profession combined services which were derived from Chinese divination, Shinto, and Buddhism. There is considerable disagreement among specialists in regard to the pattern of the existence of the *shōmonji* during the Muromachi Period.[90] Furthermore, the question of whether or not the kusemai performer and the *shōmonji* were one and the same, as Hayashiya Tatsusaburō implies,[91] has not yet been finally answered. The accounts in Zeami's writings indicate that already in the fourteenth century the kusemai was a fully developed art, and one which was practiced by professionals specializing in it. Although medieval chronicles occasionally mention the performance of kusemai by the *shōmonji,* the dancing of kusemai seems to have been an adjunct to their function, which was primarily a magico-religious one; and so it seems that these *shōmonji* may have borrowed the kusemai in order to enhance their repertoire of trade. The same can be said with regard to the proposition that the kusemai had evolved from the art of a similar sort of religious entertainer, the *senzu-manzai,* whose dances were indispensable in new-year rituals observed by both commoners and the nobility.[92] The fact that these entertainers would sometimes perform the *senzu-manzai* dance, and then the kusemai, suggests that the two dances were different, contemporaneous forms; it is difficult to accept the proposition that the *senzu-manzai* was the direct antecedent of the kusemai. *Senzu-manzai* performers frequently included nō pieces in their repertoire, and it seems that this same reasoning would be applied in investigating the origin of the nō were it not for the fact that much more is known concerning the history of the nō.

SUMMARY

It appears, in the final analysis, that the history of the plebeian performing arts of Japan can be defined only in terms of broad trends. The performing arts were developed by people of low social status who during historical times served society as diviners, exorcisers, dancers, courtesans, and performers in variety shows. Their station in society was no higher than that of haulers, boatmen, and scavengers, and they were generally despised as a social class, although not to the extent of exciting the abhorrence with which slaughterers and handlers of leathers and hides were regarded. They inhabited marginal areas such as dry river beds, or as Hayashiya has pointed out, untaxed areas called *sanjo,* which were either abandoned acreages or other areas of unfavorable terrain.[93] Many have inquired into the origins of those who engaged in the despised occupations, but no definite conclusions have been forthcoming.[94] It was within this milieu of lowly plebeians that the entertainers of medieval Japan were produced. They borrowed from one another and influenced one another in developing entertainments of increasing novelty and appeal. It is unlikely that any of the medieval plebeian arts represented a pure strain which could be traced directly to any single antecedent in an earlier period. The difficulty of defining the origin of each of these art forms is no less than that of seeking out precise patterns within an unanalyzable blend of colors. It is unlikely, furthermore, that the patterns ever existed in the precise distinction in which they are sometimes expected to be found.

THE KŌWAKA

FROM *Kusemai* TO KŌWAKA

The kusemai changed considerably during the fifteenth and sixteenth centuries, and a comparison of the kusemai of Zeami's time and what was called kusemai after the 1530's reveals that they were similar only in name. There is virtually no informa-

tion about the contents of the kusemai during the years in which
the changes occurred, so that the process of transformation remains unknown to us. But if we turn to Zeami's writings, we can
learn something about the manner in which the music of the
kusemai may have been influenced by nō music. As was mentioned previously, Kan'ami modified the music of the kusemai
into the style of the *kouta,* the popular songs of the era, and
incorporated it into the sarugaku-nō. But this modified kusemai
music in the nō had undergone further modification by the time
Zeami documented the principles of the nō some forty to fifty
years later. In the *Canon for Melodizing,* Zeami wrote:

Nowadays I frequently hear kusemai which are in the *kouta*-style and
[composed] in the style of ordinary [nō] singing. It is a style that is
exquisite, a style that is elegant and refined. Such [melodies] are
kusemai, to be sure, but they cannot be called melodies of the original
kusemai. Now, even though the melodic progression is inappropriate
[for a real kusemai song], the style is one which links words and phrases
nicely and is delightful to hear. The melodizing [of the *kuse*] today
should, therefore, be in accordance with this general style.[95]

The great public performances of sarugaku-nō held in the
capital proclaimed the success of the modified kusemai music in
the nō. There is every reason to believe that kusemai performers
would have quickly adopted this new music—a form of music
which actually represented a modification of their own music—
so long as it was considered to be an improvement upon their
own. For professional entertainers in those times sought con-
stantly to mold their performances to suit the changing tastes of
the audience.

What sets the kusemai of the sixteenth century distinctly apart
from the earlier kusemai is the text. The so-called kusemai of the
sixteenth century was dancing to the melodic recitation of
historical tales that were, on the average, several times longer
than the typical nō texts. The tales were narratives which bore
little resemblance, either structurally or stylistically, to the songs
of the early kusemai. This "kusemai" is the form of ballad-drama
which was later to be called the kōwaka. Perhaps because the
story was emphasized, notices of performances in diaries and
chronicles usually cite the titles of all the pieces presented. The

titles of the brief narratives that were the songs of the earlier kusemai were seldom, if ever, recorded.

When chroniclers wrote about this new form of art—or what we may now call the kōwaka—they referred to the dancers usually as "kusemai," or as *shōmonji* or *senzu-manzai*. The performance itself is called either "kusemai" or *mai*, but the titles of the selections presented are definitely those of pieces which have been standard in the kōwaka repertoire, and not of anything that can be associated with the earlier kusemai. The following are among the earliest references to performances of the kōwaka:

Fourth day of the Sixth Month, 1545: Next the three persons, Yama-moto (his style, Daigashira), Fujii, and Hikoshirō, danced the kusemai piece *Hyōgo no tsukishima*. Following a round of wine they danced *Takadachi*. Food was served. Then they danced *Jūbangiri*.[96]

Ninth day of the Third Month, 1546: Today Yamamoto (his style, Daigashira) performed the kusemai within the imperial palace . . . the dances were *Chōryō, Wada sakamori, Shochi-iri, Tada-Manjū,* and others.[97]

Fifth day of the First Month, 1551: The *senzu-manzai* [performers] of Kitabatake came today and [performed] the kusemai pieces *Wada sakamori, Koshigoe, Yuriwaka-shō,* and others.[98]

Twenty-sixth day of the Eighth Month, 1551: Since emissaries were re-ceived from the Shogun, Lord Yoshiteru, and Ōtomo Yoshishige, the rarest delicacies were assembled to make up courses for the feast held beside the garden hill, and the wine party continued through the day and night. Kodayū, an expert in the kōwaka style of the *mai,* danced *Shida* and *Eboshi-ori.* Everyone was most attentive, and there were no conversations of war.[99]

Eighteenth day of the Eighth Month, 1553: This evening Naramatsu, a *shōmonji* of Sakuramachi, danced the kusemai. He danced two num-bers *(Taishokan* and *Soga jūbangiri).*[100]

Eleventh day of the Fourth Month, 1554: We had been hoping privately that the kusemai performer Kōwaka-tayū (he is attached to the Shōgoji monastery; he is close to sixty) would come to dance for this occasion (Yorisuke conveyed this). Thus he was summoned to dance at the rest-house. There were five numbers . . . *Yoriwaka Tarō, Takadachi,*

Kagekiyo, Shinkyoku, and *Koshigoe.* The party seated comprised seven persons; they enjoyed listening to the music.[101]

Twenty-fourth day of the Eighth Month, 1567: Two *mai* were performed at night (*Tosa Shōshun* and *Yo-uchi Soga*). A person named Satomura danced them.[102]

After the 1550's, chroniclers seldom used "kusemai" as a referent for the kōwaka. "Kusemai" was soon replaced by such names as *mai,* kōwaka, and kōwakamai, perhaps so that this new form of art could be distinguished from what had been called kusemai up to that time. Three things are suggested by the fact that both the performers and the pieces they presented were at first referred to as "kusemai": first, that kusemai performers may have developed the kōwaka; second, that kusemai performers may have taken into their repertoire a newly-evolved form of art; or, third, that the performers—they need not have been kusemai performers— who may have evolved a new form of art from the kusemai, as well as the art itself, were initially associated in name with the kusemai.

So long as we recognize a qualitative difference in the artistic contents, the problem of names is perhaps not too important. A newly-evolved form of art is not always recognized as such, and may—if we recall the example of "sarugaku" and "nō"—continue to be associated for some time with the form out of which it has risen. Japanese specialists in this area have tended to confuse the name of the performer with the name of the artistic genre. They have automatically equated the art of Kōwaka-tayū of the fifteenth century with the kōwaka which flourished in the sixteenth and seventeenth centuries. An equation such as this should be the product of an investigation, and instead it has been used as a premise for investigations into the history of the kōwaka. The fact that the Kōwaka performers of Echizen Province were active as entertainers during the fifteenth century is attested by reliable historical sources. But there is neither evidence nor indication that these Kōwaka performers—that is, the person or persons referred to as Kōwaka-tayū—of the fifteenth century used the narratives which we know today as kōwaka texts. The Kōwaka people of Echizen Province may very well have been the performers who started this new form of art, although probably not quite so early as in the fifteenth century as is stated in the Kōwaka family records. It is indeed possible as Muroki Yatarō suggests, on the other hand, that this form of art was called kōwaka not necessarily because the Kōwaka people had created the genre, but because through the patronage of powerful lords they had become the most influential among the many groups performing in the same genre.[103]

It is only after 1545 that chronicles cite titles which are definitely those of kōwaka. A group of kusemai performers around that time may have started to specialize in a new repertoire of extended narratives which treated themes from tales of war, and the nature of their repertoire may have imparted to their performance a quality which distinguished it from the general kusemai, and made it an art of an essentially different order. We cannot compare the music and dance of the kusemai and the kōwaka, since there is no information concerning these elements of performance. The predication of a kusemai-kōwaka distinction is, therefore, based only on the fact that an entirely new style of text was introduced among "kusemai" performers during the middle of the sixteenth century.

Literary historians of Japan are rather certain that the kōwaka texts were composed in the fifteenth century, if not earlier, although they are skeptical of the claim that Momonoi Naoaki was the author. But if we are to rely on the chronicles, these texts were not used as librettos for dances until the mid-sixteenth century, and there is no positive evidence that they were written in an earlier period. If we attempt to date the kōwaka texts on the basis of literary characteristics alone, they can, of course, be placed anywhere between the fourteenth and sixteenth centuries. If we examine the themes of the original standards, we find that, with one exception, they are themes which were well known in Japan before the fifteenth century. The exception is *The Minister Yuriwaka* (*Yuriwaka daijin* *), which presents the story of the

---

* The title in Japanese occurs variously as *Yuri, Yuriwaka, Yuriwaka daijin*, and *Yoriwaka Tarō*. The name of the hero, Yuriwaka or "Young Yuri," was obviously taken from Ulysses, which in Japanese would be transliterated as either *YURISESU* or *YURISHISU*.

Odyssey in an Oriental setting. And, curiously, the presence of Homer's epic is an anachronism. Certain motifs in the *Odyssey* occur individually in the folklore of many societies, but the general plot of the epic has not been known to exist as a folk legend in any society.* As far as we know, the Homeric epics were not transmitted to Japan through China, and so we must assume that the adventures of Ulysses were made known to the Japanese by the Jesuit missionaries, the first of whom arrived in Japan in 1549. The kōwaka *The Minister Yuriwaka* was apparently written very soon after that, for it was already being performed in Kyoto in 1551. It is indeed possible that the entire repertoire of kōwaka librettos was composed around this time, for the titles of the so-called standard kōwaka, including *The Minister Yuriwaka,* appear rather suddenly and conspicuously in the chronicles during the middle of the sixteenth century. The librettos may not have been written by Momonoi Naoaki, whose life apparently spanned the greater part of the fifteenth century; but the tradition concerning the origin of the texts, as well as the general stylistic uniformity exhibited by the texts, suggest that the standard kōwaka may have been composed within a relatively short time, and, possibly, by members of a single troupe of performers.

Japanese scholars in the past have disagreed sharply over the origin of the kōwaka. Takano Tatsuyuki suggested that the original form of the kusemai—that is, the form prior to modifications made by Kan'ami—was transformed into the kōwaka as a result of innovations made by Momonoi Naoaki during the fifteenth century.[104] Origuchi Shinobu stated that the kōwaka was a rejuvenated form of the kusemai and opined that this was probably the form which was incorporated into the sarugaku-nō in the fourteenth century; he then added that the kōwaka and the kusemai were in effect identical forms.[105] Iwahashi Koyata noted that the titles of "kusemai" pieces cited in the *Tokitsugu-kyō ki* (sixteenth century) were actually those of kōwaka texts and also observed that there are many references in historical sources (fifteenth century) to Kōwaka-tayū performing the kusemai; he concluded, therefore, that the kusemai and the kōwaka

---

* The legend of Yuriwaka on Iki Island in the strait between Kyushu and Korea shares some of the motifs of the kōwaka story, but the content represents a synthesis of various types of legends and tales.

were the same thing.[106] These views are, of course, based on the assumption that the form of art known to us today as the kōwaka was developed much earlier in history than is indicated by documentary evidence. Takano accepted the tradition, as stated in the Kōwaka family records, that Momonoi Naoaki created the kōwaka; Origuchi was simply speculating, and Iwahashi confused the identity of names with the identity of content. The only scholar after Takano to question the validity of the kusemai-kōwaka equation was Fujita Tokutarō, who suspected a qualitative difference in the texts and who concluded, on this basis, that to begin with the kusemai and the kōwaka were unrelated. As evidence he cited the fact that the song which is inscribed beside the illustration of the kusemai dancer in the *Matched Poems on the Seventy-One Occupations*—he assumes that this was a typical kusemai song—differs entirely in its form from kōwaka texts.[107]

THE DECLINE OF THE KŌWAKA

The kōwaka reached its artistic apogee around the turn of the seventeenth century. Having been developed to meet the aesthetic requirements of a violent and stormy age, it quickly deteriorated once the samurai began turning to urban fads and foppery and ceased being true warriors.

The decline of the kōwaka has been ascribed by Muroki Yatarō to the loss of patronage from an entirely different audience—the plebeian populace.[108] His conclusion, which has aroused considerable interest among literary historians of Japan, is based on the assumption that artistic life and creativity do not exist apart from the "masses" (*taishū*). If this were true, we may well wonder how so many of the finer arts evolved amidst small coteries of artists and patrons, or, for that matter, how the nō drama survived the Edo Period, when it was considered to be the exclusive property of the upper class. Muroki, unfortunately, assumed that the kusemai of the early fifteenth century and the kōwaka, which thrived two centuries later, were of the same artistic order; and that there were no qualitative differences between the kōwaka performed for an exclusively samurai audience and the strain of kusemai that continued to find an audience among the plebeian populace during the early Edo Period. The latter form was usually called *maimai,* and we know little today about its contents.[109] In view of the rigidity of social stratification under the Tokugawa Government, it is rather unlikely that the *maimai,* performed popularly by professional entertainers of a despised social class, could have been identified artistically with the kōwaka, which was performed ceremonially at the court of the Tokugawa Shogun by samurai retainers of the Shogunate.

We would know very little about the kōwaka but for the accident of its survival in Ōe Village on the island of Kyushu. Since this kōwaka appears to have changed little since the time it was transplanted there from Kyoto in the late sixteenth century, it will give us some idea about the performance of the kōwaka that appealed so greatly to the samurai of that era. The kōwaka that continued to be performed at the court of the Edo shogun changed considerably during the years of peace. Having been accorded the status of samurai, the master performers of the kōwaka may have felt it below their dignity to participate in staged performances. Though theirs may have at one time been regarded as a noble art, the role of a performer was, nonetheless, that of an "entertainer" and not to be relished. The Kōwaka people in time eliminated the visual elements of performance and later even claimed that "dance" had never been a part of the kōwaka. By the nineteenth century, according to the description by the novelist Bakin, the kōwaka in Edo had been reduced to "simply singing to a beat produced by the slapping of a fan." As a mode of entertainment, this would have been consistent with the dignity of even the most dignified of samurai.

Performers of the nō were officially classed as entertainers and permitted to wear only one sword at the court of the Edo shogun,* but members of the Kōwaka family were accorded the full privileges of the samurai. Extant diagrams of the houses of the several branches of the family in Nishi-Tanaka Village reveal that they were large mansions. The mansion of a collateral house of the Kōwaka still stands in the city of Tsuruga today and reflects

---

* The fifth Tokugawa shogun, Tsunayoshi (1646–1709), for a while accorded nō performers the privilege of wearing two swords. But this was looked upon simply as another eccentricity of this unorthodox shogun.

the high status and opulence which this family must have enjoyed during the Edo Period. According to local tradition, it was customary for daimyos to halt their processions momentarily before the main gate of the mansion as a gesture of courtesy. They say that fugitives were immune even to the laws of the Shogunate if they took refuge within the mansion.

Because the Kōwaka people enjoyed considerable prestige as samurai during the Edo Period, they may have deliberately tried to suppress the history of their role in society as entertainers, for they changed the kōwaka from a formally staged performance into a relatively informal melodic recitation of tales of war. This may account partly for its decline. But there may have been another, more basic, reason. The kōwaka probably ceased to appeal to the samurai audience for which it was originally intended. Perhaps to the urbanized peacetime samurai, the melodies sounded rather provincial, the movements appeared too angular, and the tone seemed far too serious.

III: THE KŌWAKA TODAY

THE HISTORY OF ITS SURVIVAL

T H E history of the kōwaka in Kyushu begins in 1582 with the arrival from Kyoto of the master of the Daigashira School of the kōwaka. Although it has been performed continually in Kyushu over a period of nearly four centuries, few people in the past have known about it. We may recall that Bakin, who lived in Edo, was surprised when he was told that the kōwaka was still being performed by the farmers of Ōe Village. Even within Kyushu itself, the existence of the kōwaka seems to have been little known outside the locality in which it was practiced. Matsuura Seizan, lord of the Hirado Feudatory in the neighboring province of Hizen, recorded his broad knowledge of society and the arts in a voluminous miscellany of 280 chapters, but his remarks on the kōwaka in Kyushu were limited to the following: "The [kōwaka] song is extant today in [the feudatory of] the Lord of Yanagawa in Chikugo. They say that it is often sung by flippant persons. The dance is supposed to have survived there too, but I have not seen it. There are few people today who know of it." [1]

Oral traditions and the genealogical record of the Daigashira School—these are the sources for the history of the Ōe Village kōwaka.[2] In the genealogical document, the part which covers the period since 1582 is an unpretentious list of the successive masters and principal performers, and is embellished with a few vital statistics. There is little reason to doubt its authenticity.

The master of the Daigashira School, Ōsawa Yukitsugu, was summoned to Kyushu in 1582 in order to teach the kōwaka to samurai retainers of Kamachi Hyōgo-no-kami Akimune, the lord of the castle town of Yamashita.* The year 1582, however, marked

---

* The area, known today as Kitayama Village, is approximately five miles northeast of Ōe Village.

the beginning of a new phase in the general political turmoil which preceded the unification of Japan under one feudal house. Oda Nobunaga, whose star had shone the brightest, was killed by a disgruntled subordinate that year, and the scramble for power began anew. Toyotomi Hideyoshi (1536–1598) capitalized on the confusion among the former lieutenants of Nobunaga to score a quick series of victories that gave him supremacy in Central Japan. In 1587 his armies invaded the island of Kyushu in a campaign to subdue the Shimazu, one of the great feudal houses that still refused to acknowledge his suzerainty. And the house of Kamachi was among the many lesser feudal houses that fell before the onslaught.[3]

Although he no longer had a daimyo patron, Ōsawa remained in this area, and he eventually transmitted the symbols of the mastership—the genealogical document and the costumes—to Tanaka Naotane (1579–1652), the son of a former Kamachi retainer. The mastership was not hereditary, but was passed on to the disciple who was best qualified. The several masters after Ōsawa resided in the general area that is today the southern part of Fukuoka Prefecture. We do not know what social order these men belonged to, but their names suggest that they were either masterless samurai (*rōnin*) or farmer-gentry who were descended from samurai. Most of the masters listed in the Daigashira School genealogy have the full complement of names (surname, title name, and given name) as ordinarily only a samurai would have —for example, Sakurai Jizaemon Naokuni, one of the masters of the eighteenth century.

The kōwaka masters after the seventeenth century were residents of the Yanagawa Feudatory, which was ruled by the Tachibana House. In 1787 the mastership was passed on to Matsuo Masuoki, a resident of Ōe Village, and it was retained exclusively within the Matsuo family until shortly after World War II. The Tachibana lords patronized the performers of Ōe Village, and many of the samurai retainers were devotees of the kōwaka. The Yanagawa Feudatory was known for its unusually vigorous, Spartan atmosphere during the Edo Period, and this undoubtedly encouraged the kōwaka performers to practice and transmit an art which elsewhere would have been considered an unsophisticated relic of a bygone era of war. Because the provincial samurai were not tainted with tastes for urban fads, they were probably able to tolerate, if not enjoy, the rustic strains of the kōwaka melodies and the martial sentiments of its tales. According to oral tradition, one of the Tachibana lords took kōwaka performers with him to Edo and displayed their art to other daimyos. And they say that the feudatory once awarded the performers fifty pieces (*ryō*) of gold so that they might renovate their costumes and equipment.

Public performances of the kōwaka have been held annually since the late eighteenth century at the Temmangū, a Shinto shrine in Ōe Village. During the Edo Period the performance was held on the twentieth day of the First Month, which coincided with the day on which the Tachibana lord held his *yori no iwai*, or "armor celebration." And the performance was dedicated to "tranquility of the land and perpetuity of good fortune in war." Although the Yanagawa Feudatory was abolished following the restoration of imperial rule in 1868, the kōwaka of Ōe Village continued to survive, for its performers were primarily farmers who were not dependent upon a feudal stipend for their sustenance. The end of feudalism meant, however, the loss of patronage for their art.

In an era of modernity, there was little reason for people to take notice of an art form that was already considered outmoded in the previous era. In the century since it was brought to Ōe, however, the annual performance had become the most important event of the village, and a tradition had developed that the performance had a magical effect against fire and pestilence. And so the kōwaka continued to be performed annually on the twentieth of January at the request of villagers—dedicated now, however, to "a bountiful harvest"—but its end was clearly in sight. A training of at least five years was normally required of a novice before he attained proficiency as a performer. The young men of the village could scarcely be expected to devote years of arduous practice to the mastery of an art that no longer commanded an appreciative audience. It appeared that the kōwaka would become extinct with the passing of that generation of performers.

When Takano came to Ōe Village in 1907 in his quest to find the kōwaka, there were only four performers left. It was largely through him that the villagers learned about the great tradition behind the kōwaka. The fact that the kōwaka began to attract the attention of other sholars became a source of pride to the villagers. The recognition of the historical significance and the uniqueness of the art provided an incentive for its preservation. But the survival of the kōwaka was again seriously threatened when the ranks of performers were almost wholly depleted during the arduous years of World War II and the postwar occupation. But happily a new, younger generation of performers is now being trained by the few dedicated teachers of the kōwaka, and their art has been officially designated an "intangible cultural treasure" of the Japanese nation.

THE SIGNIFICANCE OF THE PERFORMANCE

The evaluation of a composite representational art requires an understanding of its principal component elements: these are usually visual, aural (both musical and speech sounds), and textual (or story). The purpose of performance is to produce an aesthetic effect through the blending of these elements. In order to evaluate a nō drama, for instance, one has to experience the mood which is created by the images and sounds that emanate from the stage. One has to hear the strains of the samisen and the singing and bellowing of the reciter in order to appreciate Chikamatsu's creations for the puppet theater. Although the texts of certain nō and puppet dramas may in themselves be literature of considerable artistic merit, they are not always appreciated as such by the Japanese. In sharp contrast to Western drama, wherein declamation is all-important and the beauty of words is to be relished, in Japan importance is given to the stylized mode of delivery in the traditional performing arts. The audience at times cares little whether a passage is verbally intelligible, though it may be one of notable literary elegance. The kōwaka is exceptional so far as the story must be conveyed to the audience without the aids of character portrayal or mimetic action. Consequently, clarity of delivery is of importance. In other respects it is the same as most other staged arts: it presents an aesthetic effect—an intellectual and emotional complex that is achieved through the blending of its visual, aural, and textual elements. If one is to describe it, he must describe, so far as is possible, all three elements.

What was the kōwaka like during its artistic efflorescence? We would like nothing better than be able to reconstruct the form as it was in the past, for the kōwaka is a form of art that belongs primarily to the sixteenth century. To do so on the basis of performances seen today must be an extremely haphazard undertaking—or, at best, one that is fraught with problems of methodology. Yet it is indeed possible that the kōwaka of Ōe Village may provide us the unusual opportunity to study a historical form of art in all its dimensions, as a composite representational art. The circumstances of its survival and transmission in Kyushu give us some basis for surmising that the kōwaka may have been transmitted with no significant loss in its aesthetic essentials.

The kōwaka texts have been transmitted faithfully. A comparison, for instance, of the Ōe Village text for *Izumi's Fortress* with another version which is dated 1593 reveals that the corruption is negligible.[4] As for the visual and aural aspects of the performance, however, we have to rely almost entirely on the performances today. There is no known documentation of the choreographic and melodic patterns. Since the musical neumes do not indicate specific tonal values or rhythmic intervals, the melodies cannot be reconstructed on the basis of the librettos. What documents there are, purporting to teach the secrets of kōwaka music, are really jumbles of musicological terms and symbols and yield no musicological information.[5] And the comparative method is of no avail, because there are extant no performing arts that are directly related to the kōwaka.[6]

The kōwaka which was transplanted in Kyushu in 1582 represented the art at its height of development, for it was in the several decades around the turn of the seventeenth century that the kōwaka was especially widespread among the samurai. The master of the Daigashira School was a *chōnin,* but the fact that he was engaged to teach the vassals of a feudal daimyo suggests that the art which he taught was suited for performance by the samurai. Members of the Daigashira School doubtlessly emulated the kōwaka as it was performed by the Kōwaka troupe of Echizen. The records of the former say that the founder of the School, Yamamoto Shirozaemon, learned his art directly from Kōwaka Yajirō Naoshige, a son of the creator of the kōwaka.[7] But the persons who prepared the genealogy of the Daigashira School evidently did not have access to the Kōwaka family records, for the names of the early Kōwaka masters they listed do not tally with those listed in the Kōwaka family documents. Yamamoto may actually have been a student of Kōwaka Yajirō, although this is not corroborated by other historical records. Nevertheless, the fact that the Daigashira School attempted to link itself with the Kōwaka family suggests that it sought to be identified artistically with the Kōwaka performers, who were the favorites of the daimyos and samurai of that era. The style of the Daigashira School of the kōwaka which was transmitted to Kyushu in 1582 was probably identical with the style of the performers of the Kōwaka family of Echizen.

The kōwaka of Ōe Village is a composite of musical and choreographic patterns that have remained unchanged since the sixteenth century. This is what the performers believe. Matsuo Rikizō, who was born in 1890, states that it had been traditional for the master to transmit the kōwaka exactly as he had learned it from the previous master. And the Matsuo of Ōe Village have been kōwaka performers since the generation of Matsuo Masuoki, who presumably learned the art in the early half of the eighteenth century. There is a strong possibility that the kōwaka was transmitted faithfully up to the time of Matsuo Masuoki, for the earlier masters enjoyed extraordinarily long lives. Ōsawa Yukitsugu, we will recall, first brought the kōwaka to Kyushu in 1582. His successor lived until 1652, and Iguchi Naokatsu, who later became a master, lived from 1639 to 1725. Thus we have the remarkable phenomenon of the style of the first master being transmitted a century and a half later by a person who is only one generation removed from him as a performer. However, it is well to bear in mind that performing artists have been known to let their art deteriorate in their old age.

Changes that may have occurred in the kōwaka since its arrival in Kyushu are more likely to be changes resulting from loss rather than from innovation. The kōwaka existed in geographical isolation, and it had ceased to evolve and develop as an art form. The performers have been farmers. They have been the custodians of an art which belonged essentially to the samurai and which had outlived its useful span of existence. There could not have been any incentive for experimentation and innovation, for the performers were transmitters of an art that had become ossified and traditionalized, and sustained artificially owing largely to the patronage of the feudal house of Tachibana.

The kōwaka does not appear to have been influenced by folk art. In fact it has little aesthetic appeal for the local populace, and few villagers ever attend the annual performance. The audience on the twentieth of January usually consists of frisky children on a "cultural" excursion from the local public schools, a few students of folk art, and scholars and university students who are interested in medieval literature or drama. But this does not disconcert the performers in the least, for they pride themselves on sustaining a noble tradition of the warrior class. The melodies of the kōwaka may have, on the other hand, been modified by the song style of the nō, for the Kita school of nō recitation (*yōkyoku*) has been influential in this region for many centuries. Even today most adult males of the agricultural communities in this area would be able to sing a few strains from a nō song if they are called upon to do so at formal social functions. Melodic patterns which are labeled *pomposo* in the translation of *Izumi's Fortress* are, indeed, constructed on melodic principles similar to those of the nō. But the neumes and terms for recitative features in the manuscript copies of kōwaka texts of the sixteenth century are similar to those employed in the nō texts. This would suggest that the melodic similarities between the kōwaka and the nō may have existed when the kōwaka was brought to Kyushu.

Though the performers may have done their best to preserve the kōwaka, there have been both changes and losses in the elements of performance. We can say so definitely with respect to the aural elements, for melodic patterns and recitational features can be checked against the neumes and terms which appear in the text. A comparison of the singing with the notated text reveals occasional inconsistencies. Whereas the same neume occurring in identical environments should be given the same musical value, very often it is not. And often two different neumes receive identical musical treatment. A simplification of melody has undoubtedly occurred in many instances, although we cannot determine to what extent. Because kōwaka melodies are strongly modal, we can probably assume that the over-all melodic feel has remained unchanged. For although changes in music are often whimsical and occur at no constant rate, musical modes and scales are molds which tend to endure.

As for the visual elements of the performance, we can only guess at the extent of loss, if any. In contrast to the intricacy of the melodic patterns, the physical movements in the kowaka are strikingly simple, comprising only four items—a stylized bow, two stationary poses, and a rhythmic strut. Only the last can be termed choreographic. There is no mimicry. Nor is there anything that may suggest levity or frivolity. The tenseness of the performers' poses and movements is the antithesis of the suppleness and grace inherent in most other forms of art which are choreographically ordered. Its sheer simplicity serves to impart to the performance a quality of purity and austerity. The simplicity is, perhaps, an end to which the creators of the kōwaka aspired and not necessarily a reflection of loss. This is, perhaps, as much as can be said in general terms about the possibility that the kōwaka today is a relic of the kōwaka of the sixteenth century.

DESCRIPTION OF THE PERFORMANCE

The staging and the costume worn by Kōwakamaru for a performance allegedly given for the retired Emperor Go-Hanazono (1419–1470; reigned 1428–1464) is described as follows in a genealogical document of the Kōwaka family:

. . . a very simple stage—that which is called a "stage with legs"—was erected in the Garden of Pines. Permission was given to raise a backdrop on which were imprinted crests of the chrysanthemum and the paulownia. A fur mat was placed where [Kōwakamaru] was to sit, and wind screens decorated with ink paintings were placed about. . . . On that day Kōwakamaru was attired in a sky-blue *hitatare* that bore a design of a crane with pine needles in its beak, and he wore a folded *eboshi*. . . . The Emperor was immensely pleased and bestowed on him rewards consisting of many bolts of silk. The backdrop with the crests of the chrysanthemum and the paulownia was given to him with the words that it may be used as proof by his descendants that his was an art of the nonprofessional [that is, a genteel art].[8]

The account is of doubtful accuracy, but the description of the costume probably fitted that used by performers during the sixteenth century. The *hitatare* is a two-piece silk garment, con-

13. The traditional cloth backdrop for kōwaka performances

sisting of a surplice-front shirt and trousers, and served as the formal attire of the samurai from the late Heian Period. The folded *eboshi* is a small black-lacquered hat that was worn by the samurai; it was also called the "samurai-*eboshi*" (fig. 1).

In Ōe Village today, the players perform in front of a dark-blue cloth backdrop that bears three large crests in white (fig. 13). In the center is the chrysanthemum with sixteen petals, the symbol of the Imperial House. On its either side are the "five-seven pau-lownia" crest * of the famed Momonoi and the "hanging wisteria," the family crest of the Kamachi of Kyushu. The wooden stage is approximately twenty feet square and stands three feet above the ground. Thatch-roofed and enclosed on three sides, it is dark even at midday. The present structure was built in the grounds of the village shrine in 1902. Before that time the performances were staged on the veranda which projects in front of the shrine building.

The performers are attired in a *suō*, which is quite similar to the *hitatare* that Kōwakamaru is said to have worn. The *suō* is made of hemp fabric and is usually decorated with a family crest, whereas the *hitatare* is a solid-color garment made of silk. The trousers they wear, however, are the "long trousers" (*nagaba-kama*), which have long legs that trail behind the wearer. Each dons the *eboshi* and wears a short sword in his waistband; and in his hand he carries the *hempuku* fan, characterized by the tip that flares outward. This is precisely the ceremonial attire pre-scribed for samurai of modest rank in the Edo Period. The

---

* "Five-seven" refers to the number of flowers on the stems which project from the three paulownia leaves. The longer central stem has seven flowers, and the two stems on the side each bear five flowers.

garments are of a hue which in Japanese is termed *ume-iro,* or "plum color"; it is a reddish brown of medium saturation. Two large white paulownia crests ornament the front of the shirt. Two white stripes—one broad and one narrow—run horizontally

14. Designs on kōwaka costumes

across the upper part of both the shirt and trouser. The sleeves
are bordered with a narrow white stripe. The stripes, incidentally,
are special embellishments that were not ordinarily used in the
samurai's ceremonial attire. The back of the shirt is adorned
with one of three bold designs (fig. 14)—an exceptionally large
paulownia crest, a carp scaling a waterwall, or an eagle seizing
a pheasant. These are purportedly designs which adorned the

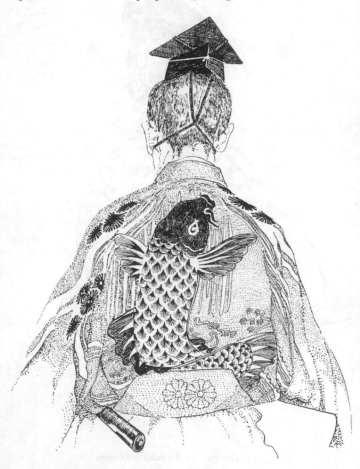

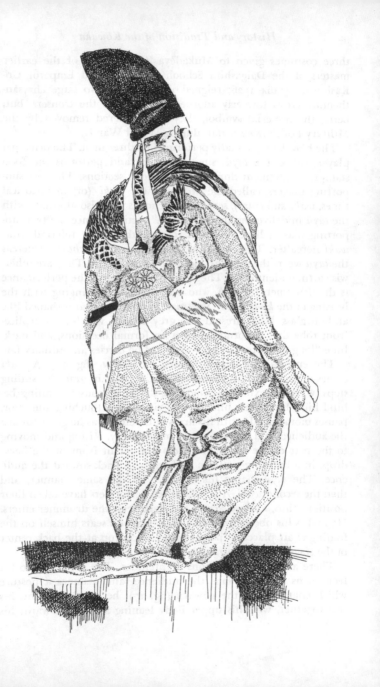

three costumes given to Mukadeya Zembei, one of the earlier
masters of the Daigashira School, by the retired Emperor Go-
Kashiwara (1464–1526; reigned 1500–1526). Two large chrysanthemum crests formerly adorned the front of the trousers, but,
being the imperial symbol, they were ordered removed by the
Military Police (*Kempeitai*) during World War II.

The kōwaka is normally performed by three men. The principal
player, called the *tayū*, sings the solos and performs the foot-
stamping movement during the climactic sections. The two supporting players, called the *shite* and the *waki* (or, in historical
times, *waki* and *tsure*), serve as the chorus and also alternate with
the *tayū* in delivering the "narrative" sections. Since the two supporting players have identical roles, both will be referred to as
waki hereafter. The two *waki* wear the samurai-*eboshi*, whereas
the *tayū* wears the upright, elongated *tate-eboshi*. They are otherwise attired identically. The other participant in the performance
is the drummer (fig. 15), who accompanies the singing with the
beating of the *ko-tsuzumi*, the small hand drum that is shaped like
an hourglass. He is dressed in a grey *kosode*, which is a surplice-
front robe that is normally worn on formal occasions, and dark-
blue "long trousers." In his waistband he carries an ordinary fan.

The entrance of the performers is stately (fig. 16). A *waki*
comes on stage first and proceeds to the front in graceful, sliding
steps, with the extended length of the long trousers trailing behind him. He lowers himself, the right knee touching the floor,
pauses momentarily with his arms outstretched as he gazes toward
the audience, and bows low and majestically. Rising and moving
to the rear of the stage, he places himself in front of the backdrop, in a kneeling position and with his back toward the audience. The *tayū* makes his entrance in the same manner, and
then the second *waki*. After the three performers have taken their
positions thus, aligned across the stage rear, the drummer enters.
He makes his obeisance to the audience and seats himself on the
folding chair placed adjacent to the backdrop at the back center
of the stage. The performance is ready to begin.

There are no introductions or preludes. The *tayū* rises to his
feet, turns about to face the audience, and assumes a posture
which characterizes the kōwaka (fig. 17): he stands upright, his
feet together, with his upper body leaning slightly forward; his

15. The drummer

arms are outstretched firmly, pointing slightly downward and forward, so that the large hanging sleeves suggest a pair of huge wings. The intense gaze of the performer is fixed on a point some fifteen feet in front of him. Although he stands motionless, he appears as a dynamic figure in which untold vigor and force are held constrained. He presents a tragic, yet heroic, image—at once tense and solemn, even ominous. Then, in a sonorous monotone, he begins the recitation of the opening narrative section.

The *tayū* assumes the pose described above also during the singing of all solo passages, while the two *waki* remain kneeling with their backs toward the audience. The narrative sections—these are spoken rather than sung—are apportioned among the three performers, who stand and face the audience in turn as they narrate. The change of narrators occurs in places in the text that are comparable to paragraph breaks in English prose—usu-

16. Entrance of the *tayū*

17. The characteristic pose in kōwaka

18. The "stepping" during the *coro risoluto*

ally when the emphasis of the narrative shifts from one character in the story to another. The opening narrative section is, however, delivered entirely by the *tayū*.

Unisonal passages are always melodic and are sung by the three performers to the accompaniment of the drum. The *tayū* and the two *waki* stand abreast, facing the audience, glide forward a few steps, and align themselves across the stage. They assume the characteristic upright pose and stand thus rigidly throughout the singing. This formal pose is broken only during the singing of the *coro risoluto* (*tsume*), the strongly rhythmic musical pattern to which the climactic sections of the texts are set. All three performers stand perfectly erect, with their arms at their sides; and the fan is unfurled and held flat against the front of the body. While the *waki* remain stationary, the *tayū* strides about the stage in cadence with the beat of the drum, lifting his knees high and stamping vigorously on the wooden floor (fig. 18). He traces an hourglass pattern as he moves about the stage. The steps are in syncopated rhythm, and the movement as a whole constitutes a distinct choreographic pattern, although there is much less bodily movement than in most dance patterns. The kōwaka is ordinarily concluded with such a section.

The recitational patterns described in the following all occur in *Izumi's Fortress*. The Western-language equivalents for the names of these patterns are intended only to be descriptive equivalents of special Japanese terms. There are the following types.

Speech:

Kotoba	*Narrative*

Solo melodies:

1. *Kakari*	*Prefatory*
2. *Iro-kakari* (Type I)	*Solo pastorale*
3. *Iro*	*Solo pomposo*
4. *Iro-kakari* (Type II)	*Solo recitativo*
5. *Kudoki*	*Solo delicato*

Melodies for unisono-chorus:

1.	*Fushi* (Type I)	*Coro melos pastorale*
2.	*Fushi* (Type II)	*Coro melos pomposo*
3.	*Tsuke*	*Coro pastorale*
4.	*Tsume*	*Coro risoluto*

The *narrative* sections of a kōwaka normally occupy from one-third to one-half of the text. In performance, the *narrative* is recited in a cadenced monotone. Words are enunciated distinctly, and punctuation breaks in the text are indicated by pauses in the recitation. Syllables fall into a syncopated rhythm that may be compared to a series of iambs. The recitation represents a styliza-

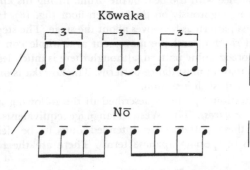

19. The kōwaka and nō: the basic meter

tion of speech in which linguistic morae are given artificial time values so that they may be forced into a predetermined metrical pattern. This meter is maintained regularly even though short syllables occur often in contiguous series—in which case syllables which are normally short are lengthened so as to fit into the pre-scribed metrical foot. The long syllable, which occurs less frequently, is usually given a time value equivalent to a quarter note. In this respect it differs from the iamb, which is a combination of a syllable that is naturally short and one that is naturally long or accented. This style of recitation is in marked contrast to that of the nō, in which the basic meter of the narrative consists of equal time units.

MELODIES OF THE KŌWAKA

The meter of the melodic sections of the kōwaka is reminiscent of that of the *narrative,* since it consists largely of rhythmic units that are similar to the syncopated foot just described. But because it is governed by melodic considerations, in addition to those which are verbal, the meter is more complex and varied. The original melodies are not conceived in measures or in notes that imply specific time values. The cadence is not quite as regular as the notation would indicate. An exception is the cadence of the *coro risoluto* (fig. 28) with which the *tayū* synchronizes his foot-stamping. The "scale" given for each melodic pattern described represents an arrangement from low to high of all the notes employed in the particular example given. It simply represents the sum of the tonal material. The principal tone—or that which recurs most frequently—is rendered as a whole note in the notations, and the ancillary tones as quarter notes. Certain melodies gravitate, as do the nō songs, around two or three fixed pitches which are separated from one another by an interval of a fourth. These pitches, which we may call "nuclear tones," [9] also are indicated by their notation as whole tones. We cannot in arbitrary fashion determine a specific mode for each of the melodic patterns occurring in the kōwaka, inasmuch as the melodies often suggest a combination of modes.

The kōwaka performers are not concerned with maintaining the same pitch from performance to performance, and so the same melody may be sung in various keys. Some historians of Japanese literature and drama have mistakenly interpreted this as evidence of change or deterioration. The notations below are given in relative pitch. Only one key signature is used so that the reader may readily compare the various melodic patterns. We should be cautious, however, lest we equate the similarity of tonal material with similarity of melodic type. The *solo pastorale* and the *solo pomposo,* to cite one example, employ identical tones but are governed by entirely different principles of melodic progression.

The *prefatory* (fig. 20) is usually quite brief, extending merely to a verbal phrase or a short sentence. Its function is to provide a transition between speech and melodic sections. The melody it introduces may be either solo or unisonal and is generally one of considerable length.

20. The *prefatory*

The *solo pastorale* (fig. 21) is always preceded by a *prefatory*. The melody is constructed on a pentatonic scale that is believed to have been widespread in folk society since ancient times, and the flavor of the melody is decidedly rustic. We do not find the melodic interval of a minor second, which strongly colors the urban music which developed in the Edo Period and which occurs in gagaku as well. In the kōwaka, the interval of a minor second occurs only in the *coro melos pastorale*. The first motif in the example given is based on a tetrachord containing three tones that is very common in traditional folk melodies. The second motif, which is repeated, is a four-note pattern that also is common in folk songs. The final motif, however, is in accord with the very different melodic principle of the *solo pomposo*.

The *solo pomposo* (fig. 22) is based on a musical principle similar to that which today governs the songs in the nō drama. Melodies of the nō song are not based on a graduated music scale but, instead, are centered about three disjunct tonal levels—the

Andante

ki_ chi_ ji_ tsu   e_ ra_   bi_   ta_ ma__   i

i_ shō   o   ki_ yo_ me   shō__   go_   n   shi

shi_ me_ n   no   da_ n   o   ka_ za_____   tte

chō_ bu_ ku   no   go_ ma   o   zo

ta_   ka_   re_   ke_____   ru

21. The *solo pastorale*

"upper," "middle," and "lower"—which are separated by an interval of a perfect fourth. The melodic line of the nō song represents a movement back and forth between the levels in accordance with three fundamental rules: (1) that a melodic skip may be made only to the next immediate level; (2) that the melodic line must be raised a major second before it can either rise from the middle to the upper level or descend from the upper to the middle level; and (3) that the melody may make direct skips between the middle and lower levels.[10] The melody of the *solo pomposo* is centered about three similar levels of tones and adheres for the most part to the above three rules. It does not, however, rise a whole tone before ascending from the middle (A) to the upper (D) level, but makes a direct leap of a perfect fourth. In the example given, the note of E in the final measure is definitely climactic and would seemingly be the upper nuclear tone rather

22. The *solo pomposo*

than the D. It would also appear that, with D supposedly the upper level, the melody had made an unorthodox ascent. But there is an exception to the second stated rule above: that because a melody which has risen to the upper level (D in this instance) must be raised a major second, or to an E, before it may descend again, it may leap directly from the middle level to the E in anticipation of the descent. This would not be permissible, however, if the melody were to linger for long at the upper level.

There is no question that the *solo pomposo* is related to the nō song, although the relationship may be an indirect one established as a result of influences received from a common exemplar, the Buddhist shōmyō. An examination of shōmyō melodies today reveals that many of them are constructed on levels of tones spaced a perfect fourth apart.[11]

The *solo recitativo* (fig. 23) is constructed on a musical principle identical with that of the *solo pomposo* except for the absence of the third, or lower, tonal level. It may represent a modification of the *solo pomposo*. It may be of interest to note a similar simplification of melody which has occurred in the nō song; in the nō,

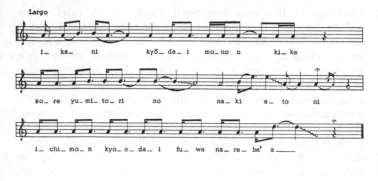

23. The *solo recitativo*

however, it is the upper tonal level that has vanished. This simplified style of song in the nō is called *tsuyogin* (literally, "strong
melody"). The *solo recitativo* and the *solo pastorale* are based
on distinctly different musical principles; yet both are labeled
iro-kakari in the libretto of *Izumi's Fortress*.

The *solo delicato* (fig. 24) occurs only once and then very
briefly during a moment of great poignancy in the story. The
text reads here, "[He realized] only that he was relieved; / He

24. The *solo delicato*

knew not of [his own imminent] death. . . . A pity!" This melody, too, is centered about three tonal levels, but it has a certain modal charm that complements the pathos evoked by the textual element. Comparing it with the melody of the *solo pomposo,* we note first of all the presence of an additional tone (C) that makes the scale hexatonic. The melody of the *solo delicato* moves more freely; in the *solo pomposo,* the melody dwells monotonously on the middle-level tone and only occasionally leaps to the other levels. An ethereal effect evident to some listeners may be due to the ear accumulating the notes of a tone cluster in the initial C followed by the two melodic skips of D-A and B-E. Passages marked *solo delicato* in other kōwaka are usually much longer, but they inevitably portray scenes of sadness.

Among the melodies for unisono-chorus, the *coro melos pastorale* (fig. 25) is the most complex musically and, also, the most

25. The *coro melos pastorale*

curious. The modal impression of this example alternates frequently between those of major- and minor-like modes (the *yō* and *in* modal scales). The motif of the first measure in notation is clearly constructed on the principle which regulates the *solo pomposo*. The second motif, occupying the entire second measure, seems to consist of three distinct segments: the first employs five tones within an interval of a fifth; the second is a common three-note pattern confined to a span of a fourth; and the third is a three-note pattern confined within a minor third. The last of these, with its semitone interval, anticipates the motif of the third measure which is in the minor-like *in* scale. The remainder of the melody is largely in the pentatonic major-like *yō* scale.

The use of the *in* scale and the relative freedom of juxtaposing motifs in different modal scales are both characteristic features of popular music that developed during the Edo Period. And so we may have here an exceptional instance of the kōwaka possibly having been influenced by newer forms of music during its period of survival in Kyushu. Despite its musical complexity, however, the *coro melos pastorale* presents a strongly rustic impression. Like the *solo pastorale,* it is always preceded by the *prefatory.*

The *coro melos pomposo* (fig. 26) is a melodic pattern which, like the *solo pomposo,* is centered on three levels of tones. The two are very similar, the only noticeable difference being that one is sung in unison, and the other by the *tayū,* or soloist. In *Izumi's Fortress* the *coro melos pomposo* occurs most frequently of all the melodic types. The passages intoned are usually between twenty and thirty lines (or phrases) long, but the melody is generally a repetition of the two patterns shown in the notation. These passages are divided into units of either three or two lines each. The three-line units are set to the three-measure melodic phrases, and the two-line units to the two-measure phrase. The *coro melos pomposo* and the *coro melos pastorale* both are labeled *fushi* in the libretto, although they represent two basically different types of melody.

The *coro pastorale* (fig. 27) occurs only once in *Izumi's Fortress.* Musically, it resembles the *solo pastorale* to the extent that the scale encompasses the pentatonic scale of the latter, so that similar motifs emerge. But the spirited, regular cadence stands in marked contrast to the slower, halting rhythm of the *solo pastorale.* This

26. The *coro melos pomposo*

melody is unique in kōwaka because of its frequent melodic leaps of an octave or more. Such soaring melodic leaps are, in fact, exceptional in traditional vocal music in general. A distinct feature is the regular alternation between phrases which are sung on a monotone and those which follow sweeping lines of movement.

In the *coro risoluto* (fig. 28), to which the climactic sections of the story are set, rhythm is of primary importance. The beat of the drum establishes a cadence to which the *tayū* synchronizes his steps as he moves about the stage. Much of the *coro risoluto* is musically divisible into fairly regular eight-beat measures. Because the tempo is so rapid, the syncopated iamb-like meter gives way to a smoother flowing series of utterances. Melodically, it is like a chant, for similar motifs are repeated over and over during much of the singing. In one instance in *Izumi's Fortress*—during the scene in which the five sons of Fujiwara Hidehira are reading a message from the Kamakura Shogun urging them to betray Yoshitsune—the *coro risoluto* becomes a strong chant that almost loses its musical quality owing to the emphatic enunciation of the words. The example in notation contains a modulatory phrase that is rather unusual in a *coro risoluto* melody.

Andante quasi allegro

ka_ mi wa Bo_ n_ ten Te_ i_ sha_ ku shi_ mo wa

shi_ da_ i Te_ n_ nō ge-ka_ i no chi ni wa

I_ se Ten_ shō_ da_ i_ ji_ n no ha_ ji_ me

ta_ te_ ma_ tsu_ ri ō_ jō no chi_ n_ ju_

Ha_ chi_ ma_ n da_ i_ bo_ sa_ tsu

27. The *coro pastorale*

28. The *coro risoluto*

PART TWO

****

The Librettos of Kōwaka

IV: THE CHARACTERISTICS
OF KŌWAKA TEXTS

THE LITERARY CHARACTERISTICS

THE kōwaka may conveniently be termed a drama, but in a limited sense, for it is a staged performance but lacks—in its form today, at least—mimicry and dialogue. The texts are true ballads although, like the celebrated *Tale of the Heike,* which seems originally to have been a ballad,[1] they are not written in formal verse. We may even say that poetic meter is rather suprisingly lacking, especially in view of the fact that the format of a libretto is a distinctive feature of kōwaka texts. These texts are primarily librettos used for staged performances in which are combined both the narrative and melodic modes of recitation. The recitative quality of the texts is implicit in their division into sections which are intended specifically to be narrated or intoned in various styles of melodic recitation. The verse structure of the melodic passages is implied by the meter in which they are cast. The format of the libretto constitutes a characteristic which is at once structural and stylistic, and the communicating force of the passages is determined largely by the mode of its recitation.

The over-all prose style of kōwaka texts in many respects resembles that of the romantic war chronicles and historical romances of the Medieval Era. There is, for example, a directness and vital force that often reminds one of the Homeric epics. Although we may note little variance in style among the individual pieces in the kōwaka repertoire, we find a discernible stylistic difference between the standard pieces, on the one hand, and the later *Miki* and *Honnōji,* on the other. And there are pieces which contrast structurally with the main body of the texts—in particular, the *New Piece (Shinkyoku),* a love story which has been taken from the *Chronicle of the Grand Pacification,* and the plotless jumble of trite literary phrases eulogizing the creation of Japan, *Nihongi*.

The narrative structure of the translated pieces, *Atsumori* and *Izumi's Fortress (Izumigajō)*, come within the scope of the convention. In *Atsumori,* the climax of the story—Kumagae's slaying of Atsumori—occurs in the middle, and the latter half of the story is an extended epilogue, telling of Kumagae's repentance, his entry into the Buddhist priesthood, and the dedication of his life to atonement for the killing. The plot of *Izumi's Fortress* unfolds in more ordinary fashion. Of the five sons of Fujiwara Hidehira, Izumi alone remains faithful to the pledge of loyalty to Yoshitsune; as a result he incurs the enmity of his brothers, and his fortress is attacked; and the story culminates in the anticipated climax—the death of Izumi, his wife, and his children. We can note a structural cleavage between kōwaka which are complete, self-contained stories and those which appear to be individual episodes of an epic series. The *Minister Yuriwaka, Shida, Kagekiyo,* and *Chang Liang* are among the pieces which present complete stories. The "Soga" and "Yoshitsune" pieces are generally episodic; but they have been enjoyed individually because the Japanese are quite familiar with the whole epics. Therefore, should the conflict in the plot remain unresolved at the end of the tale, the reader could supply the eventual resolution.

The uninitiated reader may occasionally be confounded by highly unusual twists in the plot. In *Togashi,* for instance, the tension in the story mounts as Benkei, doing his best to maintain his precarious disguise as an emissary of the Tōdaiji, continues pretending to read from a fake subscription tablet. He improvises with great eloquence, but it seems inevitable that he must falter eventually and betray himself. The plot must proceed to the anticipated resolution—the moment of reckoning in which Benkei is either seized as an impostor or freed as a result of his convincing impersonation. But the piece ends just prior to this moment. The concluding passage reads: "The [feigned] reading thus completed, he quickly rolled up the scroll and threw it back into his shoulder-trunk. This deed of Musashibō Benkei was truly a deed of no ordinary mortal." This anticlimactic ending would not perplex a Japanese, however, unless he were reading the text with an eye only to its narrative structure. Because the story of *Takadachi* is woven about the theme of Yoshitsune's last battle, it would normally be expected to culminate in the death of Yoshitsune. But the closing passages describe the heroic death of Benkei, who is the last of the stalwarts defending Yoshitsune. The uninitiated reader is again left in suspense by the surprise ending.

Such structural peculiarity becomes a weakness when the story is presented as a staged drama. When *Takadachi* was adapted for presentation as a play for the early puppet theater, the only major textual revision made was the addition of a final scene depicting Yoshitsune's death, for without it the drama would lack a much-needed catastrophe. Similarly, whenever the story of *Togashi* is dramatized in the nō, puppet, or kabuki theater, the plot is always resolved; the final scene depicts the exodus of Benkei and other members of Yoshitsune's party from the confines to Togashi's court of inquiry.

The individual character in a kōwaka, as in the Homeric epics, is seldom described by more than a short epithet or a single descriptive adjective. Characterization is not a technique that is employed consciously in the kōwaka texts. But because the major characters are always those who are well known in history or legend, the audience will automatically link their names with their stereotyped images. The passage from *Atsumori* in which Kumagae studies the youthful hero's face may, therefore, seem rather exceptional, for it reads:

. . . the side-locks were as delicate and elegant as the wings of the autumnal cicada, the fluttering brows resembled the moon over distant mountains. He was the [celebrated poet] Narihira of old, attired in a hunting shirt, brushing his sleeves under snowy skies by the wilds of Katano. Painted brows of deep-blue hue, a face of blooming fairness, garments of brocade and embroidered fabric: should an artist attempt to depict this image, how could his brush contrive to reproduce the likeness of this courtier? [2]

But the description offers no individualizing detail, so that the face depicted remains simply that of a character type, the youthful courtier. This rather extended description is used primarily to amplify the tragedy of Atsumori's death. On the whole, characters in the kōwaka are merely reënacting their roles in stories with which the audience is already familiar. In many instances only the mode of telling the story is new.

Little attention is given to the character portrayal of the individual, but the visual image of the warrior is described elaborately. The material, weave, color, and style of his garments, the various parts of his suit of armor, his weapons, and his steed—all are described in minute detail. Given a description such as the following in *Atsumori,* the audience could readily envision the magnificent figure of the Heike captain, Iga no Heinaizaemon:

The attire in which he emerged on that day was most resplendent. Next to his person he wore an all-white *katabira* shirt, and over it, he donned a blue-black military *hitatare* gown, the four cords tied loosely. His arm guards were woven in the hues of the arbutus, peach, and plum blossoms; his shin guards were finished in sandalwood, and his soft socks were made of bearskin and fitted with metallic rims of silver. He stepped into his shoes of ankle length, and then donned a right-side guard that was decorated with a lion and peonies. His suit of armor of red silk shone in its serpent-hour newness; he gripped it by the shoulder catch, lifted it high, slipped it on to the full length of the hip plates, fastened the top-straps, tied the outer sash quickly, and slipped an armor-piercer nine-and-a-half inches long into his steed-hand side. His slashing blade, a foot and eight inches long, he inserted vertically in his waistband. He secured his great sword, three feet eight inches long and with fittings made of gleaming copper, tied a cloth headband over his soft-*eboshi* hat, and strode out, using a white-handled halberd as a staff.[3]

We might compare this with Homer's equally vivid and dynamic description of Paris in the Third Book of the *Iliad:*

The godlike Alexander, husband of fair-haired Helen, put his splendid armor on his shoulders. First he fastened upon his shins the handsome greaves, fitted with silver ankle-clasps. Next, he put about his chest the breastplate of his brother Lycaon, for it fitted him. Then over his shoulders he threw his silver-studded sword of bronze, and then his great stout shield. Upon his mighty head he set the well-wrought helmet with its horsehair plume, and the plume nodded dreadfully above it. And he took a sturdy spear which fitted his hand.[4]

Characters in the kōwaka are often seen in static, picturesque poses. The heroic pose assumed by Atsumori—holding a bow with an arrow notched to the string and mounted on a prancing steed —as he addresses a poem to Kumagae is a cliché modeled on the image of the warrior so frequently depicted in picture scrolls. There is really no reason for Atsumori to wield his bow at this point in the story, or even to recite poetry, and it seems that the progression of the plot has been disrupted. But this is a literary convention which recurs throughout the romanticized histories.

With the actors frozen in picturesque poses, the reader is afforded a momentary glimpse of a scene that has become strikingly visual. The exchange of poems between combatants is also a convention, and falls agreeably on the Japanese ear. On the other hand, the narrative is occasionally enlivened by dynamic portraitures—such as that of a magnificently-clad warrior, his halberd tucked tightly under his arm, sallying forth to challenge his enemies. Battle scenes are stylized to the extreme. Following an exchange of appropriate insults, the battle is begun as some warrior of high renown lets fly an arrow that finds its mark unerringly in the man who is at the forefront of the enemy formation. The bow usually requires a pull of the combined strength of at least three men; the archer performs with a great flourish, and the arrow, although it has flown a great distance, always has sufficient force to penetrate its mark. We find similarly stylized depictions of battles in the *Chronicle of the Grand Pacification*.[5]

Many of the formal elements and conventions of the kōwaka are strikingly similar to those in the *Iliad*. Actions are so stylized that they develop easily into stock motifs. For example, the manner of Yoshitsune's death in *The Mouthed Letter (Fukumijō)*—" . . . he drew his blade quickly, gashed his belly in a crisscross, grasped his viscera, tore them out and cut them to bits. . . ."[6] —is about as conventional as the *Iliad's* " . . . he hit him in the navel, and all his bowels gushed out on the ground, and darkness veiled his eyes as he gasped."[7] Such expressions as ". . . stormed out of the fortress with blades flailing" are as conventional in the kōwaka as is ". . . fell with a crash, and his armor clanged about him" in the *Iliad*. The archaic stock introductory phrase, *saru aida* (literally, "erstwhile") in kōwaka functions simply to mark transition of thought, similar to the "now" and "so" with which many of the books in the Homeric epics begin. Long passages, particularly messages, are often repeated in their entirety in both the kōwaka and the Greek epics. The many parallels may be attributed to the fact that both the kōwaka and the Homeric epics, being essentially the products of a long oral tradition, were intended to be recited aloud. Many of the features—especially the repetitions and the recurrence of stock phrases and stereotyped passages—helped to fix the attention of listeners, though they would only contribute to tedium if the works were read silently.

The recurrence of similar character types and plot elements is one of the structural characteristics of the kōwaka. The loyal vassal is ever present. In *Iruka,* Kamatari sacrifices the life of his infant child to the success of a plot contrived in the emperor's behalf. In *Manjū,* Nakamitsu kills his own son so that his master's son may live. In *Izumi's Fortress,* Izumi no Saburō sacrifices his whole family in order to honor a pledge of loyalty to Yoshitsune. The motif in *Izumi's Fortress,* of avarice as the cause of infidelity, is recapitulated in detail in *Kamada.* In the former piece, Mina-moto no Yoritomo induces the five sons of Fujiwara Hidehira to turn against Yoshitsune by promising them a reward of five provinces. In *Kamada,* the manager of Osada Manor is tempted by a bribe of three provinces from Taira no Kiyomori to turn against the Genji leader Yoshitomo, who is his lord; and only Senjō—like Izumi no Saburō, he is the third among five sons—tries to dissuade the family from the planned treachery.

Then there are the heroic women who are even bolder, more circumspect, and more self-reliant than their gallant men. Izumi's wife has the courage to see her children deliberately killed lest Izumi's concern for their safety sway his determination to honor his pledge of loyalty; she fights alongside him, and in the end, when they are about to take their own lives, she has the presence of mind to make certain that her husband kills himself in a manner becoming a samurai. In *The Night Attack on the Hori-kawa Mansion* (*Horikawa yo-uchi*), Yoshitsune's paramour, Shi-zuka, is portrayed as a woman of similar fortitude. Yoshitsune would have perished in the surprise attack were it not for Shizuka's alertness, for she awakens him, assists him as he dons his suit of armor, and fights by his side until reinforcements arrive.

The themes of most kōwaka can be found in the romantic war chronicles and historical romances, but the versions of the kōwaka are in many instances embellished with Buddhistic sequences not found in the others. The frequent allusions to the esoteric sects of Buddhism suggest that the kōwaka texts may have been written by persons who were associated closely with Tendai or Shingon Buddhism, as *Beowulf* was written by a Christian scribe. Here we may recall the tradition that Mononoi Naoaki created the kōwaka when he was a youth living in the headquarters of the Tendai Sect on Mount Hiei. The relative abundance of such sequences might in itself be considered a structural peculiarity of the kōwaka. If we compare the story of the kōwaka *Mongaku* with the accounts of the Buddhist monk Mongaku in either the *Tale of the Heike* or the *Rise and Fall of Gempei*,[8] we see that the version of the kōwaka contains an original Buddhist-miracle sequence and, additionally, the working of a Buddhistic curse. The kōwaka *Atsumori,* unlike the versions of the romantic war chronicles,[9] describes Kumagae's religious life at length and depicts Mount Kōya, the headquarters of Shingon Buddhism. Buddhist curses are mentioned frequently in medieval literature, but such a detailed description of esoteric rituals as seen in *Izumi's Fortress* is unique.

Literary devices that are conventions in most traditional forms of Japanese prose literature are employed also in the kōwaka librettos. Among them, the *michiyuki,* a lyrical description of travel composed largely in a poetic meter of alternating five- and seven-mora phrases, is particularly favored. The michiyuki in *Atsumori,* of Kumagae's journey from Kyoto to Mount Kōya, is a delightful description of the famous sights of Kyoto, of scenic wonders along the route of travel through present-day Osaka and Wakayama prefectures, and, finally, of the spacious temple grounds on Mount Kōya. The best example of a michiyuki in the kōwaka is found in *Koshigoe.* It is an extended passage depicting the journey of the victorious Yoshitsune and the Heike captives, who are being led from Kyoto along the Eastern Sea Highway (*Tōkaidō*) to Kamakura. This brief excerpt will illustrate how the various technical devices—here, alliteration, the pivot (*kake-kotoba*), and associated words (*engo*)—are often compressed into a relatively few lines:

Nani to naru mi to	Whither my sorrowing person? "It is Narumi!"
kiku kara ni	As I hear this,
isobe no nami ni	The waves of the surf
sode nurashi	Moisten my sleeves.
Mikawa no kuni ni	When we enter
irinureba	The province of Mikawa
Yatsuhashi ni	And come upon
sashikakari . . .	Yatsuhashi . . .[10]

Naru mi (literally, "my [sorrowing] person shall become") is a pivot phrase that functions homonymically as Narumi, the place name; it links with the phrase preceding it in one meaning, and with the phrase following it in another. *Mikawa* (literally, "three rivers") and *Yatsuhashi* (literally, "eight bridges") are both proper nouns but are lyrically associated through their reference to numbers. "Moistened sleeves" is a timeworn image of sadness.

Although michiyuki passages in kōwaka are composed largely in a poetic form of alternating lines of five and seven morae, on the whole the meter is not so completely regular, nor the expressions so lyrical, as in michiyuki found in nō and jōruri texts. Such poetic passages as the "song of the four seasons" in *Atsumori* and the following poem in *Shizuka,* a similar eulogy of the seasons, are rather exceptional in the kōwaka:

Haru no iro wa	Blue-green is
aokeredo	The hue of spring;
nani tote hana wa	But flowers shall
kurenai no	Be tinged with the hue
iro ni wa idete	Of crimson:
hirakuran.	Then may they blossom.
Natsu no iro wa	Because red
akakereba	Is the hue of summer,
teru hi mo yagate	The radiant sun must, before long,
gokunetsu su.	Turn searing.
Aki no iro wa	The hue of autumn
urei nite	Is one of sorrow,
mushi no naku ne wa	So vivid
kotowari ya.	In the insects' cries.
Fuyu sarinureba	Should winter pass, [we may fete]
nehan nite	Nirvana [Day],
yuki furu yama wa	[Though] the mountains will be so white
shirotae no.	With fallen snow.[11]

Metrical passages are particularly conspicuous in the kōwaka, inasmuch as the main body of the text seldom continues in meter for long. The following passage in prose from *Izumi's Fortress* may give the reader a better idea of the general tone and style of the kōwaka:

Tadahira, having exhausted his arrows, leaped down nimbly from the gate tower and bared his weapon, and husband and wife stormed out together with blades flailing. Because Tadahira's ability was already known, the foes scattered as do leaves before a tempest, and no one dared face him. Those who fled he drove to bay. He hacked off both legs of some, and they fell prostrate; others he slashed down the center of their helmets, cleaving them like Chinese bamboo, and they fell to either side. While twenty-seven horsemen among the bold and hardy warriors were being cut down by Tadahira, seven or eight horsemen, all good warriors, were cut down to the ground by his wife. They inflicted grave injuries or minor wounds on the remaining warriors and scattered them in all directions. Then husband and wife, hand in hand, withdrew quietly to their own lines. Truly it was a feat not of ordinary mortals.[12]

Though passages may be melodically intoned, only rarely are they composed in alternating five- and seven-mora lines, and even then only in part. Lyricism in most cases is not indicated explicitly by verse form or special poetic quality, but only implied by the presence of musical neumes and of labels indicating the melodic patterns to which the passages are to be set. Kōwaka texts were published during the Edo Period in the form of ordinary prose and circulated as tales for reading. These texts belie the real kōwaka to the extent that the absence of the format of the libretto results in the loss of much of the dramatic quality of the original text; for the communicating force of a passage is determined largely by the mode of its recitation. The *prefatory*, for instance, is ordinarily a phrase or a brief sentence that serves as a prelude to a longer melodic section. But the relative importance of the words is magnified by the sonority of the *prefatory* melody and the intense feeling with which it is sung. Even a statement as undistinguished as "he accepted" acquires dramatic significance by being segmented as a *prefatory* in the libretto. A comparison of the translations of *Atsumori* and *Izumi's Fortress* will illustrate this difference. *Atsumori* is a translation of a text written in ordinary prose, whereas the translation of *Izumi's Fortress* represents a kōwaka text in the form of a libretto for recitation. The various rhetorical figures, historical and literary allusions, and the metaphor and other literary devices which occur in the kōwaka are explained in the notes to the translations.

The literary historian who knows kōwaka texts only as tales for reading will surely find it difficult to regard them as ballads if the more formal identifying textual features of the ballad are missing. The fact that the kōwaka text is a libretto means that its expressive qualities can be fully apprehended only in performance. The pathos evoked by human utterance, the musical effect of the various modes and melodic patterns, the emphasis provided by the lone accompaniment of the drum—these are tonal colorings which supply a multiple veneer of aesthetic meaning to the kōwaka and lift the artistry of the contents far above what can be expressed solely through the written word. The real artistic significance of the kōwaka text can be realized and described only if the text is analyzed and evaluated in its essential form—as a libretto, which is merely one of several interdependent elements that constitute a composite representational art.

THE THEMES OF THE FIFTY LIBRETTOS

The kōwaka might best be described as a ballad-drama with librettos consisting of epic material. Most of the fifty extant texts are stories from the latter half of the twelfth century, the Heroic Age in Japanese history. The stories are generally episodic, but many of them—for instance, the twenty pieces treating the life, both historical and legendary, of the illustrious Genji general, Minamoto no Yoshitsune (1159–1189)—are parts of coherent series that have the quality of true epics.

In the early genealogical documents of the Kōwaka family we find the titles of the thirty-six standard pieces listed in groups of twelve "long," "medium," and "short" pieces. A survey of the thirty-six texts shows that the "long" pieces occupy fifteen or more pages in print (in the *Kōwaka bukyoku shū*), the "medium" pieces between seven and fifteen, and the "short" pieces seven pages or less. Applying this criterion to the other texts, we find that the entire repertoire of fifty pieces can be classified into thirteen long, nineteen medium, and eighteen short pieces. But there is no correlation between the length of a kōwaka text and its literary content, with the one exception that all four "propitious" pieces are short. A propitious piece is one which relates an auspicious occurrence in legend or mythology—for instance, the creation myth of Japan.

Categorizing the texts by the historical periods in which the stories are set, we find that the kōwaka repertoire deals rather exclusively with the years surrounding the Gempei War. Forty of the pieces are set in the brief historical period encompassing the years between 1160 and 1193, and the events described are generally related to members of the Heike and Genji clans. In addition to the twenty which treat the life of Yoshitsune, there are seven which concern the famed vendetta of the Soga brothers and thirteen which touch upon various aspects of the struggle between the Genji and the Heike. Of the remaining ten kōwaka, one is set in the mythological era, eight in various periods between the seventh and sixteenth centuries, and one in China of the third century B.C.

The Japanese are familiar with many of the stories told in the kōwaka, and even children can recount the exploits of Yoshitsune and the Soga brothers. These stories are a part of the reservoir of historical and legendary tales that make up the epic material of the Japanese, and they are alluded to time and again both in literature and in history. Their themes have inspired many playwrights in a later age to create their greatest dramas. In the following synopses of the fifty extant kōwaka, the twenty "Yoshitsune" pieces are listed in the chronological sequence of the episodes described, and the introductory historical sketch of Yoshitsune may provide the reader with the background information he needs in order to see the twenty episodes as parts of an epic series. The seven "Soga" pieces are similarly presented. The other thirteen pieces treating this historical period are somewhat varied in theme and are listed in the chronological sequence of the episodes. For variant titles, other works which are related thematically to the kōwaka, and mentions of the themes in historical sources, the reader is referred to the Notes at the end of the text.

THE "YOSHITSUNE" PIECES

Minamoto no Yoshitsune is probably the most popular figure in all of Japanese history. He is the apotheosis of the valiant and faithful warrior. Invincible in the field, he leads his army in an unbroken series of brilliant victories over the foes of his lord, his half-brother Yoritomo. His life in many ways parallels that of the Cid, the famed Campeador of Spain's national epic. But unlike the Cid, who was "born in a good hour," Yoshitsune is the tragic hero whose star is ill-fated. The very source of his fame —his brilliance as a military commander and his personal daring as a warrior—is his tragic fate. His renown became a source of annoyance and, eventually, of resentment and hatred to the jealous Yoritomo.

The many legends about Yoshitsune have been retold as fables, nō dramas, kōwaka, and kabuki and puppet plays, and have delighted the Japanese during the many centuries since the Kamakura Period. The *Tale of the Heike* and the *Rise and Fall of Gempei* present detailed accounts of his martial exploits; but they are romantic war chronicles, and many of the episodes they contain represent popular legendary accounts or romanticized elaborations of known historical incidents. The unadorned facts of his feats are recorded in reliable historical sources for this era, the *Azuma kagami* (*Mirror of the East*), which is believed to have been recorded by an official scribe of the Kamakura Shogunate, and the *Gyokuyō* (*Gem Leaves*), the diary of Kujō Kanezane (1149–1207) which describes this era as seen through the eyes of the most influential member of the court aristocracy in Kyoto.[13]

The *Annals of Yoshitsune* is the principal source for accounts of a more legendary nature and consists mostly of descriptions of his childhood and of his later years, when he was hunted relentlessly by Yoritomo. As was noted in the introductory chapter, the *Annals,* which was written perhaps some two centuries after Yoshitsune's death, is more a historical romance than a biography. It is a blend of facts and legends but nonetheless presents an image of Yoshitsune which is as real, perhaps, as that of any historical figure who was slighted by chroniclers but whose greatness excited the imagination of posterity.

Yoshitsune was born in 1159, the year of the war known as the Heiji Disturbance, in which the Heike and the Genji were the contending principals. Minamoto no Yoshitomo (1123–1160), the father of Yoritomo and Yoshitsune, was killed in the aftermath of the war. The Genji heir Yoritomo, then in his teens, was spared and sent to live in Izu Province. The infant Yoshitsune was spared, it is told, only because the beautiful Tokiwa, mother of the three youngest of Yoshitomo's nine sons, consented to become a concubine of Taira no Kiyomori, the leader of the victorious Heike.

Yoshitsune, or Ushiwakamaru as he was called in his childhood, was sent to a temple outside Kyoto to live as a devotee to the Buddha, for he would be a potential threat to the Heike so long as he remained in the secular world. When he was sixteen, he slipped away from Kyoto and traveled north to Hiraizumi in Mutsu Province. There he was received warmly by Fujiwara Hidehira (1121–1187), whose vast domain extended over the northern one-third of Honshū.[14] He had, in the meantime, been initiated into adulthood and taken the name Minamoto no Kurō Yoshitsune. His title name, Kurō (literally, "ninth male"), indicated that he was the ninth son of Yoshitomo. Back in Kyoto soon after this, the youthful Yoshitsune bested the militant monk Benkei in personal combat. Even with the Herculean strength for which he is fabled, Benkei was helpless to cope with the fencing skill and agility of his young adversary; he surrendered and became Yoshitsune's vassal. The story of Yoshitsune's stirring conquest of Benkei may be entirely legendary, but it is described at great length in the *Annals,* and it has been retold in countless other forms.[15]

When Yoritomo took up arms against the Heike in 1180, Yoshitsune was in Hiraizumi as a guest of Fujiwara Hidehira. He hastened south to Kamakura and offered his assistance to his brother, whom he met then for the first time. Yoshitsune's first test as an army commander came in a war not against the Heike, but against his own cousin, Minamoto no Yoshinaka (1154–1184). Yoshinaka took the offensive against the Heike in 1183 with a small army of robust warriors from the mountainous region of Kiso in central Honshū, and he easily wrested the capital from the hands of the Heike. He then ruled supreme in Kyoto, but the presence there of this boorish provincial commander proved to be more noxious to the Imperial Court than did that of his Heike predecessors; and the court now turned to Yoritomo to rid the capital of this new scourge. Yoshitsune was given command of the Kamakura forces. In a display of daring strategy and inspiring leadership, he sent his 25,000 mounted warriors in a near foolhardy charge across the surging Uji River, and Yoshinaka's defenses crumbled before the spirited onrush.[16]

While the Genji were occupied thus in a war among themselves, the Heike were able to rebuild their strength in western Japan and push back to within forty miles of Kyoto. Yoshitsune acted swiftly, however, and dealt the Heike a crushing blow at Ichinotani, where their defenses had seemed impregnable. This was only three weeks after he had defeated Yoshinaka. The Imperial Court at that time conferred rewards on Genji leaders who had participated in the recent campaigns. The rewards given were in accordance with recommendations made by Yoritomo, but, strangely, Yoritomo had made no provision for Yoshitsune.[17] The Imperial Court was, nonetheless, sympathetic to Yoshitsune and awarded him a minor official post in a token gesture of recognition.

The fact that Yoshitsune accepted the post without first consulting him gave Yoritomo the pretext he needed to drop his brother from his good graces. The *Azuma kagami* states:

A messenger from Master Gen Kurō [Yoshitsune] arrived and stated the following: "On the sixth [of this month] Yoshitsune received an imperial mandate appointing him a lesser lieutenant in the Left Gate Guard. He had not sought the post. It was indicated to him, however, that the imperial favor was extended him as a matter of course since his frequent meritorious services could not be ignored; he was, therefore, unable to refuse it." This was a flagrant violation of the wishes of the Military Guard [Yoritomo]. . . . [Yoritomo suspects that] this will not be the only time when his wishes will be violated [by Yoshitsune].[18]

Although there was no doubt as to Yoshitsune's ability to command an army, or because of it perhaps, Yoritomo entrusted the leadership of the Genji army to another brother, Noriyori, and he assigned Yoshitsune to serve in Kyoto as his deputy. But when Noriyori failed to make progress in his campaign against the Heike, Yoshitsune was ordered to resume his duties as army commander. He quickly assembled a small fleet at the port of Watanabe in the Yodo River estuary and proceeded to plot the campaign personally, disregarding the advice of Kajiwara Kagetoki, who was the senior member of the staff assigned to him by Yoritomo.

The brilliance of Yoshitsune's generalship was the principal factor in the quick rout of the Heike at Yashima and the final victory in the sea battle at Dannoura, where nearly all the Heike who were prominent in the Court society of Kyoto only two years earlier were killed, drowned, or taken captive. Having achieved this triumph, Yoshitsune was surprised to learn that Yoritomo had once again turned against him. He was forbidden to enter Kamakura and even denied an audience with Yoritomo that he might answer to the charges lodged against him. From this time until he found refuge in the domain of Fujiwara Hidehira in 1187, Yoshitsune's life was in constant danger. The story of his long and perilous journey to northern Japan is Odyssean in many respects. The account of his many narrow escapes, his betrayal by the sons of his protector, and his tragic death fill the latter half of the *Annals of Yoshitsune*.

1. *Fushimi Tokiwa* (*Tokiwa at Fushimi*) is one of four kōwaka in which the main character is Yoshitsune's mother, Tokiwa. In 1160, the year after the Heiji Turbulence, Tokiwa leaves Kyoto in search of a haven for her three sons, for the Heike will surely not spare the sons of Yoshitomo. Unable to continue because of a snowstorm, Tokiwa stops at a village near the Fushimi district of Kyoto and asks for lodging at the house of an aged couple. The couple refuses at first, for there will be reprisals if it is known that they sheltered remnants of the Genji, but they are moved by pity and provide Tokiwa and her children with lodging. Tokiwa is visited there by five lowly servant women of the neighborhood. They have come to have a look at the beautiful lady from the capital, for Tokiwa's beauty is so outstanding that, with two others, she has been selected from among a thousand women to serve in the Imperial Palace. The five women are natives of five different provinces, and they entertain Tokiwa by singing and dancing the folk dances of their home provinces.[19]

2. *Nabiki Tokiwa* (*The Submission of Tokiwa*) is a sequel to *Fushimi Tokiwa*. A Kyoto merchant brings news to Tokiwa, who is living in Yamato, that Taira no Kiyomori is holding her mother captive and torturing her daily in order to learn the whereabouts of the three sons she had presented to Minamoto no Yoshitomo. Tokiwa does not question the moral precept which dictates that she must sacrifice her children in order to save her

mother. She returns to Kyoto and surrenders her sons to the Heike. Now Kiyomori becomes enamored of Tokiwa and seeks to win her affections, but Tokiwa abhors the thought of being possessed by the man who caused her husband's death. Yet she submits to Kiyomori, for by doing so she is able to save the lives of her sons.[20]

3. *Tokiwa mondō* (*Tokiwa's Disputation*) tells of an event which occurs some five years later. Ushiwakamaru, or Ushiwaka for short, is then seven years of age, and Tokiwa decides to send him to live at a Buddhist temple in order that he may prepare for the priesthood. Kurama Temple in the mountains north of Kyoto is recommended to her, and Tokiwa visits the temple one day. She enters a chapel, sits down on a platform which is reserved for only the most exalted priests, and intones the sutra. The superintendent of the temple sees this and castigates her for having dared even to enter the hallowed chapel, for women were not allowed in the temple. Tokiwa disputes the Buddhist rationale and delivers a feminist tirade, extolling womanhood and motherhood.[21]

4. *Miraiki* (*Chronicle of the Future*) is the first of the kōwaka in which Yoshitsune is the main character. While he is living at Kurama Temple, Ushiwaka is befriended by a *tengu,* a supernatural anthropomorphic being who inhabits the nearby mountains. The *tengu* teaches him the secrets of warfare and then reveals to him the auspicious future that awaits the Genji. He advises Ushiwaka to adopt the name Kurō Yoshitsune in adulthood and predicts that he and his brother Noriyori will lead the clan to victory over the Heike. The *tengu* warns Ushiwaka to be cautious lest he incur the enmity of Yoritomo or be victimized by the insidious schemes of Kajiwara Kagetoki.[22]

5. *Fue no maki* (*The Scroll* [*Containing the Tale*] *of the Flute*) is a propitious piece which tells the legend of a flute given to Ushiwaka by his mother, Tokiwa. A very long time ago, when the revered founder of Shingon Buddhism, Kūkai, was studying in China, he had cast a length of bamboo into the sea. Later, having returned to Japan, Kūkai found that very piece of bamboo

drifting by the seashore of his home province in Shikoku. The *Aoba,* or "Green Leaf," which has come into Ushiwaka's possession, is one of the three flutes made by Kūkai from that piece of bamboo. It has strange powers and protects its owner from danger and evil. Ushiwaka is delighted to be told the legend of *Aoba* from its previous owner; he writes it down in a scroll, and he presents the scroll as an offering to the Kurama Temple.[23]

6. *Kurama-de* (*Leaving Kurama*) describes Ushiwaka's uproarious departure from the capital. In 1175 Ushiwaka is warned by Tokiwa of the Heike's plot to dispose of all remnants of the Genji. Having overheard a traveling merchant, Kichiji, describe the power and wealth of Fujiwara Hidehira in northern Japan, Ushiwaka decides to join Kichiji's party and visit the Fujiwara domain. At Matsuzaka, not far from Kyoto, he encounters the traveling party of a Heike henchman named Sekihara Yoichi. When Sekihara's horse prances in a puddle and splashes Ushiwaka, Sekihara not only refuses to apologize but even orders his men to beat the youth for daring to accuse him of an impropriety. Angered by this insolence, Ushiwaka kills or maims all the men and humiliates Sekihara by trapping him in a water hole and beating him with the flat of the sword.[24]

7. *Eboshi-ori* (*The Fold of the Eboshi*), one of the longer kōwaka, combines two fabled episodes in Yoshitsune's early life— that of the unique *eboshi* which he orders from a hatmaker and that of his encounter with the feared bandit, Kumasaka Chōhan. During his journey northward, Ushiwaka stops at Kagami, some forty miles out of Kyoto, and visits a hatmaker to order an *eboshi* that he will wear in the passing rite for adulthood. He specifies that the top of the hat is to be folded to the left. The hatmaker complies, although he is indignant that a servant boy should wear the left-folded *eboshi,* which is reserved by tradition for the Minamoto. After Ushiwaka leaves, the hatmaker's wife notices that the sword which Ushiwaka has left in payment for the hat is an heirloom of the Genji. She knows such things, for her brother, Kamada Masakiyo, was a trusted vassal of Ushiwaka's father, Yoshitomo. Ushiwaka is formally "capped," or initiated into adulthood, and he adopts the name Minamoto no Kurō

Yoshitsune. The party of the merchant Kichiji arrives in Ōhaka in Mino Province and lodges there for the night. The band of Kumasaka Chōhan raids their lodging in the deep of night, but Yoshitsune has been forewarned in a dream and is prepared for them. Singlehandedly he scatters the bandits and slays Kumasaka.[25]

8. *Yamanaka Tokiwa* (*Tokiwa at Yamanaka*) relates the tragic death of Yoshitsune's mother. In the spring of 1175, Tokiwa leaves the capital in the company of a maid and embarks on a journey to Mutsu Province in order to join Yoshitsune. She travels as far as Yamanaka in Mino Province, where she and her maid are murdered by a band of robbers. Yoshitsune, in the meanwhile, is hastening to the capital, for his dreams have brought forebodings of Tokiwa's fate. On the night Tokiwa is murdered, he is lodged only eight miles away. He arrives in Yamanaka the next day only to learn of her tragedy, and he avenges her death by killing the entire band of robbers.[26]

9. *Koshigoe* takes its title from a place name in the suburb of Kamakura. This is the first of twelve pieces which treat events in Yoshitsune's later, tragic years. After the destruction of the Heike at Dannoura in 1185, Yoshitsune journeys to Kamakura in eager anticipation of rejoining his brother, Yoritomo. Yoritomo is at first overjoyed by the news, but Kajiwara Kagetoki plants suspicion in his mind with regard to Yoshitsune's loyalty. Kajiwara has quarreled fiercely with Yoshitsune over the launching of the Genji fleet prior to the Battle of Yashima, and he is fearful that Yoshitsune will take revenge on him. As a result, although Yoshitsune has come as far as Koshigoe, he is forbidden to enter Kamakura. He sends an oath of loyalty to Yoritomo, but Kajiwara intercepts it. As a final resort, he has his faithful vassal Benkei compose a letter of appeal. Benkei is praised by all for his skill with words.[27]

10. *Horikawa yo-uchi* (*The Night Attack on the Horikawa* [*Mansion*]) tells of the first active attempt made on Yoshitsune's life. Late in the year 1185, Yoshitsune is back in Kyoto and residing in a mansion in the Horikawa district. With all of western

Japan rallying to his support, he has become a formidable political power. It is Kajiwara again who warns Yoritomo of treasonable intent on the part of Yoshitsune. As a result the militant monk Shōzon is dispatched to Kyoto on a mission to kill Yoshitsune. Once in Kyoto, Shōzon is detected immediately and brought before Yoshitsune for questioning, but he is realeased when he swears an oath of loyalty to Yoshitsune and explains that he is merely leading a group of pilgrims to the Kumano Shrine. On that night Shōzon and his men attack the Horikawa Mansion. Yoshitsune is alerted by his mistress, the beautiful Shizuka, and the two hold off the assailants until Yoshitsune's vassals arrive. The attacking force is routed, and Shōzon is captured and executed.[28]

11. *Shikoku-ochi* (*Escape to Shikoku*) describes the first episode in the Odyssean wanderings of Yoshitsune. Toward the end of 1185, Yoshitsune leaves Kyoto with two hundred warriors bound for the island of Shikoku. He intends to establish his headquarters there and become the master of western Japan. His band sets sail from Osaka Bay aboard eight ships, but as they approach the Shikoku coast, they are met with a tempest raised by the spirits of the Heike who died in the Battle of Yashima. Yoshitsune's ship is blown back to Ashiya and grounded in the shallows. Here they are attacked by warriors of the local lord, for it is known that the government at Kamakura has ordered the chastisement of Yoshitsune; but Benkei and the other stalwarts defeat them handily.[29]

12. *Shizuka* is the tragedy of Yoshitsune's beautiful mistress. After parting with Yoshitsune, Shizuka lives in hiding in Kyoto, but she is betrayed by her mother's maid, who is covetous of the reward posted for her capture. But her only reward for leading Kajiwara to Shizuka's hideaway is death by drowning, for even Kajiwara is appalled by her wickedness. Shizuka is taken to Kamakura. She is carrying a child at that time, and Kajiwara urges Yoritomo to have the fetus torn out lest a son of Yoshitsune come into this world; but she is spared this cruelty through the intercession of Yoritomo's wife. She gives birth to a boy, but the infant is killed immediately. Shizuka's fame as a shirabyōshi

dancer is such that she is prevailed upon to dance at the Hachi-man Shrine. The performance is attended by Yoritomo and his court, and her singing and dancing is acclaimed by all. Although she is rewarded with a grant of land, she donates the land to the local temples and shrines and returns to Kyoto.[30]

13. *Togashi* relates the celebrated episode of the "subscription tablet" (*kanjinchō*), an episode which is very frequently drama-tized today on the stage of the traditional Japanese theater. The militant monk Benkei is the central character in this episode. In 1187, Yoshitsune is traveling northward in the company of twelve loyal vassals in order to seek a haven in the domain of Fujiwara Hidehira. They are disguised as a band of mountain-priests (*yamabushi*) allegedly on a mission to solicit subscriptions, or pledges of donations, for the Tōdaiji monastery in Nara. Traveling along the western seacoast so as to avoid Kamakura, they come to Ataka in Kaga Province. They learn that the local lord, Togashi, has been forewarned by the government at Kama-kura that Yoshitsune and his party may be traveling through his territory in the guise of mountain-priests. Benkei goes to Togashi's mansion alone to test whether or not they would be permitted passage through Ataka. Togashi is convinced that the powerful looking mountain-priest who confronts him is the renowned Benkei. When Benkei persists in his claim that he is an emissary of Tōdaiji, Togashi demands that he produce a subscription tablet. Benkei produces a blank scroll and pretends to read from it. With great eloquence, he improvises a message that is superb in its literary elegance and remarkable for the erudition it re-flects. His feat is that of no ordinary mortal.[31]

14. *Oi-sagashi* (*Search of the Shoulder-trunk*) is a sequel to *Togashi*. Having allayed Togashi's suspicion, Benkei rejoins Yoshitsune and the others. They travel up the coast to the port of Naoe in Echigo Province, whence they will continue by sea. The inhabitants become suspicious of Yoshitsune's identity and demand to inspect the contents of the shoulder-trunks the men are carrying. They find, in addition to the usual paraphernalia of mountain-priests, a suit of armor and finery belonging to Yo-shitsune's wife. They are not satisfied with Yoshitsune's explana-

tions and become exceedingly menacing, but they disperse when they meet with the boisterous fury of Benkei. Once at sea, the ship is imperiled by a storm raised by ghosts of the Heike. Benkei soothes the dead by discoursing on the principles of salvation, and the storm subsides.[32]

15. *Yashima no ikusa (The Battle of Yashima)* continues the story of Yoshitsune's journey to Mutsu Province. Yoshitsune and his party, still in the guise of mountain-priests, are now nearing their destination. Seeking shelter one evening, they chance upon a dilapidated mansion and spend the night there as guests of an aged nun. The nun is the mother of the Satō brothers, Tsuginobu and Tadanobu, who have died fighting for Yoshitsune. She suspects that her guest is Yoshitsune in disguise, and this causes her to reminisce over her two lost sons and to grieve. Taking compassion on her, Benkei tells her about the Battle of Yashima in 1185, how her son Tsuginobu used his own body as a shield and took the arrow that was intended for Yoshitsune, and how the younger Tadanobu fought valiantly to prevent the Heike from taking his brother's head as a trophy. He also relates how Tadanobu died heroically in the mountains of Yoshino, holding off Heike pursuers while Yoshitsune escaped. Yoshitsune in the end reveals his identity and consoles her.[33]

16. *Okayama* serves as an epilogue to the previous piece. Yoshitsune is now residing in Hiraizumi under the protection of Fujiwara Hidehira. The mother of the Satō brothers wishes that the surviving sons of Tsuginobu and Tadanobu could don the *eboshi* in the presence of Yoshitsune. She brings the youths to Yoshitsune, and he conducts the initiation rites and selects adulthood names for them. The mother, accompanied by her sons' widows, makes a pilgrimage through all fifty-four counties of Mutsu Province. The three women then settle in a place named Okayama, where they live out their lives.[34]

17. *Kiyoshige* relates the misadventure of two of Yoshitsune's vassals. In 1188 Yoshitsune decides to circulate a message among the various daimyos in order to enlist their political support. For his emissaries he selects Suruga no Jirō Kiyoshige and Ise no

Saburō Yoshimori, and the two men leave Mutsu Province disguised as mountain-priests. After their task in Musashi Province is completed, Kiyoshige decides to view the famed sights of Kamakura before continuing the mission. When his partner objects, he proceeds to Kamakura alone. Kiyoshige's death is a tragicomedy. His hat is blown off by a sudden gust of wind, and his samurai hairdo gives away his disguise. The bizarre sight of a mountain-priest chasing a wind-blown hat, with one hand outstretched and the other covering his pate, attracts the attention of the Kamakura warriors; and Kiyoshige dies fighting them. Yoshimori proceeds to Kyoto, and he also dies fighting when his disguise is broken.[35]

18. *Izumigajō (Izumi's Fortress)*, one of the two kōwaka presented in translation, depicts the tragedy of fratricide among the sons of Fujiwara Hidehira due to divided loyalties to Yoshitsune. When Kajiwara Kagetoki learns that Yoshitsune and Yoritomo may possibly be reconciled, he attempts to curse Yoshitsune to death. The curse affects Hidehira instead. Before he dies, Hidehira has his five sons swear an oath that they will remain faithful to Yoshitsune. Soon after Hidehira's death, his sons receive a message from Yoritomo ordering them to slay Yoshitsune; they are promised five provinces as a reward. Of the five sons, only the third, Izumi no Saburō, abides by the oath of fidelity and refuses to be swayed by Yoritomo's enticement. As a prelude to their treachery against Yoshitsune, the brothers attack Izumi's Fortress. Izumi, at the urging of his wife, kills his two infant sons lest his concern for their lives deter his resolution. He and his wife battle gallantly and in the end take their own lives.[36]

19. *Takadachi* is a glorified account of Yoshitsune's last battle. In the spring of 1189, a small force of some three hundred horsemen arrive in Hiraizumi. It is an army sent from Kamakura to help Fujiwara Yasuhira execute his treacherous plot against Yoshitsune. On the eve of the attack on his residence, the Takadachi Mansion, Yoshitsune gathers his eight remaining vassals together for a final feast. There are to be nine men fighting by his side on the morrow, however. The ninth man is Suzuki no Saburō Shigeie, who arrives that night after a journey of seventy-five days from

his native Kii Province. When Yasuhira's army attacks the following day, the nine warriors fight valiantly against overwhelming odds. Finally there is only Benkei left. He bids farewell to Yoshitsune and, although horribly wounded, slays another score of men and scatters the enemy. It is some time before the attackers dare to approach him again, only to discover that his erect body is lifeless.[37]

20. *Fukumijō* (*The Mouthed Letter*) constitutes the final chapter and epilogue to the story of Yoshitsune's life. As the battle at Takadachi nears its end, the only ones left are Yoshitsune, his wife and infant son,[38] and his wife's manservant, Kanefusa. Yoshitsune takes the blade, but only after he has seen Kanefusa kill his wife and son. The faithful Kanefusa then sets fire to the mansion and dies in the blaze. When Yoshitsune's head is delivered to Kamakura and brought before Yoritomo, a letter is found in its mouth. It is addressed to Yoritomo. Through this letter Yoshitsune protests his selfless endeavors on behalf of the Genji and accuses Kajiwara of having caused the injustices meted him. Yoritomo can only shed tears of regret. Kajiwara and his sons flee from Kamakura, and they all come to miserable ends.[39]

THE "SOGA" PIECES

The vendetta of the Soga brothers is famed as the first of the "Three Great Vendettas" in Japanese history.* On the twenty-eighth day of the Fifth Month, 1193, Soga Jūrō Sukenari and his brother, Gorō Tokimune, slew Kudō Suketsune to avenge their father's death eighteen years earlier. The killing took place inside the encampment of the Shogun Yoritomo, who was conducting a wild-game hunt in the plains below Mount Fuji. That the event created a great stir at the time is attested by the fact that the *Azuma kagami* describes the incident at some length; the chronicler has noted the great admiration with which the deed was regarded, even by the Shogun himself.[40]

The Soga brothers were not important political figures, and

---

* The others are those carried out by the forty-seven samurai retainers of the lord of the Akō Feudatory in 1702 and by Watanabe Kazuma with the assistance of the master swordsman Araki Mataemon in 1634.

their names do not appear elsewhere in chronicles of that era. As with Yoshitsune, however, the story of their lives was transmitted through many legends and tales, and sometime during the fourteenth century the various popular traditions were woven into a lengthy historical romance, the *Soga monogatari*. The biographical sketch which follows is based entirely on this romance.[41]

When their father, Kawazu Sukeyasu, was murdered by henchmen of his cousin, Kudō Suketsune, in the autumn of 1175, the Soga brothers were mere children, five and three years of age. They were known at that time by their childhood names, Ichiman and Hakoō. Young as they were, the boys vowed that they would some day avenge the death of their father; and the remainder of their short lives was to be dedicated solely to this purpose.

Kudō had some justification for his hatred of Kawazu and, particularly, of Kawazu's father, Itō Sukechika, who was the lord of Itō Manor in Izu Province. The Itō Manor belonged originally to Kudō's father; but when he died, Itō took advantage of Kudō's minority to usurp the manor. Kudō petitioned the Imperial Court in an attempt to recover his patrimony. Kudō's act did not constitute a serious transgression of the social customs of his time, but it made him liable to the vengeance of his victim's survivors. The code of the vendetta required only that a killing—whether or not it was justified mattered little—be avenged, and the avenger was to be praised for his dedicated loyalty to the deceased.

The mother of Ichiman and Hakoō soon remarried for the sake of her sons, and the brothers acquired the surname of their stepfather, Soga Sukenobu. Sukenobu was kindly and gentle and treated the two as though they were his true sons, and the brothers were now exhorted by their mother to forsake the vendetta lest their stepfather be caused to suffer. The youths, nonetheless, continued secretly to train themselves in the arts of the samurai.

Kudō could find no peace as long as Kawazu's sons were alive. Recalling that Itō Sukechika had been put to death by Yoritomo, Kudō once suggested to Yoritomo that the brothers might some day try to avenge the death of their grandfather. Yoritomo knew how dangerous the vengeful could be, for his own success was due to his determination to avenge the fallen Genji; and he promptly ordered their execution. Many of his vassals, even the dour Kajiwara, pleaded for their lives, but Yoritomo was adamant. The youths were spared in the end only because of the intercession of Hatakeyama Shigetada, whom Yoritomo respected highly.

The mother, frightened by this incident, decided to separate the brothers; for they would continue to contemplate perilous ventures so long as they remained together. And so the younger Hakoō was sent to the Hakone Shrine to prepare for entry into the Buddhist priesthood.* He left Hakone some years later when it became apparent that he would have to take the tonsure, and he became a full-fledged samurai by undergoing the capping ceremony as his brother had done some years earlier. But he was disowned by his mother for his disobedience. The brothers were now known as Jūrō and Gorō. The elder Jūrō was an exemplar among samurai—reserved, circumspect, and learned, yet skilled in the martial arts. The younger Gorō was his opposite— boisterous, quick-tempered, and with brute strength. In a contest of muscular prowess, he proved himself at least the equal of Asahina Saburō, reputedly the strongest man of this era.

When the Shogun Yoritomo staged a massive hunt in the foothills of Mount Fuji in 1193, the brothers found their opportunity to meet Kudō without his usual horde of guards. Before they departed for the site of the hunt, the brothers visited their mother for the last time. Then, armed with swords given them by the superintendent of the Hakone Shrine, they entered the hunting area to stalk Kudō. He proved to be an elusive prey, but with the covert aid of the many who were sympathetic to their cause, they were able to find his quarters. They attacked Kudō at night and slew him. Their ends attained, the brothers then crossed swords with Yoritomo's men and wounded many of them before Jūrō was finally cut down and Gorō taken captive.

On the following morning Gorō was interrogated before Yoritomo, and his story of the hardships and suffering which he and

---

* The deity of the Hakone Shrine was a product of Dual Shinto, in which Japanese Kami were regarded as local manifestations of Buddha; hence the apparent incongruity of Buddhist monks in residence in a Shinto shrine.

Jūrō endured in order to consummate the vendetta elicited the sympathy of everyone. He was executed, however, for the maiming of other innocent men could not be condoned. The Soga brothers were enshrined in the Soga-Hachiman Shrine, which was built at the foot of Mount Fuji by orders of Yoritomo. The day on which the vendetta took place, the twenty-eighth day of the Fifth Month, has been commemorated annually at that shrine.

21. *Kirikane Soga* (*The Reluctance to Slay the Soga* [*Brothers*]) relates an episode in the lives of the Soga brothers which occurred when Ichiman was eleven, and Hakoō was nine. One day when Yoritomo is reminiscing about the unsympathetic treatment he received at the hands of Itō Sukechika during his days in exile, Kudō Suketsune informs him that Itō's grandsons are being reared by Soga Sukenobu and warns that they may some day threaten his life. Yoritomo is alarmed and immediately orders their execution. The sight of the two youths arouses such pity that the chief executioner is reluctant to see them beheaded. He rides back to Kamakura and exhorts Yoritomo to spare their lives. He is joined by others at court, but to no avail. Finally Hatakeyama Shigetada, who is held in high esteem by all Genji, comes to court in order to plead for their release, but Yoritomo will not relent. He is vindictive, for the hated Itō had not only forced his wife to leave him and marry another man, but even murdered his infant son. Only when Hatakeyama threatens to take his own life rather than see such an injustice come to pass does Yoritomo consent to their release.[42]

22. *Gembuku Soga* (*The Adulthood Rites of Soga*) treats two themes—Hakoō's chance meeting with Kudō and his initiation into adulthood as a samurai. In the early spring of 1185 Yoritomo comes to worship at the Hakone Shrine, where Hakoō is serving as an apprentice monk. Hakoō knows that Kudō Suketsune, whom he has never seen, is among Yoritomo's entourage. He has someone point Kudō out to him, and he studies the face of the man who has killed his father. Kudō recognizes the son of Kawazu. He addresses Hakoō with a feigned tenderness and gives him a sword as a token of "his affection." Hakoō restrains his urge to attack Kudō then, for he is only thirteen and could not

possibly succeed in such an attempt. One day three years after that, Hakoō learns that his mother has come to Hakone in order to arrange his formal entry into the priesthood. Should Hakoō take the tonsure, the brothers realize, they can no longer hope to avenge their father's death. They leave Hakone secretly so that Hakoō may be initiated not into the priesthood but into adulthood as a samurai. They have Hōjō Tokimasa, who was a close friend of their father, conduct the initiation rites, and Hakoō is thenceforth to be known by the name of Soga no Gorō Tokimune.[43]

23. *Wada sakamori* (*Wada's Wine-feast*) is a spirited piece in which the contrasting personalities of Jūrō and Gorō are depicted vividly. After the brothers have agreed to attempt the revenge during the great hunt which will take place at the foothills of Mount Fuji during the Fifth Month of 1193, Jūrō goes alone to Oiso to bid farewell to his paramour, the beautiful Tora. While he is visiting her at her father's mansion, the famed Genji warrior Wada Yoshimori arrives there with his clansmen, and a lively party ensues. Tora joins the party reluctantly at Wada's insistence, but she ignores Wada and directs her attention only to Jūrō. Incensed by this affront, Wada abuses the gentle Jūrō. Just when trouble is about to begin, the powerful and belligerent Gorō arrives on the scene. He has been at home sharpening arrowheads but has somehow sensed that Jūrō is in difficulties. The Genji strongman, Asahina Saburō, grabs the hip plate on Gorō's suit of armor and tries to drag him into the party room, but Gorō stands firm. So strong are the two men that the hip plate is ripped apart. Gorō proceeds to intimidate Wada and his men by gesticulating menacingly and causes them to leave.[44]

24. *Kosode Soga* (*The Soga Brothers and the Kosode Shirt*) depicts the scene in which Gorō is reconciled with his mother. Before embarking on the vendetta, the Soga brothers go to visit their mother for the last time. They do not tell her about their plan. The mother has not seen Gorō from the time he violated her wishes by forsaking the priesthood. Jūrō appears before his mother alone to tell her that he is leaving for the Fuji foothills, and the mother gives him a *kosode* to protect him against the cold. Jūrō begs her to bestow a similar garment on Gorō, but she

refuses even to see him. But Gorō talks to her through a screen, speaking of his loneliness when he was sent away to Hakone as a child and of his misery in being estranged from his own mother, and she can no longer repress her own longings for her son. She forgives Gorō and gives him a *kosode*.[45]

25. *Tsurugi Sandan* (*Laud of the Sword*) tells the legend of a fabled sword used by Gorō. When the Soga brothers visit the superintendent of Hakone Shrine in order to bid him farewell, each is given a sword by him. The sword which Gorō receives is one of the two swords made in the early ninth century from the blade of a famed Indian halberd. The swords were named *Onikiri* "Demon-cutter" and *Kumokiri* "Spider-cutter" because Minamoto no Yorimitsu (tenth century) had used one of them to slay a demon, and the other to kill a monstrous spider. The spider-cutter was presented as an offering to the Kumano Shrine by Yoshitsune's grandfather. It later came into the hand of Yoshitsune, who called upon the sword's magical powers to destroy the Heike. Yoshitsune made an offering of the sword to the Hakone Shrine in 1185, when he went there to pray that he might be reconciled with Yoritomo.[46]

26. *Yo-uchi Soga* (*The Night Attack by the Soga*) is the climax to the story of the Soga brothers. All the warriors of the eastern provinces, some sixty-six thousand strong, are participating in the great hunt on the plains below Mount Fuji. The brothers search the area frantically for Kudō. When at last they chance upon him, Jūrō is thrown from his horse, and their quarry rides off into the distance. At night as they search the various quarters, Jūrō is recognized by Kudō's child, Inubōmaru. He comes face to face with Kudō but hesitates to act, for he and Gorō have agreed that neither will act without the other. When he returns later with Gorō, Kudō is gone, and all seems lost. But a man comes to them secretly from their sympathizer, Hatakeyama Shigetada, and he leads them to Kudō's quarters. They awaken Kudō that he may defend himself and slay him as he draws his sword.[47]

27. *Jūbangiri* (*Slashing the Ten* [*Challengers*]) is the final

chapter in the lives of the Soga brothers. Gorō administers the *coup de grâce* to Kudō, using the very sword which Kudō had given to him many years earlier. The brothers accept the challenge of Genji warriors who are attracted by the commotion. They cut down nine men, but the tenth man slays Jūrō. Gorō, crazed with grief, dashes into the Shogun's quarters and is finally overpowered by several men and taken captive. He is questioned by Yoritomo the next day. As he recounts the story of the grief they have borne and of the many ordeals they have suffered, everyone is moved to sympathy. During the questioning, Kudō's son, Inubōmaru dashes up to Gorō and beats him with a fan; but Gorō takes compassion on him, for he has known the torment which now possesses Inubōmaru. Although Yoritomo decrees the death penalty for Gorō as required by his own laws, he listens willingly to pleas entered in Gorō's behalf; but Gorō is executed by his own choosing. The Soga brothers are enshrined at the foot of Mount Fuji and deified by posterity.[48]

THE "GEMPEI" PIECES

The following thirteen kōwaka do not, from the standpoint of theme, necessarily fall into a sequential pattern as do those pieces which treat Yoshitsune or the Soga brothers. Taken as a series, they might be compared to the loose strings of short stories that make up the less connected and coherent of the Icelandic Sagas. Some of the pieces recount well-known episodes in the Gempei War. Others describe situations, real or imaginary, which are set in the latter half of the twelfth century.

28. *Kamada* tells of the death of the Genji chieftain, Minamoto no Yoshitomo, in the aftermath of the Heiji Disturbance of 1159. Yoshitomo, fleeing from the Heike, arrives in the Osada Manor in Owari Province. He is accompanied by two stalwart vassals, Shibuya Kin'ōmaru and Kamada Masakiyo. Kamada's father-in-law is the manorial manager, Osada. The Heike tempt Osada into slaying Yoshitomo by offering him a reward of three provinces. Blinded by greed, Osada calls his five sons together to formulate his plot of betrayal. His third son, Senjō, is appalled to learn of this diabolical undertaking and enters the priesthood

when he fails to dissuade his father and brothers. In order first to eliminate his son-in-law, Kamada, Osada plies him with wine and kills him as he lies in a stupor. Kamada's wife is so grieved that she kills her children and then commits suicide. Osada's wife, too, kills herself in protesting against her husband's cruelty. Still Osada is not to be deterred. He tricks Yoshitomo into laying aside his arms by urging him to bathe; he surrounds him with two hundred warriors and slays him.[49]

29. *Ibuki* also treats the period immediately following the Heiji Disturbance. The young Yoritomo is fleeing Kyoto together with his father, Yoshitomo, but the two become separated in a snowstorm. Yoritomo is rescued by the manager of the Kusano Manor, which is at the foot of Mount Ibuki near Lake Biwa. One day he learns that his father's head is being displayed as a war trophy in the capital, and he goes there so that he may see his father's remains and pray for his salvation. Once in Kyoto, he is captured by the Heike and sentenced to death. But he is saved from execution and exiled to Izu Province instead, because the mother of Taira no Kiyomori takes pity on him.[50]

30. *Iōgashima (The Island of Sulfur)* is a tale of the monk Shunkan and two other men who were exiled to a barren island south of Kyushu for their part in the Shishigadani affair of 1177, an abortive plot to overthrow the Heike. An amnesty is proclaimed in 1179 when it becomes known that the empress is carrying a child. Of the three men exiled to the barren island, only Shunkan is refused a pardon, for he is hated intensely by Taira no Kiyomori. Shunkan has refused to worship the deity of Kumano Shrine as the other two men have done during their exile. It is said that this is probably the cause of his misfortune.[51]

31. *Yume-awase (Portent of Dreams)* is a "felicitous" piece which tells of the prophesying of a prosperous future for the Genji. The year is perhaps 1179, when the Heike clan is at the zenith of its power. One morning Adachi Morinaga comes to Yoritomo at his residence in exile and tells him of a series of unusual dreams he has had. The dreams are interpreted by another vassal as por-

tending that Yoritomo will some day become the shogun, reign over territories even beyond Japan, and be blessed with long life.[52]

32. *Mongaku* is a tale of the monk who in 1180 encouraged Yoritomo to rise against the Heike and served as his link with the Imperial Court in Kyoto. Mongaku, the son of a former Genji commander, is canvassing the capital for subscriptions that will enable him to build a Buddha Hall at the Jingoji monastery. He boldy enters the palace of the retired Emperor Go-Shirakawa and reads the subscription tablet aloud, caring little that he is disrupting a musical program. When samurai guards attempt to eject him, Mongaku draws a dagger and kills them. For this crime he is cast into a pit to die of starvation. As a result of a Buddhist miracle, however, he is very much alive when the pit is revisited a hundred days later. Mongaku is then exiled to Ōshima,[53] an island off the coast of Izu Peninsula. One day he visits Yoritomo, who is living in exile on the peninsula, and shows him Yoshitomo's skull. Mongaku then performs a ritual to curse the Heike, and it is due to this curse, so it is said, that the Heike are to be destroyed in the years to come.[54]

33. *Tsukishima* (*The Island Construction*) tells the legend of the construction of an artificial island which was known as Kyō-no-shima (literally, "island of sutras"). In 1180 the imperial capital is moved from Kyoto to Fukuhara, the site of present-day Kobe. Taira no Kiyomori orders the construction of an island in the harbor so that ships can be moored safely. Work is interrupted for some time because of tempestuous seas, and a divination reveals that thirty men must be buried as "human pillars" in order to placate the sea god. The Heike seize travelers to use as sacrifices, and the thirtieth man to be seized is Gyōbu Kuniharu, who is traveling about the country in search of his daughter, Meigetsu. When Meigetsu learns of her father's plight, she hastens to Fukuhara together with her husband, and the two plead with Kiyomori that they be sacrificed instead. In the end, however, a youthful servant of Kiyomori offers himself in place of the thirty victims, and he is buried along with ten thousand copies of the Lotus Sutra.[55]

34. *Umazoroe* (*The Assemblage of Horsemen*) describes Yoritomo's reviewing of warriors who gathered in Izu in response to
his call to arms in 1180. Having been encouraged by Mongaku,
Yoritomo decides to rally the Genji forces in preparation for an
uprising against the Heike. He circulates a letter calling on the
various lords of nearby provinces. In all, 353 warriors arrive at
Yoritomo's encampment. All are mounted on steeds worthy of
carrying such noble warriors.[56]

35. *Kiso gansho* (*Kiso's Supplication*) depicts an act of religious
devotion by Yoritomo's cousin, Kiso Yoshinaka, on the eve of his
victory over the Heike expeditionary force in 1183. Kiso's army
of fifty thousand men and a Heike army twice its size are
positioned on either side of the Karakuri Divide on the border
between Kaga and Etchū provinces. As Kiso surveys the terrain,
he espies the crimson structure of a shinto shrine amidst the
green of the hills. He is overjoyed when he is informed that it is
the shrine of Hachiman Bodhisattva, the tutelary god of the
Genji. He has his vassal, the militant monk Kakumyō, write a
supplication for victory and tender it to the shrine.[57]

36. *Atsumori*, which is presented in translation, eulogizes the
chivalrous but tragic death of the youthful Taira no Atsumori and
the noble actions of his slayer, Kumagae Naozane. As the Heike
are taking to their ships following their defeat at Ichinotani,
Atsumori rides back to the fortress in order to retrieve his flute.
All the vessels are out at sea by the time he returns to the beach,
and so he rides his steed into the water. He responds gallantly,
however, to a challenge voiced by the formidable Kumagae and
returns to shore. Although Kumagae wants to spare Atsumori, for
he is reminded of his own son, he is forced to slay him when
he sees other Genji warriors riding toward them. Kumagae returns Atsumori's remains to the Heike, and he enters the Buddhist priesthood to spend the rest of his life praying for Atsumori's salvation. In the twilight of his life, he makes a pilgrimage
to Mount Kōya and deposits Atsumori's ashes there.[58]

37. *Nasu no Yoichi* is the stirring tale of a Genji warrior who
stakes his life and the honor of the entire Genji clan on his skill

as an archer. After their defeat at the Battle of Yashima, the Heike again take to their vessels. The entire fleet stands off shore, facing the Genji forces, which line the beach. A lone Heike vessel approaches the shore, and a woman beckons to the Genji. She is daring the Genji to show her an archer who can hit a fan which is fastened to a pole at the prow of the vessel. Nasu no Yoichi is chosen to represent the six thousand Genji warriors. As Yoichi rides into the sea, he prays silently to Hachiman Bodhisattva, and miraculously the wind subsides, and the target is steady. His arrow hits the fan near the hinge and sends it fluttering into the sea. The roar of approval from the Heike vessels resounds over the water.[59]

38. *Hamaide (Beach Outing)* is a short "felicitous" piece which describes a festive outing held near Kamakura by Yoritomo and his vassals. They have just received official appointments from the Imperial Court, and this is cause for celebration. Following two days of festivities, the party boards a ship and sails to the nearby island of Enoshima, which is likened to the mythical Mount Hōrai. Bugaku dances are performed on a stage that has been erected on the deck of the ship.[60]

39. *Kuketsu no kai (The Nine-holed Shell)* is also a "felicitous" piece and is a sequel to *Hamaide*. It is only a few paragraphs long. During the outing at Enoshima, Yoritomo orders that fresh shellfish be brought up from the sea and served to him. The younger warriors vie with one another to bring up shellfish and seaweed, and they are rewarded for their catches. Chichibu no Rokurō, the son of Hatakeyama Shigetada, remains submerged for more than two hours. He finally comes to the surface with thirty large shellfish attached to his body. For this miraculous feat, Yoritomo rewards him with a large fief in Hitachi Province.[61]

40. *Kagekiyo* is a fictional account of the persistent endeavors on the part of Taira no Kagekiyo to avenge the Heike by assassinating Yoritomo. Kagekiyo makes thirty-seven attempts on Yoritomo's life, but each time his disguise is broken by Hatakeyama Shigetada and he is forced to flee. When Yoritomo posts a reward for his capture, Kagekiyo is betrayed by the courtesan Akoō, by

whom he has had two children. But instead of being rewarded, Akoō is drowned as punishment for her heartlessness. Kagekiyo surrenders himself to Yoritomo when he learns that his father-in-law has been imprisoned in his stead. He breaks out of prison once simply to prove that he cannot be held a captive against his own will, and then surrenders again. Finally he is executed, or so it seems. Kagekiyo is still alive, for the bodhisattva Avalokiteśvara of Kiyomizu Temple has taken his place at the execution. Yoritomo hears about this miracle and orders Kagekiyo's release. Kagekiyo then gouges out his own eyes lest the sight of Yoritomo arouse hatred in him again. The deity of Kiyomizu Temple restores his sight, and Kagekiyo lives out his life peacefully on an estate granted him by Yoritomo.[62]

MISCELLANEOUS PIECES

41. *Nihongi* (*Chronicle of Japan*), the title of which is taken from the first official history of Japan compiled in 720, is a short "felicitous" piece based on mythology. Concepts in Chinese cosmology and in Buddhism are infused in the story of the creation of Japan by the deities Izanagi and Izanami. India is compared to the moon, and China to a star, and Japan is extolled as the land of the sun.

42. *Chōryō* (*Chang Liang*) is the only kōwaka treating a non-Japanese theme. It is based on the legend about Chang Liang, a hero of the Early Han Period (206–6 B.C.), being taught the secrets of warfare by the mythical figure, Huang-shih-kung. Chang Liang comes to a marvelous bridge made of emeralds and gold, having been guided there by revelations made to him by the Eleven-faced Avalokiteśvara. When an old man whom he meets on the bridge drops his shoe into the gorge below, Chang proves his courage by diving into the water and combating a giant water serpent in order to retrieve the shoe. The old man is really Avalokiteśvara in disguise, and he takes Chang on a flight through the heavens to the Buddhist paradise. The Buddha gives Chang a fan, a whip, and a scroll containing many secrets, and he tells Chang about the origin of wine and about its wonderful properties.

Through the magical powers of the fan and the whip, Chang is able to return to his home in an instant.[63]

43. *Iruka* is a romanticized account of the slaying of Soga Iruka in 645 by Fujiwara Kamatari (614–669), the founder of the courtly Fujiwara family. When Kamatari is a child, he is given a sickle by a fox, an animal which in Oriental folklore is said to possess supernatural powers, and he keeps it with him always. As an adult he becomes a high court official. Kamatari receives an imperial mandate to slay Iruka, who has grown so powerful that he threatens to usurp the throne. Iruka is wary, however, and does not give Kamatari the opportunity to come near him, even after he receives Kamatari's beautiful adopted daughter as his consort. Kamatari then feigns blindness and maintains this pretense for three years. One day his infant child falls into the fireplace, and Kamatari gropes about blindly while the child is burned to death; and Iruka is at last convinced of Kamatari's blindness. Soon after that Kamatari is able to approach Iruka by pretending that he has mistaken his seat, and he strikes off Iruka's head with the sickle.[64]

44. *Taishokan* (*The Great Woven Cap*) is an imaginary tale. The Great Woven Cap was worn by the highest official of the land in accordance with the system of caps instituted in 647. Kamatari was the minister of state at that time, and *Taishokan* came to be regarded as his epithet. Kamatari's daughter, Kōhaku, is so famed for her beauty that she is sought as a consort by the Emperor T'ai-tsung of T'ang China. As empress of China she is adored by the citizenry. When Kamatari begins the construction of the Kōfukuji in Nara, Kōhaku sends him numerous treasures with which to adorn the temple. The ship bearing the gifts is guarded by the general Unsō and three hundred men. The ruler of the underwater realm, the Dragon King, covets these treasures, but his attempts to seize them are thwarted by Unsō's bravery and the protective powers of the Buddha. The Dragon King sends his beautiful princess to beguile Unsō, and she is able to make off with the priceless *Mukei* gem. Kamatari is determined to recover the precious stone. Knowing that the gem is heavily guarded, he entices the denizens of the Dragon Palace to the

surface by staging a spectacular show of music and dancing aboard a ship. A woman diver, who is Kamatari's paramour, swims into the unguarded palace and retrieves the gem. Although she is pursued by a dragon, she manages to cut open her breast and conceal the gem before she is killed. The gem is removed from her lifeless form and taken to Nara, where it is placed in the forehead of the Buddha's statue in the Kōfukuji.[65]

45. *Yuriwaka daijin (The Minister Yuriwaka)* is an imaginary tale of a truly Odyssean adventure. The son of the minister at the court of Emperor Saga, Yuriwaka himself becomes the Left Minister when he is seventeen. In 816 a Mongol fleet carrying forty thousand men invades Kyushu. The Shinto gods on the High Celestial Plain hold council, and they call on Yuriwaka to lead an army of three hundred thousand men against the invaders. The Mongols are awed by the sight of his army and flee. Yuriwaka, who is now the governor of Kyushu, takes a huge fleet across the straits and after three years' campaigning succeeds in destroying the Mongol fleet. On the return voyage, the victorious fleet stops for a short while at a small desolate island called Genkaijima. Yoriwaka goes ashore to rest. As he lies in deep slumber, the Beppu brothers set sail with the fleet and return home to reap the harvest of victory for themselves. The brothers not only take over Yuriwaka's governorship but even attempt to possess his wife. Yuriwaka's wife clings to the belief that her husband is still alive, and her belief is confirmed one day when a pet falcon she releases returns with a leaf bearing a message written in Yuriwaka's blood. When Yuriwaka finally returns to Kyushu, he is treated as an oddity because of his wild appearance. No one recognizes him, not even his loyal vassal, Kadowaki. During a New Year's gathering of his former vassals, Yuriwaka reveals his identity by stringing and drawing a steel bow which only he has the strength to use. The Beppu brothers are meted out their deserts, and Yuriwaka is restored to his former station of honor.[66]

46. *Manjū* is a tale which eulogizes the selfless loyalty of Fujiwara Nakamitsu to his lord, Minamoto no Mitsunaka (912?–997?), the Genji chieftain who was known also as Manjū of Tada Manor. As Manjū approaches old age, he becomes increasingly concerned

about his afterlife in the Buddhist realm, and he bids his young son, Bijo, to enter the priesthood and pray for his salvation. Bijo, however, does not wish to forsake his samurai heritage. At the temple he spends his days playing games of war, and after three years he still cannot recite a single word in a sutra. Manjū is so incensed that he orders his vassal Nakamitsu to slay Bijo. Nakamitus cannot disobey his lord, but neither can he bring himself to slay the son of his lord. He solves this dilemma by killing his own son and presenting his head, wrapped in cloth, as evidence that he has carried out the order. He sends Bijo secretly to Mount Hiei to enter the priesthood. Some years later, Bijo returns to the Tada Manor in the company of his eminent teacher. He learns that his mother has grieved so over his supposed death that she has lost her eyesight. Her sight is restored as a result of his prayers, and the family is happily reunited.[67]

47. *Shida* tells the story of an intrafamily intrigue in the tenth century. The hero, Shida Kotarō, is a mere child when his father dies. A short time later, a man named Oyama Yukishige enters the household as the bridegroom for Kotarō's sister. Because Oyama proves himself an exemplary son-in-law, the mother gives him half of Shida Manor. She does this against the advice of the loyal vassal, Ukishima. Once Oyama acquires this right of ownership, he changes abruptly. He dispossesses the widow of her half of the manor, expels her and Kotarō, and, for good measure, has the widow cursed to death. The young Kotarō enlists the aid of Ukishima and attempts to oust Oyama; but Ukishima is killed, and Kotarō captured. Although Kotarō escapes with the help of a sympathetic vassal, he falls into the hands of a slave trader and is sold into bondage. After many vicissitudes he has the good fortune to be adopted by a samurai in Mutsu Province. When the governor of Mutsu hears of Kotarō's misfortune, he grants him the powers of governorship for a period of three years so that he may right the injustices. The usurper Oyama receives his due punishment, and Kotarō eventually prospers as the lord of eight eastern provinces.[68]

48. *Shinkyoku* (*New Piece*) is unique as a kōwaka inasmuch as it is basically a love story. Prince Takanaga (1311–1337) falls in

love with a girl who resembles a lovely but imaginary woman he once saw in a painting. She has a suitor, but he withdraws graciously in deference to the prince. During the war between the court of Emperor Go-Daigo and the Kamakura Shogunate, the prince moves temporarily to Shikoku. He sends his vassal Shōhata to Kyoto to escort the princess to Shikoku, but during the journey she is abducted and taken out to sea. Shōhata kills himself that he may acquire the powers of the dead to save his mistress. When he assails the abductor's ship with a tempest and shows himself in his ghostly form, the terrified crew casts the princess adrift in a small boat. She is washed ashore on a small island and cared for by the inhabitants until she is reunited with the prince.[69]

49. *Miki* is one of the two kōwaka written especially to eulogize Hideyoshi. Hence it was written much later than the other texts in the repertoire. In 1578 Oda Nobunaga sends his commanders on armed expeditions to various parts of the country in an effort to achieve the political unification of Japan. Hideyoshi is assigned to campaign in the western provinces. Bessho Nagaharu, the lord of Harima Province, consolidates his forces in the Miki Fortress and puts up a stiff resistance; but Hideyoshi's army surrounds the fortress, and the war remains stalemated thus for two years. Reinforcements sent by the lord of Aki Province fail to break through the encirclement, and provisions cannot reach the defenders. Bessho surrenders the fortress in order to save his vassals from starvation; he begs Hideyoshi to spare the lives of his vassals and then kills himself and his family. Hideyoshi is merciful and treats Bessho's vassals with magnanimity.[70]

50. *Honnōji* describes the event in history which served to catapult Hideyoshi to a position of supreme power. In 1582 Hideyoshi is campaigning on Nobunaga's behalf against the great Mōri clan of western Japan. He floods the Takamatsu Fortress, the Mōri outpost in Bitchū Province, thereby cutting off its supplies, and waits patiently for starvation to reduce the garrison. Nobunaga, who is in Kyoto, orders the commander Akechi Mitsuhide to take an army of reinforcement to help Hideyoshi. Akechi instead attacks Honnōji, the temple where Nobunaga is quartered, and kills his lord. When Hideyoshi receives this news, he immediately ac-

cepts the surrender of the Takamatsu Fortress, hastens back to the capital with his army, and annihilates Akechi and his followers. The feat of Hideyoshi is all the more remarkable when we recall that Han Kao-tzu fought more than seventy battles before he finally destroyed his arch foe, Hsiang Yü.[71]

V: A NARRATIVE: *Atsumori*

T H E diverse textual styles of the kōwaka are represented in the translations of *Atsumori* and *Izumi's Fortress*. The translation of *Atsumori* represents a kōwaka text that has been transcribed or published in prose narrative, as a tale for reading. The translation of *Izumi's Fortress,* on the other hand, represents the style of a text written as a libretto for recitation.

The text of *Atsumori* on which the translation is based is from the Daigashira Sahei Collection, and is believed to have been transcribed during the sixteenth century; it is contained in the *Kōwaka-bukyoku shū*.[1] Another version of this text contained in the *Mai no hon*[2] is more convenient to read, because the editor has supplied Chinese graphs for many words which are rendered only syllabically in the manuscript text. But the text appears to be corrupt in parts.

THE HISTORICAL SETTING

The tale of *Atsumori* is set against a background of the final series of wars between the Genji and the Heike during the years 1180–1185. The story of the decline of the once-powerful Heike and their ultimate conquest by the Genji is described vividly and artistically in the *Tale of the Heike;* it is recounted in even greater detail, although with less artistry, in the *Rise and Fall of Gempei.* The basic facts concerning most of the events described in the war tales can be found as entries in the *Azuma kagami* and the *Gyokuyō.*

Atsumori is the tale of the tragic encounter between the youthful Taira no Atsumori (1169–1184) and the Genji warrior Kumagae no Jirō Naozane at the Battle of Ichinotani in 1184—a battle in which the Heike suffered a disastrous defeat and were forced to flee out to sea. Atsumori was a member of a clan which prided itself on its strength as a warring group, but he grew up amidst the aristocratic surroundings of the court society in Kyoto and knew little about the ways of the samurai. He was yet too young to hold an official post, and his skill as a flutist was his only renown. In spite of his gentility and his youth, he responded gallantly to a challenge to combat and rode back to meet an adversary who was well known for his prowess in battle. The story of his tragic death and of Kumagae's repentance has been retold in literature,[3] and is one of the best-known episodes of the Gempei War.

The Battle of Ichinotani was a prelude to the sea battle at Dannoura in 1185, in which the Heike were to receive their final crushing defeat. Ichinotani was located on the coast of the Inland Sea, a few miles west of the present city of Kobe. The Heike had been ousted from Kyoto in 1183 and had fled to western Japan, but they took advantage of an intraclan strife among the Genji to reorganize their forces, and they were now advancing again toward the capital. They built a fortress at Ichinotani which seemed impregnable, for their powerful fleet commanded the sea to the front and a precipitous slope rose to the rear. Their land forces were deployed as far up the coast as Ikuta, which is today within the city of Kobe.

By the fifth day of the Second Month in 1184, Yoshitsune's elder brother Noriyori was moving toward Ikuta with an army of 56,000 men; Yoshitsune himself, with an army of 20,000, was marching inland in order to attack the stronghold of Ichinotani from the rear. As described in the *Azuma kagami*,[4] the main body of Yoshitsune's force circled down to the coast road and commenced a frontal assault on the Ichinotani fortress in the early hours of the seventh day, and Kumagae was the one who led the initial charge. Yoshitsune in the meantime led a handpicked group of some seventy warriors up to the high ground known as Hiyodorigoe, which overlooked Ichinotani,[5] and he charged his band of horsemen down the sheer precipice to catch the Heike completely by surprise. The battle began at six o'clock in the morning and was over by noon. Most of the surviving Heike had by this time taken to their vessels, and Genji warriors were searching the area for stragglers who had failed to escape out to sea. And it is at this point in the story of the war between the Genji and the Heike that the episode of *Atsumori* unfolds.

THE TRANSLATION

To begin,[6] on the occasion of the Battle of Ichinotani, the Heike lost in all sixteen samurai commanders of their clan.[7] Among them, the one who especially inspired sad reflections[8] was the Grandee-without-Post[9] Atsumori, who was the son of Tsunemori, the younger brother of the Nation's Overseer [Kiyomori].[10] Indeed, he inspired sad reflections. His attire on that day was of greater resplendence than usual. He wore a fine, bright crimson undergarment that gave off a scent of plum blossoms, a *hitatare*[11] [shirt and trouser] of soft silk[12] woven with strands of various hues to depict the herbage of an autumnal field, a hand guard on his bow hand,* a pair of shin guards, a full-length suit of armor[13] [with plates] that darkened at the bottom into a deep purple,[14] a sword with fittings made of gleaming gold, sixteen dyed-feathered arrows inserted [in a quiver], and a bow closely wound with wisteria vine. He took a saddle which was finished in gold-speckled lacquer and embellished with overlays of silver circles, placed it on a steed with a coat of bluish-gray that bore coin-like splotches, and he mounted it nimbly. Even the horse he rode and the very braid of his suit of armor appeared truly magnificent. Atsumori accompanied the Lord Eminent [the Emperor Antoku] down to the beach together with those of his clan, but he had left his transverse flute made of Chinese bamboo in the Inner Palace †
—a mishap that augured his expiring fortune. Had he gone on, forsaking the flute, the matter would have been of little consequence. Yet he reasoned that to leave the flute behind would be a discredit to the clan . . . a folly in a young courtier.[15] He went back to retrieve it, but by the time he had gone thither and returned, the grand vessels[16] had pushed out far to sea. Ah, how piteous, Atsumori! He fled in the direction of Shioya[17] and let the steed run of its own will.

---

*"Bow hand" (*yunde*), or the hand that grips the bow, and "steed hand" (*mete*), or the hand that grips the reins, are used figuratively to denote "left hand" and "right hand."

† Inner Palace (*Dairi*) refers to the emperor's living quarters within the Imperial Palace. The Heike had taken the infant Emperor Antoku (1178–1185; reigned 1180–1185) with them in their flight from the capital; hence the reference to an Inner Palace at Ichinotani.

Just at this moment, Kumagae no Jirō Naozane, a resident of the province of Musashi and banner head of the Shi Band,[18] came [riding] along the surf. Although he had led the charge this time at Ichinotani, he was most chagrined that he had not received any noteworthy feat. "The glory [that could be mine]," he thought, "if only a worthy foe would pass by, so that I could press up to him and grapple with him to take him alive." When he espied Atsumori, he was delighted, indeed.

"You, in flight over there! I take it that you are a worthy commander of the Heike! Come back and let us contend! Who is this warrior who speaks thus, you would say? I am a resident of the province of Musashi, the banner head of the Shi Band, Kumagae no Jirō Naozane! As a foe, I am a worthy one! Would you wrongly show your enemy the tasseled cord and reverse plate of your armor?[19] Come back! Come back!"[20] And he pursued him.

Ah, how piteous, Atsumori! Hearing that it was Kumagae, he knew that he could not escape; but he fled, letting the steed run of its own will.

Just at that moment, Atsumori glanced out toward the sea and saw a grand vessel afloat very close [to shore]. Thinking that he would signal the vessel to stand in that he might board it, he pulled out from his waist a fan emblazoned with a crimson disc and waved it toward the vessel out at sea, signaling to it. The lord Kadowaki[21] looked to those in the vessel—there were many, indeed—and commanded, "See whether the warrior wearing an arrow cushion* who signals to this vessel is the Head-of-the-Left-Stable Yukimori or the Grandee-without-Post Atsumori." The Wicked Shichibyōe[22] complied. "Where now?" he exclaimed, as he rose to stand at the boat's edge, using his halberd as a staff. He removed his helmet and stared intently.

"How piteous! How could he have failed to board a grand vessel? It is the son of Tsunemori, the Grandee-without-Post Atsumori. The suit of armor he wears, the coat of his horse . . . there is no mistake. How piteous!"

"If it is Astumori, take this vessel nearer and rescue him," the lord Kadowaki said, when he heard this.

---

* A *horo,* a large globular cushion carried on the back as a protection against arrows.

The water-master and helmsman complied. They reset the oars and the tiller and attempted to take the vessel toward the surf. But on this day the waves were again surging as if to remind one of the boreal winds which had blown vigorously during the past two or three days. The wind was furious, and the waves [coiled] like mighty serpents. Foaming swells—like mountains of snow—washed the deck planks* and raised grains of sand to the heavens. The smaller boats could not be steered freely toward the direction of either the bow hand or the steed hand, and so the greater part of the forces had taken to the fine large vessels. Buffeted by the enfolding waves, the grand vessel moved forward gradually, but she seemed unable to draw closer to shore. Atsumori observed this and decided instead to swim his horse to the vessel that he might board it. He hung on tightly to the reins of his steed and rode into the sea, but he could barely stay above the water as he swam his horse.[23] How piteous, Atsumori! Had he been a seasoned warrior,[24] he would have ridden down on the croup, calling out to the horse from time to time; his horse—a superb specimen—would have reached the grand vessel far out at sea with little difficulty. "Above all, I must not be separated from my horse," he reasoned . . . a tragic folly of an inexperienced warrior. And he rode on top of the mane, stepping firmly in the stirrups and clutching the reins, barely staying above the water as he swam his horse. The horse—superb specimen though it was—was buffeted by enfolding waves and appeared to be failing. And Kumagae saw this.

"Foolhardy Heike!" he shouted. "The grand vessel out at sea is drifting farther away. And with the sea so tempestuous and the wind so violent, what can you do? Come back, and let us fight. It shall not be otherwise, for I will send forth a middle-inserted [arrow]."[25] He fitted an arrow into his bow and drew it slowly. And Atsumori saw this.

"If a rusty arrow should perchance find its mark in me, this would be a disgrace to the clan," he reasoned. He pulled the reins and turned his steed around. As they reached the shallows, the steed pranced, kicking up beads of water. Atsumori fitted a

---

* These were platforms for the oarsmen or pole-pushers and were located either along the edge of the vessel or across the afterdeck.

hollow-pointed [arrow] [26] with dyed feathers into his bow, and
he recited the following:

> *The catalpa bow:*
> *When you nock an arrow*
> *And draw it back,*
> *Do you know, my lord,*
> *How to slacken the pull?**

Now Kumagae, too, was a bow-handler with a [prudent] mind,[27]
and he was touched. He kicked away the stirrups and returned the
following poem:

> *In target practice*
> *The "A" arrow missed,*
> *So I had thought;*
> *But a voice cried, "A hit!"*
> *And so I halted.* †

He recited thus and awaited Atsumori.

Now,[28] Atsumori threw his bow and arrow aside and drew his
sword. "Take this!" he cried, and he struck. Kumagae parried
lightly, regained his stance, and struck back hard. They struck
hard at each other—two blows, three blows. Since the contest
would not be decided this way, they threw their weapons aside
so that they could come closer and grapple. They pulled each
other by the armor sleeves,[29] came to tight grips, and plunged
to the ground between their horses. Ah, how piteous, Atsumori!
Though his heart was bold and courageous, he was no match for
the seasoned warrior Kumagae, who easily pinned him down.

---

* *Azusayumi / ya o sashihakete / hiku toki wa / kaesu koto o ba / shiru ka
zo mo kimi.* "The catalpa bow" (*azusayumi*) is a semi-imagistic ornamental
epithet (*makura-kotoba*) used in poems treating themes of archery or ideas or
movements that can be associated metaphorically with archery.

† *Itatsuki no / haya hazuren to / omoishi ni / ya to iu koe ni / tachi zo
todomaru.* During target practice, an archer holds two arrows in his right hand
and shoots them in quick succession; the first arrow is called "'A' arrow"
(*haya*), and the second the "'B' arrow" (*otoya*). The *ya* (literally, "arrow") in
the fourth line is the target tender's call to indicate a "hit"; here it is used
with a double meaning, for *ya* is also a common hailing call. Kumagae is
comparing his verbal challenge metaphorically to the shooting of a practice
shot, and he is saying, again metaphorically, that he has acknowledged Atsumori's response to his challenge.

Kumagae tore off Atsumori's helmet and threw it aside; he drew a blade from his waist and was about to take Atsumori's head. But he felt it odd that the resistance should be so frail, and he looked downward to behold the countenance of his foe. The face was lightly powdered, the teeth dyed black, the eyebrows drawn thickly; he was unmistakably a person of palace rank,[30] his age fourteen or fifteen, perhaps. Because he looked so pitiable, Kumagae slackened his hold.

"To say true, courtier," he asked, "you are the noble scion of what personage of the Heike? Speak your name."

Ah, how piteous, Atsumori! Pinioned by the seasoned warrior Kumagae and breathing with great agony, he spoke:

"Truly, I had heard that you, Kumagae, were renowned in the ways of both the literati and the samurai. Why then do you say things which do not accord with the laws of battle? I am a subject of the emperor of the subcelestial realm; I am one who frequents the room of the dwellers amidst the clouds,[31] one who is accomplished in the ways of poetry and music.[32] In the two or three years since we left the imperial capital amidst [emotions of] yearning, the fortune of our clan having expired, I have come to know roughly the code of the samurai's daring. I had learned that one spoke his name during the thick of battle as warriors swarmed toward one another's position; that warriors, bearing quivers emptied of arrows and holding blades shorn of their sword guards, spoke their names by calling out, 'I am so and so of such and such a province,' and that they fought to the finish using weapons or by grappling. But here I lie pinioned by my foe. I have never before heard of a code that tells one to speak his name [while looking up to his adversary] from below. Ah, I understand, Kumagae. You want me to speak my name so that you can take my head to show to your master, Yoshitsune. That is well and good, not a thing unknown in this world. Take my head, then, and show it to your master, Yoshitsune; perhaps he will recognize it. Should he not recognize it, then show it to Kaba no Kanja.* Should Kaba no Kanja not recognize it, then turn it toward the

* A popular sobriquet for Minamoto no Noriyori, an elder brother of Yoshitsune.

Heike captives—there should be many—let them see it, and then inquire of them. Should they not recognize it, then consider it a head of a person of no renown whatever and leave it among the grass. After you have thrown it away, it will concern you no more, Kumagae."

Kumagae heard him.

"How well you know the code of the samurai's daring, courtier. We are the sorrowful ones of this world. When we comply with our lord's wishes and endeavor to advance ourselves, we dispute with our parents, war against our sons, and only create wrongs that we did not foresee. This is the custom among the samurai. [The pleasure of entertaining] a guest for a half day under the blossoms, or a friend for an evening while viewing the moon; the enjoyment of the clear wind, of the moon viewed from a tower, of the scattering of blossoms, the falling of leaves [33]—all are decreed, they say, by a marvelous fate that is not an effect of our present life. Although there were many men in this battle, it was I, Kumagae, whom you encountered. Accept this as a fate ordained in a previous life [34] and speak your name. Though I shall take your head, I will pray for your soul in the afterworld. This I will do in my faithfulness to serve you." [35]

Atsumori heard this.

"I did not think I would speak my name, but your concern for [my life in] the afterworld has so gladdened me that I shall speak my name for you to hear. For whom do you take me? I am the third son of Kadowaki no Tsunemori, who is the younger brother of the venerated Jōkai.* I still bear the temporary title of Without-Post; I am the Grandee Atsumori, my age sixteen. This is my first time in battle. That is all you need to know. Take my head quickly, Kumagae!"

Kumagae heard him.

"Then you, courtier, are a descendant of the Emperor Kammu.[36] And your age is sixteen? My heir Kojirō [Naoie] is sixteen years of age. Then you are both the same age. The worth-less Kojirō is homely and dark-skinned, and I regard him an un-

---

* Refers to Taira no Kiyomori. Jōkai is the Buddhist name he acquired when he took the tonsure in 1168.

feeling eastern barbarian; but when I think that he is my own, I am moved to pity. Ah, how merciless [I have been]! At the front gate of Ichinotani this morning, an arrow released by the foe Marei caught Naoie in the left upper arm. When he turned to me and said, 'Pull the arrow for me,' I wanted to ask him whether the wound was painful or slight. As a bow-handler of great renown, I thought that I dared not let either friend or foe hear me utter such a [tender] inquiry. I glared at him and said, 'What an unworthy one you are, Naoie! If that arm is seriously wounded,[37] then stay and put the blade to your belly. If it is only a slight wound, then seek out the foe and die fighting. Make our fort your pillow [in death] and disgrace not the name of the Shi Band.' He understood this, and cast one longing glance toward me before running off into the enemy position.

"I know not of his fate since then. Should I, Kumagae, be suffered to live on and return to the province of Musashi and meet Naoie's mother, how his thin-haired [38] mother will grieve when I tell her that he was slain. And how that Tsunemori, too, must be grieving, having left this youthful lord of blooming fairness alone at the water's edge."

If Tsunemori's sorrow and Naozane's thought were compared to things [in nature], they would be like the [constantly] shifting levels [39] of flowing water. It was so piteous that Kumagae again gazed downward and beheld Atsumori's countenance: the side-locks were as delicate and elegant as the wings of the autumnal cicada, the fluttering brows resembled the moon over distant mountains.[40] He was the Narihira of old, brushing the sleeves of his hunting shirt under snowy skies by the wilds of Katano.* Painted brows of deep-blue hue, a face of blooming fairness,[41] [garments of] brocade and embroidered fabric: should [an artist] attempt to depict this image, how could his brush contrive to reproduce the likeness of this courtier?

"Though I may receive a prize for having taken the head of this lord, would it keep a thousand years? Would I live a myriad years?

---

* An allusion to Ariwara no Narihira (825–880), who was famed as a poet and romanticized as a lover. Katano, some ten miles south of the city of Kyoto, was an imperial hunting reserve during the Heian Period.

Let me spare this lord so that it will be told through the ages to come." Thus did he ponder.

"Listen, Atsumori. Tell those of the Heike that you grappled at the water's edge with one known as Kumagae of Musashi but were spared because you reminded him of his own son Naoie."

He helped him up, brushed away the dust on his suit of armor, and lifted him onto his horse. Naozane, too, mounted his horse. After they had ridden some five *chō* westward, he glanced back and saw Mekada, Mabuchi, Iba, and Mitsui—commanders all of the Omi-Province Genji—at the head of five hundred horsemen, flying the banner of the four-eyed crest [42] and riding in pursuit of them. He scanned the direction of his bow hand and saw Narita and Hirayama positioned there. From his steed-hand side the lord Dohi with seven riders came in pursuit. [Watching them from] the hill above was the Genji scion [43] Kurō [Yoshitsune], with Musashibō Benkei, Hitachibō Kaizon, Kamei, Kataoka, Ise, and Suruga in close attendance.

"Kumagae was wrestling with a foe but has spared him," they all clamored. "This looks like treason.[44] If Kumagae has treasonable intent, slay him too!" And they vied with one another to pursue him.

If this lord in his plight were compared to things [in nature], he would be like a bird in a cage or an icefish caught in the barrier-net.[45] There was no escape. "Rather than let him perish at the hands of others, I, Naozane, would see him killed by my own hand, for I shall pray for his soul in the afterworld." He again grasped Atsumori tightly, and they plunged to the ground. How piteous! He struck off his head quickly and held it high.[46] And [ferocious as] a demon though he was, Kumagae wept helplessly.[47]

Kumagae checked his tears and pushed and shoved the remains variously; inserted [48] in the fold of the armor he saw a transverse flute of Chinese bamboo. And at his steed-hand side he noticed a scroll. What is this? He unrolled it hastily and looked at it. Ah, how piteous! Atsumori, during moments of pensiveness, had inscribed words [expressing his emotions] on leaving the capital.

[This story goes back to the time] when this lord was residing in the capital. The damsel of the noble Inspector and Great

Councilor Sukekata [49] had turned thirteen, and she was the fairest of all in the subcelestial realm. Atsumori [once] played the flute in the orchestral ensemble which performed each month in the Palace of the August Chamber * of Ninnaji. She played the *koto* in the same ensemble, and Atsumori loved her from the moment he first saw her. He wrote poems about her, and he sent her letters. As the letters multiplied, they began to meet as lovers. They had been lovers only three days when the Heike departed from the metropolis of blossoms that was the imperial capital, bound for the surging waters of the western sea. Ah, how piteous, Atsumori! His person was in the province of Settsu at Ichinotani, but his heart yearned only for the capital. He composed this, perhaps as he reminisced—a song of the four seasons, which he had written down:

> *First there is the morn*
> * of azure brightness,* †
> *When the bush warbler,*
> * Skipping amidst hedges and trees,*
> *Graces the wilds with the elegance*
> * Of its soft warble.*
> *Mist is encountered*
> * On the path through the wilds;*
> *Beyond, there are blossoms:*
> * How exquisite they must be—*
> *The folds of cherry blossoms,*
> * The eightfold cherry blossoms.* ‡
> *Then there will come*
> * The summer skies*
> *Of the ninety summer days,* [50] *the three retreats,* §
> * Wisterias grown ever thickly,*
> *And the cuckoo.*
> * Nocturnal flames to repel the mosquitoes—*
> *As they burn low, I feel*

* A sobriquet for the chief priest of the Ninnaji monastery, who was by custom an imperial prince.

† An epithet for early spring.

‡ A variety which has multiple layers of petals.

§ "Three retreats" (*sambuku*), an epithet for "summer," refers to the days during which one must hide himself in order to escape the searing heat.

> *The torment of my love.*
> *Then will come autumn*
> *With yellow chrysanthemums,*
> *Orchids and touchwood,*[51]
> *Deer on mountains high,*[52]
> *The red maples of Tatsuta River,*[53]
> *The crickets about the pillow.*
> *Bush clovers* [54] *will be in bloom:*
> *Have you not heard?*
> *When the wintry evenings come,*
> *The dark winter, the white snow,*
> *The rivulets in the mountains,*
> *And the paths, too,*
> *Will be white, they say.*
> *But the whiteness will disappear,*
> *Leaving no traces.*

I saw disappear in the distance the treetops [55] *of the home for which I long, and I lie forgotten* [56] *now beside the moss-covered road at Ichinotani. The youngest child of Tsunemori, the Grandee-without-Post Atsumori.*

Thus he had written.

As Kumagae perceived one thing and beheld another, his tears flowed all the more. Having entrusted Atsumori's remains to his henchmen, he brought the head, the flute, and the scroll before his commander [Yoshitsune], and he related what had happened.

"How incredible!" the commander said, when he beheld the trophies. "I recognize this flute. The *Saeda* and the *Semiore,* the two [foremost] flutes of the subcelestial realm, were in the possession of Prince Takakura [57] when he plotted a rebellion some years ago. He presented the *Semiore* to the Mii monastery as a good work for the bodhisattva Maitreya, but they say that he kept the *Saeda* until the very end. When he was slain at Mount Kōmyō in Minase, this flute passed into the hands of the Heike. I have heard that members of the Heike who were accomplished on the flute were called forth [at that time], and that Atsumori, although of tender years, was deemed the most accomplished on the flute and was given the *Saeda*. The faraway sound of a flute was heard in Ichinotani this morning, coming from the office of the Inner Palace. So he was the one who played!" Tears flowed from the commander's eyes. Tears were shed by all the others, whether or not they had known him.

"The illustrious commander Kumagae has acted nobly with respect to Atsumori. As a reward for this feat you shall have the Nagai Manor in the province of Musashi. Hasten to install yourself there." Thus did Yoshitsune speak. His henchmen rejoiced in anticipation of a [triumphant] entry into the new fief, but what thoughts did Kumagae entertain?

> *To become a man,*
> *A truly worthy man—*
> *Only to this I aspired;*
> *It was not to be, and now . . .*
> *Sleeves dyed in the black of ink.**

Thus did he versify and leave the presence of Yoshitsune.

"I would not leave Atsumori's remains on ground trodden by steeds of the common Genji soldier. If I were to deliver it [to the Heike], would I be guilty of an offense? No, I must deliver it," he reasoned. He went down to Shioya, fitted out a small vessel, and commanded three of his men—a samurai and two servant-men—to bear the letter which he wrote and deliver the body to the shores of Yashima.†

The Heike fled from Ichinotani on the seventh day of the Second Month in the First Year of Genryaku [1184]. Sailing along inshore waters and hopping from island to island, they reached the shores of Yashima in the early morning of the thirteenth. The vessel which Kumagae had sent also arrived at the shores of Yashima on that same day. But because they were foes, Kumagae's men stopped the vessel at a far distance and called aloud:

"We have come from the Genji side on a personal errand for Kumagae. We have a matter to convey to the esteemed Iga no Heinaizaemon-no-jō,[58] who is of the entourage of the lord Kadowaki."

---

* Disillusioned with the ideals of the samurai, Kumagae intends to seek spiritual solace through the priesthood. "Sleeves dyed in the black of ink" is a synecdoche representing the black robe of the Buddhist clergy, and a metonym for "priesthood."

† A promontory on the northeast corner of Shikoku Island, facing the Inland Sea. It is two miles east of the city of Takamatsu.

Ah, how piteous, these Heike! Having fled from Ichinotani and come such a great distance over the sea, they did not expect to encounter Genji forces. Their recent grief . . . then travel by sea with the tiller and waves as pillows for repose,[59] their dreams broken by winds sweeping through the pines . . . the lingering . . . the uncertainty of life . . . surely they had been kept in torment and in melancholy thoughts.[60] They were forlorn, indeed, when they heard the cry, "A Genji vessel!" They quickened their oars, each striving to outrun the other in flight, and not a single Heike was willing to meet with the Genji of the eastern provinces.

"How unbecoming, my lords," the Minister [61] said, when he saw this. "They say that the world has reached its period of twilight, that the time has come for Buddhist laws to expire.[62] Even if Fan K'uai* were to come across the waters from a foreign land, how much would one expect from a vessel so small? One of you! Go meet them and hear them!"

Heinaizaemon complied. "It is only proper; I shall go hear them," he said, and slipped quickly into the cabin [to change]. The attire in which he emerged on that day was most resplendent. Next to his person he wore an all-white *katabira* [undershirt],[63] and [over it], a blue-black military *hitatare* gown,[64] the four cords tied loosely. His arm guards were woven in the hues of the arbutus, peach, and plum blossoms,[65] his shin guards were finished in sandalwood, and his soft socks were made of bearskin and fitted with metallic rims of silver. He stepped into his shoes of ankle length,[66] and then donned a right-side guard [67] [decorated] with a lion and peonies. His suit of armor of red-silk braid shone in its serpent-hour [newness];[68] he gripped it by the shoulder catch, lifted it high, slipped it on to the full length of the hip plates, fastened [the top-straps], tied the outer sash quickly, and slipped an armor-piercer nine-and-a-half inches long [69] into his steed-hand side. His slashing blade,[70] a foot and eight inches long, he inserted vertically [in his waistband]. He secured his great sword, three feet eight inches long and [with

---

* The Japanese considered Fan K'uai (d. 189 B.C.) the archetype of the Chinese military hero. He was renowned particularly for his daring rescue of Liu Pang, founder of the Han Dynasty, during a perilous encounter with Hsiang Yü. For his biography, see the *Han-shu, ch.* 41 (K'ai-ming ed., I, 461d–462b).

fittings] made of gleaming copper, tied a cloth headband over his soft-*eboshi*,[71] and [strode out] with a white-handled halberd as a staff. He lowered a small craft and boarded it together with seven or eight henchmen, who were no less than his equal [in valor]; with shields affixed in front, they pressed forward, stirring the waves. Here was an image of the might which Fan K'uai must have presented.

Heinaizaemon called aloud to the vessel escorting [Atsumori's body]: "What matter do you convey from the Genji on a personal errand for Kumagae?"

The escorts replied: "Atsumori died by Kumagae's hand. Kumagae thought it so piteous that [he bade us] bring you Atsumori's remains and his arms and weapons and, also, gifts. Transfer them quickly to your grand vessel."

"How strange," Motokuni said,* when he heard this. "I had understood that Atsumori was at Naruto in Awa Province aboard a vessel of the clan. How could he have been slain? It must be a lie!"

The escorts replied, "You may have reasons for your suspicions, but you need only to peer into this vessel to know the truth."

"They are right," Motokuni reflected, and he brought his craft up to the escorting vessel. When he peered down into the escorting vessel, leaning on his halberd, he saw a richly-embroidered *hitatare*, and wrapped in it were what appeared to be Atsumori's remains. He saw a full-length armor [with plates] which darkened at the bottom into deep purple, a sword [with fittings] made of gleaming gold, sixteen dyed-feathered arrows inserted [in a quiver], and a bow closely wound with wisteria vine. There was no mistake. Motokuni was so overcome with sorrow that he threw his halberd aside, boarded the escorting vessel, and threw himself on Atsumori's remains. Though he would grieve, tears would not come; though he would cry, his voice would not sound. It was only after some time that Motokuni spoke, his tears streaming.

"How piteous, this lord. I presented him with this full-length armor when he was leaving Ichinotani. So like an adult he seemed when he said to me, 'If only the world would again be the world

* Obviously refers to Iga no Heinaizaemon, although Iga's given name was Ienaga.

of our clan and the [turbulent] winds of the four seas would subside, I would reward you, Motokuni, with a new fief; and how greatly you would rejoice.' When he said this, my pleasure knew no bounds. Now when I face reality, I am bewildered. I said that you, Atsumori, had boarded a vessel of the clan, although you had not, and that you were at Naruto in Awa. How deluded my heart has been! Let me hear you say, 'Is that you, Motokuni?' Speak to me again!" And he sobbed weakly. The escorts sympathized. Indeed, one should [grieve], for there is good reason. And they all shed tears.

"We are entrusted with an errand," the escorts said. "Quickly! Carry his remains to the grand vessel."

"Indeed! Lost in my thoughts, I have been remiss," Motokuni replied, when he heard them. He took Atsumori's remains aboard his craft and rowed back to the large vessel and related the incident.

"What? Atsumori slain?" Both Tsunemori and the lord Kadowaki exclaimed.

"Yes, sires."

"How strange," they said. "The wind had carried word to us that Atsumori had boarded a vessel of the clan and that he was at Naruto in Awa. How happy we were! Now we learn that he fell into the hands of Kumagae and was slain." And they were in tears.

As for the court ladies, the Emperor's mother and the principal female officials,[72] one hundred and sixty in all, came out to the edge of the vessel, holding the hems of their skirts. They embraced his remains and wailed. "Is this dream, or is it reality?" Were we to seek a parallel [to their grieving], when the Venerated Śākyamuni entered Nirvana [73] in the Second Month, the ten great disciples, the sixteen arhats,[74] and even the fifty-two species [of life] grieved the parting of ways. Theirs must have been such a grief.

It was only after some time that the father, Tsunemori, spoke, his tears flowing. "Ah, how cruel, Atsumori! When we were leaving Ichinotani, you stood there, so forlorn, looking back in the direction of our home. It was only to hearten you that I spoke [harshly]: 'How unbecoming, Atsumori! You are one who should [be the first to] leave the house which for three generation was [acclaimed] an *Enju* Gate * and to bury your body in the wilds and mountains.† Thus would your fame rise as high as the abode of the clouds in the high heaven. You should be ashamed even to have our own henchmen see you thus.' You came down to the water's edge as if you were not greatly disturbed. When you turned back, saying that you had left the flute behind, I tried to ride back with you; but we were separated by friends and foes, and I was never to see you again. These articles of remembrance were conveyed to us through the compassion of Kumagae. The empty remains and these articles of remembrance are for me to see today. After the morrow, to whom can I speak of my longings? How can I be consoled? Is this not so?" He writhed in the agony of his lament, and the people of the Heike wept still more.

After some time, [Tsunemori] called for the missive which Kumagae had forwarded. He himself was a high commander, and he expected that perhaps Yoshitsune had sent this missive. The messenger knew not of this matter and could say only that it was [intended for] the lord Kadowaki. Since the missive was addressed to Iga no Heinaizaemon, however, he bade Ienaga read the letter. Heinaizaemon obeyed. He knelt on the deck planks, held the missive high, and read it aloud.

I, Kumagae, address you respectfully.

I met this lord by chance, and, although I was determined to settle the contest with dispatch, I suddenly became forgetful that he was of the hateful enemy. The daring of my martial skill vanished, and I was even offering him my protection and care when numerous forces assailed us at once. They were to the east and to the west. They were many, and we were few. Even Fan K'uai was mindful of the skills of Chang Liang.‡ It happens that I, Naozane, was born into a house of the bow and the horse. I have merely been scurrying about [the regions] west

---

* A sobriquet for the three high ministers of the imperial court. The *enju* (*huai* in Chinese) is the *Sophora japonica*. According to tradition, the three high ministers of the Chou Dynasty (11th to 3rd century B.C.) of China were seated in court in positions indicated by three *huai* trees, and they were referred to figuratively as the "three *huai*" or "*huai* gate."

† Figuratively, to die on the battlefield.

‡ Chang Liang (d. 168 B.C.), another of the famed adherents of the founder of the Han Dynasty, was also a celebrated figure in Japanese literature. This passage alludes possibly to an episode described in Chang Liang's biography (*Han-shu*, ch. 41; see K'ai-ming ed., I, 458c) in which Chang convinces Kao-tzu of the logic of Fan K'uai's suggestion; Fan K'uai had argued that it would be a folly to remain in Hsien-yang, resting on the laurels of having occupied the

of the capital,[75] prolonging my life. Having spent countless [76] eves at
the forefront of battle positions, I have garnered more laurels than
I deserve. Yet this occasion was a sorrowful one indeed. That this lord
and I, Naozane, became deeply entwined in an accursed bond [77] is
truly grievous; it is truly tormenting. If only this cruel bond could be
dissolved, we might be freed forever of the fetters of life and death
and achieve the bond of one lotus.* I shall notify all of the place of
my solitary abode where I shall pray earnestly for the deliverance of
his soul.[78] May the truth [of this statement] be attested by what you
shall hear in the future. Proclaim this among those of your clan. I
address you respectfully. The seventh day of the Second Month, the
First Year of Genryaku.

> From the resident of Musashi Province, Kumagae no Jirō
> Naozane; to the Esteemed Iga no Heinaizaemon-no-jō, of
> the entourage of the Lord Kadowaki.

Those of the clan—dwellers amidst the clouds, nobles and
ministers—echoed their praise in unison. Truly, in the distant
provinces † all one hears about Kumagae is that he is the demon
of Naraka,[79] a barbarian. But his compassion runs deep. And the
skill of his prose! The grace of his calligraphy! A warrior as
benign as he must be dignified with a reply. A letter in reply
from the Minister was written in the personal hand of Tsunemori.

The messengers accepted the letter and rowed back in haste
to Ichinotani in order to show it to Kumagae. "Without the fortunes of the bow and arrow, never would I, Kumagae, be able to
lay my eyes on the personal hand of Tsunemori." He raised it aloft
thrice and then unfolded it to read. The missive stated:

We have received Atsumori's bodily remains and other remembrances.
Why should our thoughts ever return to the metropolis of blossoms,
which we had left behind? Those who flourish must decline—this is
the way of our ephemeral [world]. Those who meet must part—this is
the way of this defiled land.[80] Did not the Venerated Śākyamuni part
with his son Rāhula? After we left [Ichinotani] on the seventh day of

---

former Ch'in capital. Here Kumagae is describing his despair by alluding to
the fact that even Fan K'uai was helpless without the eloquence of Chang
Liang.

  * The lotus blossom is a symbol of Buddhahood, or salvation. Kumagae expresses his hope that the ill-fated association between Atsumori and himself
will not extend into their future existence, and that they will be reborn together in the Buddhist Paradise.

  † That is, provinces which are distant from Kumagae's home province.

this month, I did not see the unworthy one [81] although swallows came and spoke of him. Although the returning geese brought tidings as they traversed the skies with wings aligned,* I did not hear his voice. In my longing to learn his whereabouts, I looked up to the heavens, prostrated myself on the earth, and prayed for tidings. I waited for Radiant Kami to acknowledge my prayers, for the Buddha to perceive [my longings]; and in seven days this came to pass. Within myself I practiced faith; without, tears of emotion moistened my sleeves. Hence it came that I was able to see again the son who was born to me. Without my praising the felicitous and euphoric [nature of the deities], never could I have seen him again. The summit of Mount Sumeru † is low, and the grey-green sea is shallow [in comparison with my gratitude]. Were I to endeavor to repay this debt, the past would be far distant; were I to attempt to respond to it, the future would be long indeed.[82] A myriad details remain that cannot be encompassed in writing.

> This in reply to Kumagae of Musashi.

Thus did the missive read.

Now,[83] Kumagae scrutinized [his inner heart]; the spirit of the bodhi had been evoked.

"I hear that we are to attack Yashima in Sanuki [Province] on the sixteenth day of this month," he mused. "If I were to remain with others in this world of sorrow, I, Kumagae, should again experience such moments of grief. I have become aware that this world is not a permanent abode, aware that [life] is less certain than beads of dew on the leaves and grass or the [reflection of the] moon that dwells on the water. One may poeticize the blossoms of Chin-ku, but flourishing blossoms are the first to be swept away by winds of impermanence; those who enjoyed the moon from the South Tower were secreted amidst the ever-changing clouds even before the moon was hidden from view.[84]

"Should man, after his fifty years, scan the subcelestial realm, all will prove a dream, an illusion; to acquire life and perish not . . . this cannot be. Lest I have regrets, I must make these thoughts the source of my bodhi." ‡ His mind was set.

---

* The image of geese flying in formation symbolizes a family together, and is an ironic reminder of the sadness of being separated from his own son.

† The mythical mountain which, according to Buddhist scriptures, is the central hub of the world.

‡ Kumagae is stating here that these reflections shall serve as the source of his inspiration to seek enlightenment through Buddhism.

He journeyed in haste to the capital, where he beheld Atsumori's head [which was on display]. So deep was his grief that
he stole it off the prison gate and returned with it to his lodging,
and there had a bonze conduct memorial rites. He saw the head
vanish into smoke of impermanence, and he took the ashes and
carried them about his neck. "To what use shall I put this
spindle-tree bow?" he pondered. "It has served to abet my courage
until this day and enabled me to conceal my frailty from others."
He cut it into three pieces and made three stupas to serve as a
bridge to the Pure Land.[85] He left his lodging and lived in
Kurodani amidst the [hills of] Higashiyama.[86] His Eminence
Hōnen [87] having consented to be his teacher, he severed his hair
at the roots and cast it toward the west, and he changed his name
to Renshōbō.[88]

> In place of sleeves of flowers,*
>   Sleeves dyed in the black of ink.
> In a remote hamlet,
>   An ink-black robe.
> Now will I don it,
>   Useless [though it may be].
> This have I become—
>   But for whom?
> For one who has vanished
>   Like a body of dew
> That is toppled by the wind;
>   And I have no regrets.

Renshō stayed at Kurodani, reciting prayers. One day, however, Renshō thought to himself that he would like to view
Mount Kōya, which rises in the province of Kii. He took his leave
of His Eminence [Hōnen] and left Kurodani while the night was
yet deep.

There were many famed sites [in view] as he departed from the
capital. Scanning Higashiyama, he saw the monasteries of Seikanji, Imakumano, Kiyomizu, Yasaka, and Chōrakuji.[89] The
temple named Kiyomizu was [established] at the behest of

---

* "Sleeves of flowers" figuratively denotes "lay garments" and contrasts with
the "sleeves dyed in the black of ink" of the Buddhist clergy.

Emperor Saga; it was fashioned by Sumitomo and built by Tamuramaro. It was constructed in the year 807.[90] A pledge made to
the Thousand-armed [Avalokiteśvara] promises more than do
vows made to a myriad Buddhas.[91] "May Atsumori's soul quickly
attain bodhi," he prayed.

Scanning the west, he saw the Hall of the Valley and the Hall
of the Peak at the foothill of the Mountain of the Aged in
Tamba.[92] Looking back northward, he saw the grave markers of
Rendaino and Funaoka Hill, which were beyond the Inner
Wilds;[93] and his tears would not cease to flow. Scanning the south,
he saw the East Temple, the West Temple, the Four Mounds.[94]

> Though the years may go by,
> These do not age.

He viewed the Mutsuda river bed, passed by the Takara Temple
of Yamazaki and the Sekido Cloister, descended the Yahata Hill,
and traversed the fields of Katano, where Prince Koretaka had
hunted.[95]

> Pheasants of the forbidden wilds *
> Must cherish their young.

He passed by the Udono inns surrounded with thick fences of
twigs, came to the fields of Itoda, made obeisances in prayer to
the King-Child of Kubotsu, and then went to worship at Tennōji.[96]

The temple named Tennōji was [established] at the behest of
Prince Shōtoku. Although the Seven Wonders may be time-
honored, their marvels can never be exhausted; that the flow of
the Turtle Well never ceases is a wonder.[97] He made obeisances
in prayer. Then he came to Amano; the Great-Luminous-Deity is
the pacifier-protector of [Mount] Kōya.[98] "Let this bonze be
received into the Mount," he prayed earnestly, and he arrived
anon at Mount Kōya.

The venerated Mount Kōya is four hundred *ri* distant from the
Imperial pale; it is a deserted ground, distant from villages and
hamlets.[99] The eightfold peaks [100] [which surround] eight valleys

---

* Alludes to the fields of Katano, which during the Heian Period were
"forbidden" grounds—that is, an imperial hunting reserve.

rise loftily, and the bluffs are high. The summer winds sigh through the branches, and the glow of the evening sun is peaceful. [The path] from the temple on the height opposite the valley of the Portrait Hall represents Mahāvairocana and the one hundred and eighty venerated deities of the Realm of the Womb-store.[101] [The path] from the Great Tower to the Cloister of the Interior represents the thirty-seven venerated deities of Mahāvairocana. The principal venerated deities of the Golden Hall are Akṣobhya, Ratnaśa, and Amitābha; these [statues] were carved by the Great Teacher.[102] That which is called the Great Tower is a bejeweled tower sixteen *jō* high,* modeled on the Iron Tower of the Southern Celestial [Region] [103] and shaped like the *hanri* of the Tuṣita Heaven.[104] The upper [story of the tower] houses a thousand images of Amitābha, the middle houses the Twenty-eight Followers of the Thousand-armed [Avalokiteśvara], and the lower the Twelve Deities of Bhaiṣajyaguru, the "Teacher of Medicine." [105] The multitude—even the wicked lot—regardless of which existence or world they are in, may see their sins expiated and behold the Three Venerated [Buddhas], who come to welcome them [to the Pure Land].[106] So marvelous! And he prostrated himself in prayer.

Then he proceeded to the Cloister of the Interior. The bleached bones beside the path were as numerous as scattered sand, and Renshō prayed more intently. [At last] he came to the Cloister of the Interior, where he deposited Atsumori's ashes. Then on the side of the Valley of Lotus Blossoms he built a hermitage which he named Chishiki Cloister. He picked flowers from the peaks and cupped the arghya water [107] in his hands. The ritual thus completed, he died at the age of eighty-three.[108]

He was mighty in wickedness but equally strong in goodness—a man renowned in the ways of both the literati and the samurai. We know not of the houses of China, but in Japan—and there is no one who feels otherwise—there was no warrior as worthy as he.

---

* Approximately 160 feet.

VI: A LIBRETTO: *Izumi's Fortress*

T H E text of *Izumi's Fortress* on which the translation is based
was transcribed by Takano Tatsuyuki in 1925 from a manuscript copy then being used by the performers of Ōe Village; it
has been published, partly annotated, in Shimazu's *A New Collection of Tales of Near Antiquity (Kinko shōsetsu shinsan).*[1] This
text contains a number of obvious omissions and corruptions;
but because it is a libretto, its contents reflect the recitational features of the actual performance. Emendations in this text (it is referred to in the notes to Chapter VI as Text A) were based on
comparisons with the version in the Daigashira Sahei Collection
(Text B),[2] and a third version (Text C),[3] which was transcribed
probably during the 1620's. Instances of significant variation
among the texts are pointed out in the annotation. Conjectural
emendations and the eclectic fusion of passages have, as a rule,
been avoided.

THE HISTORICAL SETTING

Izumi's Fortress is one of the twenty kōwaka which treat dramatic
highlights in the life of Minamoto no Yoshitsune. The setting is
Hiraizumi, the glittering metropolis that was the hub of the expansive domain of the Fujiwara clan in northern Japan, and the
time, late in the year 1187. The main character in the story is
Fujiwara Tadahira, who was more commonly known by his
"capped name"[4] of Izumi no Saburō. The principal theme is
Izumi's sacrifice of his own life and his wife and children in up-
holding his pledge of loyalty to Yoshitsune. Although Yoshitsune
is seldom in the foreground, the story evolves about him; he is the
key to the plot. The story of *Izumi's Fortress*—if we consider it a
segment of the great epic that is the life of Yoshitsune—occurs as
the prelude to the grand catastrophe, the death of Yoshitsune.

The Fujiwara clan that held sway over northern Japan in the

late Heian Period may have been related to the courtly Fujiwara clan of Kyoto.[5] The clan came into prominence as a local political power in the generation of Fujiwara Kiyohira (1056–1128). During the series of armed conflicts in the 1080's known as the Later Three-Year War, Fujiwara Kiyohira sided with the Genji general Minamoto no Yoshiie (1041–1108), who, as Governor of Mutsu Province and Head of the Ainu Pacification Office (*Chinjufu-shōgun*),[6] was charged with the task of quelling disturbances in his area of jurisdiction. This war began as an intrafamily feud within the Kiyohara clan, but the fact that Fujiwara Kiyohira was related to the Kiyohara did not deter him from warring against them. The Fujiwara emerged from the war victorious, and as the only important power in northern Japan. Within a time span of three generations, the clan achieved control of Mutsu and Dewa provinces, giving it a domain that occupied one-third of Honshū. Kiyohira's grandson, Hidehira (1121–1187), was appointed Governor and *Chinjufu-shōgun* of Mutsu by the Imperial Court in Kyoto, thus acquiring titulary rights to administer the domain of which he was already the effective suzerain.

In Hiraizumi the Fujiwara lords endeavored to build a metropolis that would mirror the splendor of the imperial capital. The great Buddhist monasteries which they built boasted hundreds of edifices, and the magnificence of the Gold-colored Hall (*Konjikidō*) was fabled even in Kyoto.[7] Yoshitsune sought refuge in Hiraizumi, for even Yoritomo—although he was acclaimed the leader of the island empire—would not dare to invade the domain of Fujiwara Hidehira which stood to the north a virtual empire in itself.

According to the romantic war chronicles, Yoritomo's hatred for Yoshitsune was inspired principally by the venomous tongue of his trusted advisor, Kajiwara Kagetoki. Kajiwara nursed a deep grudge against Yoshitsune as a result of the fabled incident of the "backward oar" (*sakaro*) which took place at the launching of the Genji fleet prior to the Battle of Yashima in 1185. As it is described in the *Rise and Fall of Gempei*,[8] Kajiwara suggested to Yoshitsune that the vessels be equipped with "backward oars" at the prow so that they would be able to advance or retreat with equal facility. To Yoshitsune's remark, "How can a battle be won if one prepares beforehand for retreat?" Kajiwara retorted: "A field marshal must safeguard his own self in order to destroy the enemy; this is the measure of the efficacy of his strategy. The so-called boar-warrior forgets all else in his single-mindedness to strike down only the enemy to his front. This can be dangerous. It is only your youth that lets you speak thus." Infuriated by the affront, Yoshitsune inferred that Kajiwara's attitude was that of a coward, and in the end he said abusively, "When you become field marshal, use a hundred backward oars, even a thousand, so that you may save yourself by fleeing; but a backward oar is an ill-omened thing, and I will not hear of it on a vessel of mine." Bloodshed was narrowly averted as bystanders held the two apart.

Kajiwara was with the Heike when Yoritomo initiated his campaign against the Heike in 1180. In the Battle of Ishibashi-yama at the foothills of Mount Fuji in that year, Yoritomo's meager army was almost annihilated, and he was able to escape only because Kajiwara led the Heike troops away from a hollow tree trunk in which he knew Yoritomo was hiding.[9] The grateful Yoritomo, once he rose to power, treated Kajiwara with great deference and regarded him as a trusted confidant. It was probably Kajiwara who planted the seeds of suspicion in Yoritomo's mind with respect to the alleged infidelity on the part of Yoshitsune. The *Azuma kagami* records one specific instance—this occurred shortly after the battles of Yashima and Dannoura—in which Kajiwara advised Yoritomo that Yoshitsune's existence endangered the solidarity of the Genji clan.[10]

Izumigajō treats the last phase of Yoshitsune's life. The story begins as Fujiwara Hidehira, afflicted by a fatal curse imposed by Kajiwara Kagetoki, enjoins his five sons to remain steadfast in their loyalty to Yoshitsune.

THE TRANSLATION

Narrative:

Now,[11] it seemed only yesterday[12] that Hōgan[13] [Yoshitsune] moved into the Takadachi Palace,[14] but soon it would be three years.[15] The *nyūdō* Hidehira[16] stood by him and watched over him, and all the greater and lesser lords of the fifty-four counties of the Interior Region[17] were now partisan to this Lord. Guards alternated so that they stood by him and watched over him at all times.[18]

This [state of affairs] did not remain hidden from Kantō. Kajiwara got wind of it quickly, and he summoned his heir Genta Kagesue and his second son Heiji.

"Hōgan has now gone down [19] to the Interior Region. His power and influence wax by the day, double with [each passing] month. What is more, I hear that the Eminent Mongaku of [Mount] Takao [20] and Tōkōbō of Kurama [Temple] [21] met the other day at the cloister of the Karma Master of Nara [22] and secretly discussed their intention of mending relations between the brothers [Yoritomo and Yoshitsune]. Since there is agreement,[23] it is certain that they will eventually be reconciled.

Prefatory:

> Should this come to pass . . . ah, Hōgan!

Coro melos pastorale:

> At Watanabe-Fukushima [24] in the province of Tsu . . .
> How could he forget even this day
> The grudge over the 'backward oar.'
> In such an eventuality,
> We, father and sons, shall be
> Dragged to the fore to be slain . . .
> This is only too clear.
> What's to be done?" So saying,
> He knew only worry and anguish.

Narrative:

"It is as you say," Genta said when he heard this. "There could be no greater danger to our house than for this lord to abide in Kamakura. It is customary today as in days of old to seek the aid of Buddhas and Kami against a foe with whom one is powerless to cope. Though it may be of no avail, you must at least attempt the cursing [25] of Hōgan."

"Indeed," Kajiwara mused.

He hastened to the superintendent of Wakamiya, the monk superior,[26] and implored him to accept the task of cursing Hōgan.

The monk superior was [at first] steadfast in his refusal, but he
relented when Kajiwara pleaded with deadly earnestness, and . . .

Prefatory:

> He accepted.

Solo pastorale:

> Having selected an auspicious day,
> He purified a place [27] and solemnized it,
> Decorated the altars of the four directions,
> And burned the homa fire [28] for the cursing [ritual].

Coro risoluto:

Now,[29] there are four [types of] altars [30]—altars for warding off
adversity, for increasing one's fortune, for revering, and for
cursing.[31] The [rite for] warding off adversity is performed with
the altar toward the east. [The rite for] increasing one's fortune
is performed facing the south; [the rite for] revering is performed
facing the west; and [the rite for] cursing is performed
facing the north.[32] The sight of the offerings [33] was fearsome to
behold. The sapwood [he used] was of the mountain hydrangea;
as incense for burning, the skeleton of a venomous snake. For
the food-offering he heaped a meal of ash and dirt; for arghya
water * he took the fluid that dripped [34] out of a white serpent.
The rites were changed with the days—the method of Kṣitigarba [35] during the first seven days, and the method of Amitābha
during the second seven days. With the coming of the third seven
days, he took [the offerings] and swallowed [36] them. With his
hands he formed the symbols for binding [the victim] in both
body and spirit.[37] He made vows unto the Luminous-King
Ucchuṣma and Vajrakumāra [38] and prayed on still another seven
days.

"If this method should fail, then take the life of this monk
superior!"

He beat his chest with a single-pointed vajra.[39] He then gashed
his head with a three-pronged vajra, sprinkled over the homa
flame the blood that flowed,[40] and, rubbing the loud-rattling
rosary between his palms, he prayed on with rapt fury. Such fury

---

* A Buddhist offering of water that has been scented with blossoms.

did he exhibit that Yamāntaka's "Ox of the Wise"[41] that stood
to the west [of the altar] started with a bellow and turned to the
north, folded its forelegs, and collapsed. Encouraged by this,
the devotee [took to the methods of] the One-word *Kinrin,* the
Five Altars, the Six-word *Karitei,* the Eight-word Mañjuśrī,
Acala's Life-prolongation, and the Luminous-King Yamāntaka.[42]
As he commenced [the rite for] binding [the victim] both in body
and spirit, he prayed on with even greater fury. Such fury did
he exhibit that, when [the first of] the fourth seven days dawned,
a black cloud hovered over the altar, fresh blood coated the blade
of [the Luminous-King] Acala, and a grisly head tumbled off the
altar . . . gave a biting grin . . . and expired. The task thus
completed, he tore down the altar.

Narrative:
Be grateful [Kajiwara]! The Buddha may be boundless in his
mercy, but [he allowed the evil] prayers to take effect. However,
[the curse] was not visited on Hōgan. It afflicted instead the
person of Hidehira, who [now] lay prostrate on his sickbed and
appeared to be near his end.

  Now, Hidehira had six children. He had five sons—the eldest
being Nishikido no Tarō, the next being Date no Jirō, the third,
Izumi no Saburō, and then Shirō Motoyoshi and Hizume no
Gorō. His youngest was a damsel. When it appeared that he was
near his end, the five brothers . . .

Prefatory:
    He called to his pillowside.

Solo pomposo:
    "Now, brothers all, hear this:
    Should the clan, the brothers, be in discord
    Once [your father], this bow-handler, is gone

Coro melos pomposo:
    The house shall surely be torn asunder.
    Let the elder brother comfort the younger,
    Let the younger abide by his elder;
    Regard His Lordship with reverence,
    And the people with deep tenderness.

And change not in the least,
After Hidehira's passing,
The worship of the Kami, the sacrifices."

Narrative:

"Izumi no Saburō! Go to the Takadachi Palace and escort His Lordship [hither], for in my final moments I have matters which I wish to convey to him."

Tadahira complied. He hastened to the Takadachi Palace and delivered this message. Hōgan was greatly startled, and he repaired to Hidehira's residence accompanied by two escorts, Ise no Saburō Yoshimori and Kamei no Rokurō Shigekiyo. Hidehira was overjoyed. He raised himself with the help of his five sons. He washed his hands, rinsed his mouth, donned only the upper part of his *hitatare*,[43] and met with the lord.

"It is only this that I ask of Your Lordship," he said. "I, Hidehira, have consummated my ties with the Sahā [Realm] and shall embark on my journey to the Dusky Circuit, the Yellow Spring.[44] My children are many, but since they are all tender in years, I wish Your Lordship's kind indulgence to bear witness as I apportion my landholdings [among them]. I would like to designate Nishikido no Tarō the heir since he is the eldest of the brothers, but as Your Lordship knows, of the sons and grandsons [of the family] of Hidehira, the senior scion [alone] may not receive the heirship.[45] I therefore confer the heirship of the family upon Date no Jirō, and I bequeath to him the county of Date, the county of Shinobu . . . [a total of] fifteen counties in the Eastern Sea Circuit to which the heir has a rightful claim. I bequeath to Nishikido no Tarō the county of Katsuta, the counties of Shibata, Kumoi, Ansen . . . fifteen counties in the Western Sea Circuit. To Izumi no Saburō [I bequeath] the seven counties of Matsushima, to Shirō Motoyoshi the six counties of Shiogama; and the county of Hizume . . .

Prefatory:

I bequeath to the youngest of my sons.[46]

Solo recitativo:

The two counties of Takekuma and Seikai

I bequeath to [my] youngest, the damsel.
The county of Katada is the widow's share.

Coro melos pomposo:

> And now, the twelve counties of Dewa,
> Though it be a petty province,
> I present to Your Lordship.
> I beg you, regard it only
> As grazing land for your steeds.
> Oh, the sorrow of parting, My Lord!
> It is not my true wish
> To see Your Lordship thus [in such straits].
> Acquiesce in [the course of] this world,
> That it may be endurable.
> Once Hidehira has expired,
> There will surely be
> An insidious resolve from the lord at Kamakura*
> To bid you slay [47] His Lordship.
> Should you acknowledge it as just
> And be disloyal to this lord,
> Then may you incur the malevolence of Kami,
> May the lineage of Hidehira come to an end.
> Why cannot this world be
> As one wishes it to be?
> That you might be reconciled with your brother,
> That I might attend you at Kamakura . . .
> I have wished for this so,
> But now all is in vain.
> Only this preys yet on my mind."
> In a failure of restraint, his tears flowed.

Narrative:

"Pray set your mind at rest," [48] the sons said, heeding [Hidehira].
They stated that they were assuredly without perfidy toward His
Lordship.

"How gratifying!" Hidehira exclaimed, when he heard [their

---

* That is, Yoritomo.

reply]. "Should you be so determined, then write an oath [49] and show it to me while I still draw breath in this existence."

"An easy matter," they said. They obtained [50] Goō [charm slips] from the Great Luminous Deity of Matsushima,[51] and . . .

Prefatory:

> Following the eldest, Nishikido,
> Each [of the brothers] wrote his oath.

Solo pastorale:

> Now,
> The intent [manifest] in the written oath was:

> "Hachiman Tarō Yoshiie [52]
> Came down to these provinces,
> And attacked and destroyed Abe no Sadatō;
> And upon our ancestor, Mitachi no Gontarō Kiyohira,
> Did he confer the *shugo*[-ship] of this province.[53]
> Since that time, for three generations—
> [Through] his son Kojirō Motohira to Hidehira today—
> The provinces have been serenely tranquil;
> And we have been blessed to receive
> Mandates of the Lord of the Only Celestial [Realm].*
> We have acquired renown as a house of the bow and arrow.
> For all this [54] we are indebted to this House [of Mina-
> moto].
> Are we not, then,
> Equally [55] indebted to this lord?
> Should this [oath] be violated . . .

Coro pastorale:

> On high, the Brahman-Heaven [King] [56]
> And the Śakra-Heaven Lord;[57]
> Below, the Four Great Celestial Kings;[58]
> And, in the world [that lies] below,
> The Great Heaven-Illuming Deity of Ise,[59]
> The Great Hachiman Bodhisattva,[60]
> Who is pacifier-guardian of the regal city,

---

* The emperor.

The Kami of Kashima, Katori, Suwa, and Atsuta,
The Great Luminous Deity of Matsushima,
Who is the Kami of our clan,
And all the greater and lesser Kami,
Whether of Heaven or earth,
[Worshipped] in the sixty-six provinces—
May their wrath be visited upon us.[61]
Should we be treacherous to this lord,
May the line of Hidehira expire;
May our fortunes with the bow and arrow
Suffer lasting decline in this existence;
May we sink down to Naraka in the next existence
To be immured within the ice of the Scarlet-Lotus hell,
The ice of the Great Scarlet-Lotus hell;[62]
And may there be no realm [of existence]
In which we may rise again.
The written oath is as stated herein.
The twenty-third day of the Twelfth Month,
The Fourth Year of Bunji.
Nishikido no Tarō. His Seal."

Thus did he write.
Then the younger brothers, too, wrote their oaths,
And each affixed his seal. [The sight was enough]
To make the hair on the body stand on end.[63]

Narrative:
"The oaths seem commendable," Hidehira said, after he inspected them. "Now, the oath of the heir Yasuhira shall be reposited in the Treasure Hall[64] [of the shrine] of the Great Luminous Deity of Matsushima, Nishikido's oath shall be presented to His Lordship. The oath of Izumi no Saburō I will . . .

Prefatory:
Carry with me to the Dusky Circuit as a testimony."

Coro melos pastorale:
He affixed it to the charm worn next to his person.
"The other two oaths must be burnt to ashes

And within your bodies [65] reposited secure."
"We shall heed you," they replied.
They burnt it to ashes, which they mixed into water,
And the brothers, all five,
Drank of it in turn.[66]
Of deeds such as this, precedents are few.[67]

Narrative:

Hidehira spoke: "Having witnessed this, my mind has been set at rest.[68] There is a thing called 'the pronouncement of the final moment' [which is allowed] a man who is dying. In my pronouncement I shall speak of the business of war. When Hidehira dies, there will surely come an insidious resolve from Sir Kamakura to command the slaying of Hōgan. Reply to the first emissary. Slay the second emissary.

Prefatory:

Should a third time come to pass,
The forces of Kamakura shall rise."

Coro risoluto:

"Should the winds bear news that chastising forces are being sent down, deploy your troops [widely but] maintain contact among them. Shut down the great fortress gate of Date, plant a barrier at the Kamewari slope, and, with my five sons as generals and Benkei of the West Tower [69] as war commissioner,[70] make glorious war. Should the troops be annihilated, fire the Takadachi Palace and transfer His Lordship to the rock grotto of Tatsukoku or to the summit of Kiriyama. Should the five of you hold out in the strongholds of Semboku, Kanazawa, Torinoumi, Katsuta, Murata—our forty-eight fortresses—and persist in a defensive war for five years, or even ten, it is inconceivable that the Kamakura forces would maintain so long a siege. Then, the times will change, and amity between the brothers will finally be restored. Should this come to pass, all of you will be summoned up to Kantō as samurai who were loyal to Kurō, and you will be rewarded for your feats and merits. Even in death, this Hidehira will abide in the shade of the grass, a shield of black metal,[71] and will protect you, my children!" Thus did he speak, his voice highly sonorous. But more and more . . .

Coro melos pomposo:

> His strength ebbed;
> And the lord and the children all
> Shed tears.

Narrative:

> "There is yet much that I wish to say, but, I am so
>   weary . . .

Prefatory:

> Let me be a while in repose . . ."

Solo pomposo:

> With these his final words, at dawn,
> On the twenty-fourth day of the Twelfth Month,
> In the Fourth Year of Bunji [72]—

Coro melos pomposo:

> They say [he] was ninety-eight [73]—
> He expired as does the morning dew.
> The children and the clan congregated;
> That they grieved—this is needless to say.
> The one who grieved most of all was
> He who sojourned at the Takadachi Palace,
> He who was without karmic results [74] . . . Yoshitsune.
> Even in dream he could not recall
> His father, from whom he had parted
> In the springtime of his second year.
> He felt, in parting now with Hidehira,
> As though he had lost both parents.
> "If only I, Yoshitsune, had station in the world,
> I would bestow any favor [on Hidehira].
> This notwithstanding, it is from Hidehira
> That I have received instead.
> For this, more than all else, I am ashamed.
> What is to become of my sorrowing person!"
> With tears streaming, he did lament.
> "Yet, no greater debt have I than [to Hidehira]."
> Donning his shaded [garments], he escorted

> [The remains] to the edge of the wilds.[75]
> Yoshitsune was [unblest] so, only because
> His karmic dues had expired—so it was said.

Narrative:

Each son requested seven days [during which] he, in his own
way, prayed for the soul's deliverance. The thirty-fifth day [after
passing] being the day for attending Yama-rāja's Court of Inquiry[76] . . .

Prefatory:

> Yoshitsune said, "Let me pray for the deliverance of his
> soul."

Solo recitativo:

> He intoned the sutras himself,
> Engaged numerous monks to conduct the rites;
> And in divers ways did he comfort the soul.
> Though he abided in the shade of the grass,
> How Hidehira must have rejoiced.

Narrative:

On the Forty-ninth Day,[77] the superintendent of Matsushima[78]
was summoned, and memorial rites held; and discourses on the
[Buddha's] Law lasted a full seven days.[79]

Then, just as their father Hidehira had forewarned, not to
belie anticipation, there was delivered to the residence of Nishikido—though the Hundredth Day[80] had yet to pass—an insidious resolve from the lord at Kamakura, commanding the slaying
of Hōgan. The five brothers unfolded [the missive] and read it.

Prefatory:

> This missive[81] stated:

Solo pastorale:[82]

> "There is no cause for the band of the Interior[83]
> To become enemies with Yoritomo
> By allying itself with Yoshitsune,
> Who is without station in this world.
> Should you change your hearts forthwith,
> And take Yoshitsune's head . . .

Coro risoluto:

and send it forth to Kantō, you shall be rewarded with the five provinces of Kōzuke, Shimotsuke, Kai, Shinano, and Musashi.[84] The *zuryō*-[ship] [85] of these same provinces I presume that you covet. The message is as stated herein. The first day of the Third Month, the Fifth Year of Bunji. Minamoto no Yoritomo. His Seal."

Narrative:

"Were we to take as our lord this Yoshitsune, who as Yoritomo stated is without station in this world, we would be dismounting our steeds * when we need not do so; this would be a bitter fate. Let us slay this lord and share Kōzuke, Shimotsuke, Kai, Shinano, and Musashi—the five provinces that will be awarded to us." Thus spoke the eldest, Nishikido. [The brothers] concurred, except the third son, Izumi no Saburō Tadahira. Izume spoke amidst tears and with [his head bowed low so that] the tip of his *eboshi* touched the ground:

"Our father, Hidehira, was indeed [86] contented when he died since he had had us inscribe the oaths. And now, so soon after [his death], we are conspiring to mutiny. Should this act cause our father to be cast down to Naraka, how could we escape the decree of Heaven.[87]

Prefatory:

Persist not in such thoughts.

Coro melos pastorale:

If you cannot accept this,
Then let Tadahira go.
Hereafter, we shall meet no more."
He quitted the matted room [88] and departed.
There was none who did not praise [his action].

Narrative:

Tadahira returned to his residence, and he exclaimed before his wife, "Such a dishonorable affair!" To her [query of] "What is

---

* Figuratively, "to be vanquished in war."

this now?" he replied: "My brothers have become enemies [of Yoshitsune] and conspire to slay His Lordship. Such an ignoble . . .

Prefatory:

> Affair that has come to pass!"

Solo recitativo:

> His wife heard him, and she said:
> "Oh, an ignoble affair is this!
> Left behind [in this world] by Tadahira,
> And now, though time has scarcely elapsed,
> He is an enemy to the brothers.
> What, then, will become of His Lordship?
> Though I am merely a woman,
> I shall go to the Takadachi Palace
> And attend upon His Lordship.
> What thoughts have you, Tadahira?

Narrative:

Hearing her, Izumi said: "Only this.[89] There are indications that my brothers may attack the Takadachi Palace this very night. I must send reinforcements quickly." He selected twenty-seven stalwart warriors and . . .

Prefatory:

> Dispatched them to the Takadachi Palace.

Solo delicato:

> [He realized] only that he was relieved;
> He knew not of [his own imminent] death. . . . A pity!

Narrative:

Now, the four brothers remaining at Nishikido's residence [conferred].

"Nonetheless," [one of them said], "Izumi no Saburō left this matted room in anger [90] when he failed to thwart [our plan]. We cannot wait any longer.[91] As a blood sacrifice to the ninety-eight thousand Kami of war, let us make Izumi take the blade to his belly."

"Rightly so!" [another said].

They provided Terui, Kanazawa, and Torinoumi with more than three thousand horsemen, and [this army] advanced on Izumi's Fortress. Izumi's Fortress was surrounded on the three sides by the Koromo River, and on the fourth side by a moat that had been excavated and planted with pointed shafts. Although the utmost precaution had been taken, the assaulting troops were familiar with the inside [of the fortress]; and because of the suddenness [of the attack], they were able to press up to the first and second fortress gates, where they let their battle cries resound. The warriors in the fortress were caught unawares.[92]

When Izumi saw that [his men] were bewildered and in an uproar, he uttered: "Since I spoke to you of the significance[93] of my father's bequeathed words, not even in dream did I think that you would behave so pitiably." He gave the order: "One of you! Ask them who is the commander[94] of the attacking force!"

Seki no Shirō complied. He wore his great sword, carried his arrows, grasped his bow, and ran up to [the top of] the main-gate tower[95] and shouted loudly: "Are you the chastisers sent forth by [the Emperor of] the Subcelestial Realm? You could not be! Is this due to personal rancor that you harbor, or is this brigandage! Suspicious indeed! Call out your name that I may hear it!"

The commander of the attacking force, Terui no Tarō, heard this and replied: "I know not of the cause of this uprising. On orders of the Heir [Yasuhira], we—Terui, Kanazawa, and Torinoumi—were given three thousand horsemen, and we have come this far. Take [the blade to] your belly, Tadahira! The rest of you, remove your helmets!* The Heir is the master of us all; surrender to him and save your lives!"

A ringing laugh pealed forth from Seki no Shirō as he listened.

"So that is the practice among the likes of you! To abandon one's master at the end of his path[96] and surrender . . . is there such a way? See if you can take this!" He nocked a sharply-pointed arrow, drew it well back, and released it. Torinoumi no Saburō had moved up to the front ranks, and the arrow caught him in the chest; and, its force still unspent, it went through him.

* A euphemism for "surrender."

The attackers, being of the same clan, praised [this feat] with the shouts of "Well done! Well done!"

Now, the Takadachi Palace was situated eighteen *chō*[97] away from Izumi's Fortress, and the din of war cries and archers' shouts could be heard close by.[98] Hōgan summoned Musashi [Benkei].

"That war cries are heard in the direction of Izumi's Fortress must surely mean that he has been slain by his brothers. Such is to be the fate of this Yoshitsune!"[99] And he commanded, "Go quickly and reinforce them!"

Benkei complied. [He set out with] thirty-five riders from among the samurai of the [Takadachi] Palace along with the twenty-seven henchmen of Izumi [who had been sent there earlier from Izumi's Fortress].

Prefatory:

> Coming upon a narrow paddy-way,
> They urged their steeds and rode on.

Coro risoluto:

While they were on their way, Musashi [suddenly] called out: "Wait awhile, all of you! This battle is surely one in which Izumi will betray our lord only to gratify his ruthless ambition. Soon an assaulting force will also ride against the palace of Takadachi, and we must not be cut off. Let us return to the palace and protect His Lordship!"[100] And they turned back.[101] The events coursed thus only because Tadahira's fortunes were at an end.

Izumi's henchmen said, "It is the path's end for our master, and so we shall take our leave. Farewell!" They whipped their steeds furiously and hastened on [to Izumi's Fortress].

Terui no Tarō espied them. "Lo! Reinforcements are coming from Takadachi Palace!" [The troops] leaped to either side [as the riders] cleaved through their lines to join those within [the fortress].

Now, Terui no Tarō said, "I feel utterly disgraced to have allowed so much time to go by without taking a mere fortress. I, Takanao,[102] shall lead you! Should anyone regard himself worthy, let him follow me!" With his halberd at his side, he was at the forefront of the charge. Who were the warriors that followed him?

Miwa no Rokurō, Udo no Tōji, and Aida no Hyōe led the seventy-five horsemen who stormed in with blades flailing. [They were met by] Sugihashi and Takano and twenty-seven horsemen from among the warriors in the fortress who came charging out with blades flailing and fought [with fury] since they were at the end of their path. Although these men were [now divided as] friend and foe, some were [related as] uncles and nephews, some as brothers; and they were more ashamed [to display cowardice before one another] than before total strangers. Clashing swords [103] cleaved the sword-guards, and blade-tips spewed forth flames. Retreating not a step, they fought [with fury] since they were at the end of their path. The attackers lost Aida, Nakamura, and the Furuhori brothers. Of the warriors from the fortress, seventeen horsemen were felled and lay side by side beside the moat; and the others, wounded and spent, withdrew back into the fortress. Because the attacking force was one of surging vigor [104] and was able to bring in fresh troops for each assault, the first and second fortress gates were torn down. And [the besieged now] held out in the inner fort.

Narrative:

Now, Izumi no Saburō Tadahira had refrained even from donning his armor, saying that he must not wage battle against his own brothers; but now all his friends had been killed in battle. Hearing that [the besiegers] were already storming into the fortress, he donned only his brief-armor [105] and leaped out on the broad veranda. His wife saw this, and . . .

Prefatory:

    She grasped the sleeve of his aiming [arm].*

Solo recitativo:

    "Should ever a bow-handler [in battle]
    Be concerned with thoughts [of those he] left behind,
    His death must be inglorious . . .
    Have you not been told?
    Would you go, leaving your sons

---

* "Archery-aiming" (*imuke*) refers to the left hand or arm.

To become what they will?
Whatever you may do, handle this
As you see fit, Tadahira."

Narrative:

"Truly, you have spoken [wisely]," Izumi said, when he heard this, and he came back. He placed on his bow-hand and his steed-hand knees his sons, who were five and seven years of age, and he stroked and smoothed their trailing locks.

Solo recitativo:

"Ah, how cruel, my young ones!
To be born into the bond of father and son,
And after being together too briefly,
To die by your father's hand . . .
How cruel! [106]
Hold me not in vengeful malice
Though your death shall be at my hands.

Coro melos pomposo:

Hold only your uncles in vengeful malice.
Although my wish is to spare you,
Your uncles are rapacious and unprincipled.
Would they deign to spare you?
Better to meet [death at] your father's hands.
Cross in grief the Death-journey [Mountain] and Three-way [River],[107]
And go to Yama-rāja's Court of Inquiry.
Invoke the name of the Buddha, my young ones."
When, amidst tears, he urged them thus,
They put their tender hands together,
Though their hearts were not discerning.
And, as they repeated four or five times,
"Amida-butsu . . . mida-butsu . . ."
His vision dimmed and his heart quailed.
"I must not let my heart be weak."
Quickly he drew the sword from his side,
And grabbed the elder Hanawaka,
Thrust him through twice and laid him prone.

> The young Hanamitsu saw this.
> "Oh, you are fearful, my father!
> Pray spare me!" he cried.
> As he bounded up and tried to flee
> Whither his mother stayed,
> Izumi seized fast his trailing locks:
> "It is only after you have gone
> That your parents and elder brother may go."
> A mere thrust of the blade,
> And he laid him prone on the same pillow.
> Holding himself fast, he wept.
> He was to be pitied for the [suffering] in his heart.[108]

Solo Recitativo: [109]

> The mother had watched the scene unfold.
> "Alas, a deed with no precedent!"
> Clinging to the brothers in embrace,
> "Stay awhile my young ones," she said.
> "I shall arrive anon and take your hands.
> Together we shall cross Death-journey [Mountain] and
> Three-way [River]."
> She sank [to the floor] weeping, and thus did she remain.

Narrative:

Now, Tadahira rose briskly whence he sat.

"Oh, the sorrow of parting, my wife! Our bond of husband and wife is only as of this moment. I take leave of you. Farewell!"

He quickly entered the one-space room,[110] took his suit of armor of red-silk braid which still shone in its serpent-hour [newness], and slipped it on to the full length of the hip plates; he tied the top-straps and outer sash tightly, wore his great sword, carried his arrows, took his bow, and sallied out into the greater garden.

The wife saw this and called out to him: "Wait, Tadahira! Since the autumn of your eighteenth year, my fourteenth, not for a moment have we been apart."

Coro risoluto:

"Would you forsake me now? Wait awhile, I pray." She quickly entered the one-spaced room. She seized a scarlet double-silk gown and put it on. Then she took belly-girding armor [111] of yellow-green hue, slipped it on to the full length of the hip plates, and tied the top-straps and outer sash tightly. She tucked a white-handled halberd under her arms, and, together with Izumi, stormed out with blades flailing. There was little to wonder at in her boldness of heart, for she was the younger sister of Satō Tsuginobu, who accompanied Yoshitsune into the Battle of Yashima in the western provinces and expired when he was hit by the arrow of the Governor of Noto.[112] Tadahira was renowned [113] within the fifty-four counties of the Interior Region as a man of great strength and boldness. As he ascended the tower, his wife secured the fortress gate. She carried aloft a heavy shield and advanced toward the main fortress gate in order to gain a breathing spell for the wounded troops of their side—a truly estimable deed.

Narrative:

Now, from the top of the gate tower Tadahira shouted loudly: "So Terui, Kanazawa, and Torinoumi are the ones who have come here to attack me! I do not deign to speak to persons unworthy as you, but heed well [what I shall say] and repeat it [to my brothers]. How can they escape retribution for [having betrayed] our father's dying wish and [violated] the oath? For [having forgotten] the enduring debt of gratitude to the master, continuous through three generations, for all these [wrongs], how can they escape the decree of Heaven? Ah,[114] how this Tadahira would covet another life to live! One life I would offer in service to His Lordship. The other I would sustain [only because] I want to witness the [wretched] end that is promised to my brothers. The arrows which I release now are not arrows intended for you, but for my brothers . . .

Prefatory:

A single arrow of vengeful malice . . .

Coro risoluto:

"Take this!" So saying, he took up [an arrow] thirteen grips long, nocked it quickly in a [bow with a] pull of three men's strength, drew it back fully, and released it suddenly and with a great flourish. Kanazawa no Kurō, who had moved up to the front

ranks, was caught by it squarely in the chest plate. The arrow
went through him, penetrating the black plate, and sparks flew as
it lodged in the bow-hand lapel of the helmet worn by Bamba
no Hyōe, who was standing behind. Thus begun, he broke open
the bundles of arrows and spread them about. Picking and load-
ing [arrows in rapid succession], he shot with abandon. Some
eighteen horsemen among the bold and hardy warriors were
quickly felled, and the enemy fell back to escape the arrow's range.
Tadahira, having exhausted his arrows, leaped down nimbly
from the gate and bared his weapon, and husband and wife
stormed out together with blades flailing. Because Tadahira's
ability was already known, [the foes] scattered as do leaves before
a tempest, and no one dared face him. Those who fled [115] he drove
to bay. He hacked off both legs of some, and they fell prostrate;
others he slashed down the center of their helmets, cleaving them
like Chinese bamboo, and they fell to either side. While twenty-
seven horsemen among the bold and hardy warriors were being
cut down by Tadahira, seven or eight horsemen, all good warriors,
were cut down to the ground [116] by his wife. They inflicted grave
injuries or minor wounds on the remaining warriors and scattered
them in all directions. Then husband and wife, hand in hand,
withdrew quietly to their own lines . . . [truly] a feat not of
ordinary mortals.

Narrative: [117]
In all, more than two hundred horsemen of the attacking force
died in battle. Of the warriors from the fortress, more than fifty
horsemen died in battle, and those who were not slain were
either wounded or had taken to flight. Only the two youths Tsukiōmaru and Takeōmaru now remained. Tadahira summoned the
two and said to them, "Shoot defensive arrows [to stave off the
attackers] so that I may take the blade to my belly with quietness
of mind." Takeōmaru scurried up the main-gate tower and fought
a [furious] defensive battle, for he was at the end of his path.
Tsukiōmaru took out a flint and steel and bamboo matches [118]
and struck them again and again [to ignite the matches]. He set
fire to the wind screens and partitions [119] and drove the blaze so
as to darken the sky itself. [120]

Now, Tadahira remained slumped beside the bodies of his children. "Now go, my wife, [so that you may be] together with the children," he said, and he was about to put her to death.

Solo recitativo:

> The wife clung to his sword.
> "This is unwise, Tadahira!
> It is not that I grudge my own life.
> For, however a woman shall die,
> There is no question of decorum.
> You, above all, are a bow-handler of renown.

Coro melos pomposo:

> Should you kill yourself poorly,
> Your remains shall suffer disgrace.
> Take the blade to your belly,
> [That I may witness your death.]
> And then shall I follow."

Coro risoluto:

No sooner did Izumi hear this than he said, "Truly, here again you have spoken [wisely].[121] Tadahira shall, then, take the blade." He drew his sword from his waist and plunged it into his steed-hand side; pulling out the blade and changing his hold, he struck it into the base of his heart and pressed it down to the edge of his trousers. He grasped his viscera, tore them out, and cut them to bits; and he repeated, "How is this! How is this!" No sooner had his wife witnessed this than she said, "You have taken the blade with dignity. Stay awhile, I pray." She took Izumi's sword, mouthed the tip of the blade, and threw herself onto the floor. The wife was [then] twenty-nine, and Tadahira, thirty-three. The others, too, vanished amidst the same smoke. This was, indeed, an occurrence with few precedents, and the eminent and the humble, the gentle and the lowborn, alike felt compassion for [the torment that was] in Tadahira's heart.

THE EPILOGUE

The sequel to *Izumigajō* is the kōwaka *Takadachi*, which tells the story of the Fujiwara brothers' attack on the Takadachi Palace and the gallant death of Yoshitsune and his vassals.[122] It was only after Hidehira died that Kamakura plotted actively to conquer the Fujiwara. The maxim that a house divided must fall, which Hidehira had endeavored to impress upon his sons, was one with which Yoritomo was exceedingly familiar. Although Fujiwara Yasuhira slew Yoshitsune and sent his head to Kamakura as evidence, Yoritomo was not to be placated, for he was intent upon bringing the vast domain of the Fujiwara under his control as the final step in the unification of all of Japan. The campaign against the Fujiwara was initiated in the early part of the Eighth Month of 1189, and it was scarcely a month later that Yasuhira's head was brought to Yoritomo's encampment as a trophy of victory.[123]

APPENDIX

****

APPENDIX

APPENDIX

A NOTE ON THE DISTINCTION
BETWEEN *SANGAKU* AND *SARUGAKU*

The term "sarugaku" is an enigma to many who have studied the
medieval performing arts, for it is used as a referent for three
different things. First, many scholars believe that "sarugaku" is
a phonetic corruption of "sangaku," and they often use the
two terms interchangeably. "Sangaku" is the Japanese pronunciation for the Chinese *san-yüeh* and specifically denotes the
collection of exotic magical and acrobatic acts which was imported from T'ang China during the seventh century. Second, because "sarugaku" does not appear in historical records until the
middle of the tenth century,[1] it is often used to denote a latter-
day version of the sangaku—one which evolved in Japan and
acquired some of the characteristics of indigenous forms of art.
And, finally, "sarugaku" refers also to the early nō drama. The
term "nō" came into use sometime during the fourteenth century
as a designation for staged performances of a more serious nature,
presented through dialogue, singing, dancing, and mimetic action.
Sarugaku players discarded their previous repertoire of farcical
acts and specialized in the nō. But their art was usually called
"sarugaku," so that from the Muromachi Period, "sarugaku" has
implied the nō. The term "nō" did not replace "sarugaku" until
the Modern Era. For the sake of clarity in discussion, therefore,
it is best that the term "sarugaku" be reserved as a designation
for the farcical variety show of the period prior to the development of the nō.

The differences between sangaku and sarugaku are not nearly
so distinct as those between sarugaku and the nō; in fact, there is
some question as to whether or not there was any actual difference. "Sarugaku" first appeared in the tenth century and was
used interchangeably with "Sangaku"; a common alternant form
of "Sarugaku" was "sarugō." In programs of "sumō-wrestling

festivals" (*sumō sechie*), however, sangaku and sarugaku were
frequently listed as separate numbers. "Sangaku" were performed
as interludes between wrestling matches, whereas an item entitled
"sarugaku" or "sarugō" was performed as one of the numbers in
the program of bugaku which usually followed the matches.[2] This
"sarugaku" appears fairly regularly as a number in such bugaku
programs during the late Heian Period.[3]

What is not entirely clear today is the content of the number
entitled "sarugaku." Nose Asaji believes that this "sarugaku"
was actually a sangaku number performed by musicians from
the Headquarters of the Imperial Guards (*Konoe-fu*); he states
that it can best be described as "sangaku belonging to the order
of the bugaku."[4] But Nose did not determine whether or not
there were any qualitative differences between the "sangaku
belonging to the order of the bugaku" and ordinary sangaku.
Hayashiya Tatsusaburō has been more explicit with regard to the
number entitled "sarugaku": ". . . it can be safely assumed that
this 'sarugaku' represented that part in the sangaku [repertoire]
which had been transformed into a song-dance."[5] Inasmuch as
this "sarugaku" was included in programs of bugaku, we might
assume that it was a designation for a number which was chiefly
choreographic, contrasting with the mimicking and contortive
antics which typified the sangaku. Yet there are records which
would obviate such an assumption.

From the description of the sumō-wrestling festival given in
the *Proceedings of the Ōe House* (*Gōke shidai*), a commentary on
rites and ceremonies of the Heian Period written in 1111, we learn
something about the contents of the "sarugaku" in the bugaku
program. The number comprised such acts as tricks on stilts,
legerdemain, and a dance by midgets.[8] In this instance at least,
"sarugaku" was not anything that could be called a choreographic
piece of the order of the bugaku.

The bugaku programs at sumō-wrestling festivals consisted
always of two parts. The first part comprised Dances of the Left,
which were those classed as dances of China and India; the second part comprised Dances of the Right, or those classed as
dances of Korea and Po-hai (southeastern Manchuria). Whenever
the number entitled "sarugaku" was included in the bugaku
program, it always occurred as the final selection in the Dances
of the Left. Occasionally, however, we find *zatsugei*, or "miscellaneous acts," listed in the place of "sarugaku." It seems that the
"sarugaku" in question also could be a variety show of sorts.

In support of his thesis that "sarugaku" probably represented a bugaku-like choreographic number, Hayashiya cited the fact that *Kikkan,* which was normally performed as the final selection of the Dances of the Right, was also of vulgar origin. And he suggested that "sarugaku," being the corresponding selection in the Dances of the Left, perhaps also represented a transformation of a vulgar number into a choreographic piece of a more elegant order. *A Record of Music Houses (Gakkaroku),* written in 1690, cites *Kikkan* as a bugaku piece of which only the music is extant; [7] there is no mention of "sarugaku" as a bugaku piece. The value of Hayashiya's evidence thus rests on the assumption of complete regularity in the structure of the program.

Still unexplained, however, is why "sangaku" and "sarugaku" were listed separately in the same program so as to suggest that there were qualitative differences. We can only surmise what differences there may have been. The sangaku repertoire may have been divided so that dances and acts of agility were performed during the bugaku program as "sarugaku," and some other category of acts—farcical plays, perhaps—were presented as "sangaku" during interludes between wrestling matches. There is the possibility, too, that "sangaku" referred to original Chinese *san-yüeh* acts, and "sarugaku" only to acts which evolved in Japan; for not one of the more than a dozen "sangaku" titles given in *Shinzei's Illustrations of Ancient Performing Arts (Shinzei kogaku zu)* corresponds with titles of "sarugaku" acts listed in the *Record of the New Sarugaku (Shin sarugaku ki).* This fact may reflect a distinction which stemmed from a difference in professional tradition.

The distinction between "sangaku" and "sarugaku," evidently, was not generally recognized even by the people of those times. All that can be said with certainty on the basis of available evidence is that the sangaku was a variety show originally imported from the T'ang China and performed for the enjoyment of the aristocracy; that it filtered down into the milieu of plebeian entertainment during the eighth century to provide the basis for popular variety shows which were to flourish in the latter half of the Heian Period; that "sarugaku" has been in use since the tenth century, along with "sangaku," as a designation for such variety shows; and that there may have been a subtle distinction between sangaku and sarugaku at one time, but a distinction not so pronounced as to prevent the two terms from being used interchangeably.

NOTES

****

Abbreviations Used in the Notes

KBS   *Kōwaka-bukyoku shū,* ed. Sasano Ken, 2 vols. (Tokyo: Daiichi shobō, 1943).

KKKS   *Kokusho kankō kai sōsho,* 260 vols. (Tokyo: Kokusho kankō kai, 1905–1922).

KS   *Kōchū kokubun sōsho,* 18 vols. (Tokyo: Hakubunkan, 1912–1915).

KT   *Shintei-zōho Kokushi taikei,* ed. Kuroita Katsumi, 59 vols. (of projected 60 vols.) to date. (Tokyo: Kokushi taikei kankō kai, 1929–1962).

NB   *Shinshaku Nihon bungaku sōsho,* 24 vols. (Tokyo: Nihon bungaku sōsho kankō kai, 1921–1930).

NK   *Nihon koten bungaku taikei,* 58 vols. (of projected 66 vols.) to date. (Tokyo: Iwanami shoten, 1957——).

TASJ   *Transactions of the Asiatic Society of Japan*

NOTES

I: INTRODUCTION

1 The two Chinese characters which make up the given name can each be read two different ways, so that there are four possible readings for this name: Nao-aki, Nao-akira, Tada-aki, and Tada-akira. Biographical dictionaries have settled on Naoaki as a matter of probability.

2 The given name, Naotsune, may also be read Tadatsune. Older biographical dictionaries usually list the latter.

3 *Kabu ongaku ryakushi* [*A Condensed History of the Song, Dance, and Music*], 2 vols. (Tokyo, 1888), II, 19b–22a.

4 See *Nihon zuihitsu zenshū*, III, (Tokyo, 1929), 462–463 (or *KBS*, I, 78–79). *Nimaze no ki* [*Potpourri of Records*] is a miscellany composed by the novelist Takizawa Bakin (1767–1848). The *eboshi* is a hat made of black-lacquered paper; the shape differed according to the social station of the wearer. The *tsuzumi* is a hand drum that is shaped like an hourglass.

5 Takano's earliest study, the manuscript of which he wrote in 1907, appears in his *Kabu ongyoku kōsetsu* [*A Study of the Song, Dance, and Music*] (Tokyo, 1915), pp. 223–246. His most extensive treatment appears as a chapter, with the title "A Study of the *kōwaka-bukyoku*," in *Nihon bungaku kōza*, 15 vols. (Tokyo: Shinchōsa, 1932), VII, 171–244. A similar treatment appears in his *Nihon engeki shi* [*A History of the Japanese Theater*], 3 vols. (Tokyo, 1947–1949), II, 89–132. For a convenient summary, see his *Nihon kayō shi* [*A History of the Japanese Song*] (Tokyo, 1926), pp. 583–607.

6 *Uno Mondo nikki,* entry of the 19th day, Fifth Month, 1582 (cited in *KBS*, I, 33). This incident is described in greater detail and with greater imagination in both the *Nobunaga-kō ki* [*Annals of the Lord Nobunaga*], in *Kaitei shiseki shūran*, XIX (Tokyo, 1901), 250–251 (or *KBS*, I, 34), and the *Kawasumi Taikō ki* [*The Kawasumi Annals of Taikō Hideyoshi*], in *Kaitei shiseki shūran*, XIX, 5 (or *KBS*, I, 34).

7 Tsunoda Ichirō, "The Implications of Drama in the Beginnings of the Jōruri Puppet Play," *Nihon bungaku,* no. 51 (March, 1957), 15.

8 These studies are: (1) Iwahashi Koyata, *Nihon geinō shi* [*A His-*

tory of the Performing Arts of Japan] (Tokyo, 1951), pp. 44–73. The author had earlier published the results of his inquiry into the relationship between the kōwaka and the kusemai, a problem first suggested by Takano, in a three-part article entitled "Kusemai" in *Geibun*, XI, nos. 1, 2, and 3 (January, February, and March 1920), 52–70, 32–46, and 39–54, respectively. (2) Fujita Tokutarō, *Kodai kayō no kenkyū* [*A Study of the Song of the Ancient Era*] (Tokyo, 1934), pp. 283–332. The author had published his findings earlier in the article "Concerning the Founder of the Kōwaka and Its Repertoire," *Kokugo to kokubungaku*, VI, no. 9 (September, 1929), 28-53. (3) Nose Asaji, *Nōgaku kenkyū* [*A Study of the Nō*] (Tokyo, 1952), pp. 296–315. This particular section was first drafted in 1935. (4) Origuchi Shinobu, *Nihon geinō-shi nōto* [*Notes on the History of the Performing Arts of Japan*], published posthumously (Tokyo, 1957), pp. 174–213.

⁹ This view was expressed by Iwahashi and, later, by Nose, and it served as a premise for a more recent study, Muroki Yatarō, "The Kōwaka and the Maimai," *Kokugo to kokubungaku*, XXXIV, no. 8 (August, 1957), 35–43.

¹⁰ They are: Atsumi Kaoru, "The Songful Characteristics of the Kōwaka-bukyoku," *Kiyō* (Aichi Kenritsu Joshi Tanki Daigaku), no. 5 (1954), 20–23; and Inoura Yoshinobu, "The Lineage and the Artistic Style of the Daigashira School of Kōwaka," *Kokugo to kokubungaku*, XXXV, no. 4 (April, 1958), 51–62.

¹¹ Kawatake Shigetoshi, *Nihon engeki zenshi* (Tokyo, 1959), pp. 212–217.

¹² See *KBS*, I, 157–159, 378–379.

¹³ The word *bukyoku* was evidently in wide use by the beginning of the seventeenth century, for it is listed in the Japanese-Portuguese dictionary that was published in Japan in 1603 (see *KBS*, I, 77–78). The word properly referred to the entirety of the performance rather than to the text alone.

¹⁴ This anthology was compiled and printed sometime after the middle of the seventeenth century. A later edition bore the title of *Otogi bunko* [*A Library of Fables*]. With the exception of "Booklet of the Cat" (*Neko no sōshi*), which was written after 1602, the tales in this anthology date back into the Muromachi Period.

¹⁵ Ichiko Teiji, the foremost authority on this category, suggests "medieval fiction" (*chūsei shōsetsu*) as a generic designation for short tales of the period approximately between 1330 and 1600. He does this in order to eliminate the confusion between *otogi-zōshi*, the genre, and *Otogi-zōshi*, the anthology. See his *Chūsei shōsetsu no kenkyū* [*A Study of Medieval Fiction*] (Tokyo, 1955), pp. 1–24.

¹⁶ The texts for the kōwaka *Takadachi* and *Kosode Soga* appear virtually unaltered in collections of early jōruri; see *Tokugawa bungei ruijū*, 12 vols. (Tokyo, 1914–1915), VIII, 1–17 and 34–44. According to Takano Tatsuyuki, the kōwaka *Fushimi Tokiwa*, *Eboshi-ori*, *Horikawa yo-uchi*, *Yashima no ikusa*, *Wada sakamori*, *Taishokan*, and *Yuriwaka*

daijin were also used as texts for the early puppet theater; see his *Jōruri shi* [*A History of the Jōruri*] (Tokyo, 1900), pp. 20–21.

[17] Historians of the theater are at variance with regard to where to draw the line between the "old" and "new" jōruri. The prevailing view, endorsed by Fujii Otoo and with some reservations by Wakatsuki Yasuji, the acknowledged grand historian of the jōruri, is that the term *ko-jōruri* refers to two things: (1) the styles of jōruri recitation that were prevalent before the development of the *Gidayū-bushi*, the recitative style devised by Takemoto Gidayū (1651–1714) and acclaimed initially through the performance of *Shusse Kagekiyo* [*Kagekiyo's Success in Life*], the first of many pieces written for him by Chikamatsu Monzaemon (1653–1724); and (2) in terms of dramatic literature, the jōruri texts used by reciters who practiced the styles of recitation that flourished before the emergence of the *Gidayū-bushi*. This composite definition of old-jōruri is difficult to maintain, because the marked cleavage in recitative styles is not paralleled by an equally marked contrast in literary styles between the so-called old and new texts. The dilemma of beginning the "new" with Chikamatsu's first major hit is made greater by the fact that a definite stylistic cleavage exists between his earlier works and the products—notably the *sewamono*, or "domestic plays"—of his more mature years as a playwright. These are some of the difficulties posed by the attempt to mark the division between the "old" and "new" jōruri texts at any particular time or with any particular author or work. (See also note 24 below.)

[18] In some old-jōruri pieces the narrator announces himself, using the first person, precisely in the manner of the self-introduction of the *waki* at the beginning of nō dramas. This device was incorporated deliberately by jōruri reciters in order to facilitate the dramatization of texts which were written originally in the third-person narrative.

[19] Ichiko, *Chūsei shōsetsu*, pp. 388–389

[20] A typical classification finds such suborders as children's fables, parables, parodies on love stories, parodies on war tales, tales of heroes, tales of religious experiences, tales with the stepchild theme, tales about vendettas, love, filial piety, and others. A classification which Ichiko Teiji devised seems better systematized. He sets up six major classes: tales of the court nobility, tales of Buddhist monks, tales of samurai, tales of commoners, tales of foreign lands, and miscellaneous tales. The division is, thus, based primarily on social locale. He further subdivides these classes according to themes.

[21] Two of the earliest *kana-zōshi* tales written in the Edo Period, *Uraminosuke* (post–1609) and *Chikusai* (ca 1621) were initially printed in movable type and contained no illustrations; see Matsuda Osamu, "The Genesis of *Chikusai*," *Kokugo kokubun*, XXVI, no. 3 (March, 1957), 1–10. The early booklets were generally printed in movable type, were seldom illustrated—much less in color—and were made in various sizes (the large-leafed booklets measured approximately eleven inches in height and seven inches in width). Most of the *kana-zōshi*

208

Notes

extant today are the large-leafed, illustrated woodblock editions which became popular in the Kan'ei Period (1624–1643); these are usually illustrated in color, although often only in red and green.

22 The kōwaka selections *Eboshi-ori* and *Kagekiyo*, printed in the format of the *kana-zōshi*, are included in *Kana-zōshi*, ed. Mizutani Yumihiko, 2 vols. (Tokyo, 1919), a collection of partial reproductions of original *kana-zōshi* covers, illustrations, and texts.

23 For the text of *Imagawa Ryōshun*, a drama which Chikamatsu is believed to have written for the reciter Uji Kaga-no-jō (1635–1711), see *Tokugawa bungei ruijū*, VIII, 491–515. A comparison with the text of the kōwaka *Izumi's Fortress* (see *KBS*, II, 300–411) reveals numerous examples of stylistic parallels.

24 When plays which treat themes out of contemporary plebeian society are brought within the order of old-jōruri, the defect of a literary category delimited by boundaries of time rather than literary content becomes quite evident. For example, *Keisei niga-byakudō* [*The Courtesans' Immaculate Path betwixt the Two Rivers of Agony*] (first performed in 1705 or earlier) is classed as an old-jōruri. But the theme, the setting, and speech idiom are far out of keeping with the characteristics of the typical old-jōruri; they are much closer, in fact, to the *keiseimono*, or "plays about the demimonde," of the "new" jōruri.

25 For the text of *Takadachi*, see *KBS*, II, 418–438. For the text of *Takadachi godan*, see *Tokugawa bungei ruijū*, VIII, 1–17.

II: THE HISTORY OF THE KŌWAKA

1 Throughout the Edo Period the ancestral name of Momonoi, rather than Kōwaka, was inscribed on the tombstones of members of this family. The Kōwaka family officially adopted the surname of Momonoi in the Meiji Period, and at that time many resettled in the Tokyo-Yokohama area. Only a few remain in the original area today.

2 This biographical sketch of Momonoi Naotsune is standard history. Descriptions in the biographical dictionaries are usually based on the *Dai Nihon shi* (compiled during 1657–1906), which is considered a reliable secondary source for data on warfare.

3 This document is reproduced in *KBS*, I, 213–221. The given name of the Kōwaka founder is listed as Yasunao rather than Naoaki. According to reliable histories, Momonoi Naokazu died not in 1414, but in 1370. In the *Shiryō sōran*, IV, 774, this event is listed as an occurrence of the 16th day of the Third Month, 1370: "The *shugo* of Etchū Province, Shiba Yoshimasa, and Togashi Masaie took the field at Nagasawa, attacked the forces of Momonoi Naotsune and Naokazu, and defeated them." In the *Kaei sandai ki* [*Chronicle of Three Generations in the Floral Quarters*], which is believed to have been compiled by an official scribe of the Ashikaga Shogunate, the entry under the same date reads: "At the battle of Nagasawa, [Momonoi] Naokazu and those under his command were killed." See *Gunsho ruijū*, XVI, 751.

⁴ *KBS*, I, 212–213. The year of the siege of Matsukura Fortress, however, is given as 1369.

⁵ *KBS*, I, 171–177.

⁶ *KBS*, I, 250–252 and 281–284.

⁷ *KBS*, I, 221–223.

⁸ *KBS*, I, 223–250.

⁹ *KBS*, I, 263–274.

¹⁰ This painting, currently housed in the Tokyo National Museum, has been appraised as a work either of Tosa Mitsunobu or of an artist of the same school of art in approximately the same period.

¹¹ *KBS*, I, 202.

¹² There is an interesting parallel in the case of the author of the *Dream of the Red Chamber (Hung-lou-meng)*, Ts'ao Chan (ca. 1715–1764), whom historical sources listed as the son of Ts'ao Yin, now believed to have died in 1712. Hu Shih has shown on the basis of new evidence that the father of Ts'ao Chan was a figure of minor historical importance, and that Ts'ao Yin, poet and bibliophile, was actually his grandfather; see his "A Critical Study of the *Hung-lou-meng*," *Hu Shih wen-ts'un* (10th ed.; Shanghai, 1927), III, 210–212. In the Kanze school of the nō, Zeami's brilliant son, Motomasa (d. 1432), is deliberately omitted from the formal list of grand masters; he, too, might have become a genealogical nonentity were it not for the wealth of documentary evidence.

¹³ See his article, "Kōwaka-bukyoku kenkyū," *Nihon bungaku kōza* (Tokyo: Shinchōsha, 1932), VII, 176.

¹⁴ *Nihon rekishi daijiten*, 20 vols. (Tokyo, 1956–1959), XVIII, 126. In a separate entry entitled "Momonoi-shi," the author of this article cites Naokazu, rather than Naotomo, as the name of Naoaki's father.

¹⁵ *Han-shu pu-chu*, ed. Wang Hsien-ch'ien (K'ai-ming Edition), I, 380a.

¹⁶ Cited in Henry George Farmer, "The Music of Ancient Mesopotamia," *Ancient and Oriental Music*, ed. Egon Wellesz, *The New Oxford History of Music*, I (London, 1957), 276.

¹⁷ According to traditional theory, the sound produced on a bamboo pitch pipe of prescribed length (set at nine *ts'un*, or "inches," since the Han Period) was called *huang-chung*, or "yellow bell," and it served as the basic note. The other notes were determined by being sounded on shorter lengths of bamboo. The formula, as described in the "Essay on Pitch and Calendar" in the *History of the Former Han Dynasty* (see *Han-shu pu-chu*, I, 373b), is that the second pipe is two-thirds the length of the first, the third pipe is four-thirds the length of the second, the fourth pipe is two-thirds the length of the third, and so on. The first five notes determined in this manner constitute a pentatonic mode. The twelve tones produced through this formula are approximately equivalent to the twelve tones of the Western chromatic scale. Acoustically, the process yields a series of alternating ascending fifths and descending fourths. The Japanese foot rule called the *kanejaku* is precisely the same length today as it was during the Heian Period.

The basic note of gagaku has been produced on a pitch pipe which measures nine *sun* ("inches") on this foot rule; the pitch produced is 292.7 cycles, which is very close to the 290.3 cycles of the note of "D" in Western music.

18 Tanabe Hisao, *Nihon no ongaku* [*Music of Japan*] (3rd ed.; Tokyo, 1957), p 118.

19 The five notes of the pentatonic mode are named, in ascending order, *kyū* (Chinese: *kung*), *shō* (*shang*), *kaku* (*chüeh*), *chi* (*chih*), and *u* (*yü*). The octave of the ground note is, again, the *kyū*. The notes are in the relationship of D-E-F#-A-B. A raised alternant is indicated by the affix *ei* (*ying*), or "sharp," and a lowered alternant by the affix *hen* (*pien*), or "flat." The two auxiliary notes in the Chinese heptatonic scale are called *pien-chih* ("flatted A") and *pien-kung* ("flatted D") and indicate an A-flat and a D-flat. The auxiliary notes in the gagaku *ryo* scale are actually *ei-kaku* ("sharped F#") and *ei-u* ("sharped B"), or G and C. Similar conclusions are presented in Hirade Hisao's article on gagaku in the *Ongaku jiten,* 5 vols. (Tokyo: Heibonsha, 1959–1960), I, 530.

20 Yamanoi Motokiyo, "The Scale of the Fūzoku," *Geinō,* new ser. 3. X (October, 1961), 11–13.

21 Yamanoi Motokiyo, "The Ryo and Ritsu Modes in Gagaku," *Geinō,* new ser. 3, XII (December, 1961), 5–8.

22 *Gagaku,* recorded by the Court Music Lover's Society of the Imperial Household Agency Court Music Division, King Record LKB-1001 (King Record Co., Ltd., Tokyo).

23 Eta Harich-Schneider has noted the following modifications: (1) Melodies have been simplified through the reduction of embellishments which have graced the melodies since the Heian Period; (2) the use of Western notation is causing microtones to disappear and is bringing about a new regularity in rhythmic patterns. See her article, "The Remolding of *Gagaku* under the Meiji Restoration," *TASJ,* ser. 3, V (December, 1957), 84–105.

24 *Kokushi-taikei Rikkokushi* [*The Kokushi-taikei Edition of the Six National Histories*] (2nd ed.; Tokyo, 1918), I, 461.

25 The term "gigaku" is represented either by a pair of Chinese characters which mean, literally, "skill-music," or by another pair which denote "songstress-music." But in the ancient Japanese chronicles these digraphs were read *Kure no uta-mai* and were intended to convey the meaning "music of Wu." The name *Kure,* to the ancient Japanese, usually meant China as a whole rather than the region of the state of Wu, so that the term "gigaku" actually denoted "music of China."

26 Since the gigaku was imported through Korea, we may assume that the flute used was originally the six-holed "Korean flute" (*Koma-bue*), which is at least three inches shorter than the six-holed kagura flute. The hip drum (*yōko*) is suspended in front of the drummer at hip level. It is a larger version of the *tsuzumi,* the hourglass drum which is used in present-day Japanese drama. This drum was also called

san no tsuzumi ("third-sized *tsuzumi*") and *Kure no tsuzumi* ("Chinese *tsuzumi*").

27 The *Kyōkunshō,* written by the gagaku musician Koma Chikazane (1177–1242), is a collection of facts and traditions about the ancient forms of dance and music, and is one of the most important sources for the history of early Japanese music. The edition referred to is in *Zoku gunsho ruijū,* XIX, part 1, 172–373.

28 The content of the number called "Kongō" is not described. Although in this instance it is listed after "Karora," programs of other gigaku performances cite the two numbers in reverse order. See Hazuka Keimei, "A study of Gigaku," *Tōa ongaku ronsō [A Collection of Treatises on the Music of East Asia],* ed. Kishibe Shigeo (Tokyo, 1943), p. 539.

29 *Ichikotsu* is the name of one of the twelve tones in gagaku music; it is close in pitch to the note "D" in Western music. In the *ichikotsu* key, the ground note *(kyū)* of the scale is at the *ichikotsu* pitch; the principal tones, in ascending order, approximate the pitches of D, E, F#, A, and B.

30 *Zoku gunsho ruijū,* XIX, part 1, 253–254. The fourth sentence may also be interpreted as follows: "Finally, slapping their phalli with their fans and casting suggestive glances. . . ."

31 On the basis of a study of the eleven extant plays of Aristophanes, the foremost composer of Old Comedy, Roy C. Flickinger has noted the following general structure. The performance begins with a verbal prologue; this is followed by the parodus, or entrance song of the chorus. There ensues a "dramatized debate" between two actors, each supported by a semichorus, then the parabasis in which the chorus addresses the audience on matters totally unrelated to the preceding scene, and then a series of histrionic scenes separated by brief choral odes. Finally there is the exodus, or recessional of the chorus. See his *The Greek Theater and Its Drama* (Chicago, 1918), pp. 40–42.

32 Takano Tatsuyuki, *Nihon kayō shi [A History of the Japanese Song]* (Tokyo, 1925), pp. 467–488.

33 *Zeami jūrokubu shū hyōshaku [Sixteen-Part Anthology of Zeami, Annotated],* ed. Nose Asaji, 2 vols. (5th ed.; Tokyo, 1960), II 535.

34 Yoshida Tōgo, "The Origin of the Nō and a Phase of Its Evolution," *Nōgaku,* III, no. 3 (March, 1905), 29–33.

35 See Hayashi Kenzō, "A Study of Gigaku Music," *Nanto bukkyō,* no. 8 (1960), 75–99.

36 *Zeami jūrokubu shū,* II, 278. In another work, the *Kakyō [Floral Mirror]* (1424), Zeami discusses the differences in choreographic techniques used in performing the five different pieces which make up a complete program; see *Zeami jūrokubu shū,* I, 321–322.

37 The *biwa* (Chinese: *p'i-p'a*) came into China through two routes. The four-stringed, pear-shaped, bent-neck *biwa* originated in Persia and arrived in China during the Han Period; this is the type used in Japanese gagaku. The five-stringed, club-shaped, straight-neck *biwa* was

developed in India and arrived in China through Gandhara during the
fifth century. A third type, with a round body, was developed in China.
All three types were imported into Japan from China. See Kishibe
Shigeo, "The origin of the *p'i-p'a*, with particular reference to the five-
stringed *p'i-p'a* preserved in the Shōsōin," *TASJ*, ser. 2, XIX (December, 1940), 259–304.

38 The similarity is unquestioned in the shōmyō of the Shingon Sect.
See Iwahara Teishin, *Nanzan-shinryū shōmyō kyōten* [*Canon of the
Shingon-Sect Shōmyō*], 2 vols. (Kōyasan, 1938), I, 58–61; also, Nakagawa
Zenkyō, "An Outline of the Shingon-Sect Shōmyō," *Bukkyō ongaku no
kenkyū* [*A Study of Buddhist Music*] (*Tōyō ongaku kenkyū*, combined
nos. 12 and 13 [September, 1954]), p. 127 ff. In the shōmyō of the Tendai
Sect, according to its foremost authority, Yoshida Tsunezō, the *ryo*
scale is structurally similar to the *ryo* scale of gagaku; the *ritsu* is apparently a five-tone scale, but its structure is not clearly defined in the
theoretical writings on which the author bases his description; see his
article, "An Outline Study of Shōmyō," *Bukkyō ongaku no kenkyū*,
pp. 10–20.

39 Whereas the twelve tones of the Chinese musical system are approximately equivalent in value to the twelve semitones in the Western
chromatic scale, the minimal unit in Indian music, according to the
classical theory formulated in the second century B.C., is a microtone
which is termed *śruti*. These *śruti* are, moreover, unequal units which
seem to vary between 24 and 90 cents (the semitone of the Western
chromatic scale is 100 cents); and they are combined variously to form
a seven-note scale. The enigma of the *śruti* is discussed in detail in
Arnold Bake, "The Music of India," *Ancient and Oriental Music,* pp.
195–227, and Kanekazu Kimotsuki, The Analysis of Sound-Wave [sic]"
(written in English), *Bukkyō ongaku no kenkyū*, pp. 11–46.

40 See Atsumi Kaoru, *Heike monogatari no kisoteki kenkyū* [*A Fundamental Study of the Tale of the Heike*] (Tokyo, 1962), pp. 2–15. See pp.
25–33 for a discussion of the author of the *Tale of the Heike.*

41 Tomikura Tokujirō states that these bards were neither blind nor
of the despised class of entertainers to which the blind monks belonged.
He describes them as eloquent members of the Buddhist intelligentsia.
See his article, "The Role of Biwa-playing Monks," *Kokubungaku
kaishaku to kanshō*, XXV, no. 13 (November, 1960), 76–79.

42 Honda discusses specific instances in "Melodies of Buddhist Incantations in Traditional Songs," *Bukkyō ongaku no kenkyū*, pp. 173–188.

43 Yoshida, "An Outline Study of Shōmyō," pp. 12–13 and 19.

44 *T'ung-tien,* ed. Tu Yu (735–812), in *Shih-t'ung* (Edition: Shanghai,
1925), I, 763c. That the term *san-yüeh* denoted a specific type of music
in very early history is evidenced by a passage in "Ch'un-kuan" ["Spring
Officials"] 3, *Chou-kuan* [*Officials of the Chou Dynasty*], which states,
"The Yak-tail man (*mao-jen*) manages instructions in dancing to the
scattered music (*san-yüeh*) and dancing to the barbarian music (*i-yüeh*)."

45 *Shih-t'ung,* I, 764a.

46 *Shih-t'ung,* I, 764b. The Servitors' Midst (*lang-chung*) was, starting in the Ch'in Period, one of the four subordinate offices of the Enjoiner of the Servitors' Midst (*lang-chung-ling*). Servitors were the functionaries in the Imperial Palace charged with guarding the doors and gates and maintaining the carriages and mounts.

47 This fact is cited in a note in the "Po-kuan-chih" ["Treatise on the One Hundred Officials"], *chüan* 48 of the *Hsin T'ang-shu* [*The New History of the T'ang Dynasty*] (K'ai-ming Edition), V, 3744d. Two types of performers are listed: *san-yüeh* and *chang-nei san-yüeh.* The latter, according to Kishibe Shigeo, probably refers to performers who were stationed within the Imperial Palace; see his *Tōdai ongaku no rekishiteki kenkyū* [*A Historical Study of the Music of the T'ang Period*], I (Tokyo, 1960), 164.

48 The Sangaku House is not listed in the formal table of government organization. Its official existence is implied, however, by the statement concerning its abolishment in the *Shoku Nihongi,* entered under the Seventh Month, 782.

49 Kawatake Shigetoshi has suggested that the abolishment was due not to the decline of sangaku but, on the contrary, to the fact that it had become established as a popular form of entertainment. The Sangaku House was abolished, he says, because "there was no danger of its becoming extinct despite the lack of a special institution for its fosterage." See his *Nihon engeki zenshi* (Tokyo, 1959), p. 64.

50 The earliest mention of "sarugaku" occurs in the *Nihon kiryaku* [*Abridged Chronicle of Japan*] (eleventh century). The entry for the 2nd day, Eighth Month, 965, states simply, "The sarugaku [troupe] was summoned before the Clear-Placid Palace (*Seiryōden*); the Emperor viewed it." But according to *Bugaku yōroku* [*A Record of Important Facts on Bugaku*], a piece called "sarugaku" was included in a program of bugaku as early as the year 936. The *Bugaku yōroku,* which was probably written during the twelfth century, contains lists of pieces performed in bugaku programs that were held as a part of Buddhist ceremonies between the years 928 and 1174; the edition consulted is in *Gunsho ruijū,* XII, 149–174.

51 Such programming is described in the *Shōyūki,* the diary of Fujiwara Sanesuke (957–1046), in entries for the following dates: 29th day, Seventh Month, 1005; the first day, Eighth Month, 1013; 28th day, Seventh Month, 1019; and 28th day, Seventh Month, 1023. See *Shiryō tsūran,* I, 199 and 339, and II, 272–273 and 365.

52 This work is ascribed to Fujiwara Michinori (d. 1159), who styled himself Shinzei after he took the tonsure. A photographic reproduction of a hand-copied edition of 1449 is available in *Nihon koten zenshū,* ser. 2, Vol. XIX.

53 *Gunsho ruijū,* VI, 991.

54 Chu-ju is a country of midgets that is described as follows in the "Tung-i chuan" ["Record of the Eastern Barbarian"] in the *Hou-Han-shu* [*History of the Later Han Dynasty*] (K'ai-ming Edition), I, 897b:

"The Chu-ju nation lies more than 4,000 *li* to the south of the Queen Nation; its people are between three and four feet tall." Queen Nation apparently refers to Japan.

[55] *Meigō ōrai* [*Correspondences with Akihira*], in *Gunsho ruijū*, VI (Tokyo, 1904), 1047. This work is known also by the title *Unshū shōsoku* [*News for Izumo Province*].

[56] In the *Sarugaku dangi*, Zeami wrote: "Itchū, Kan'ami, Dōami, and Kiami were the founders of this school. Kan'ami had said, 'Itchū taught me my style.' Dōami, too, was a disciple of Itchū." See *Zeami jūrokubu shū*, II, 297–298.

[57] For extant enkyoku texts, see *Nihon kayō shūsei*, V, 23–171.

[58] Among terms used today both in nō recitation (*yōkyoku*) and in shōmyō are *yuri* (literally, "slow tremolo"), *mawashi* (literally, "turn"), and *haru* (literally, "expand"). *Yuri* actually refers to grace notes, similar to the mordent and the turn in Western music. *Mawashi* in shōmyō indicates a downward glide from a high note; in *yōkyoku*, however, it indicates a melodic glide of an upward fourth followed by a downward fifth. *Haru* in shōmyō indicates a crescendo preceding a melodic descent to a very low note; in *yōkyoku* it indicates a melodic skip of an upward fourth.

[59] *Sarugaku dangi* in *Zeami jūrobuku shū*, II, 307–308.

[60] Nose Asaji, "The Antecedent Arts of the Nō," *Nōgaku zensho*, ed. Nogami Toyoichirō (Tokyo, 1953), II, 1.

[61] This is recorded in the first chapter of the *Ryōjin hishō kuden shū* [*Secret Selection of Songs: The Collection of Oral Traditions*], written by the retired Emperor Go-Shirakawa (1127–1192). The pertinent passage is cited in Ogata Kamekichi, *Chūsei geinō-bunkashi ron* [*A Thesis on the Cultural History of Medieval Performing Arts*] (Tokyo, 1957), p. 420.

[62] Entry for the Eighth Month, 1008, *Murasaki Shikibu nikki* [*The Diary of Murasaki Shikibu*] (1010), in *NK*, XIX (Tokyo, 1958), 445.

[63] The *Ryōjin hishō* is mentioned in many literary works of the Medieval Era and is known to have comprised twenty chapters, but only the second chapter and fragments of the first are extant.

[64] From chapter 5 ("Moon-viewing") of the *Heike monogatari*. See *NB*, ser. 1, IX, 253.

[65] For a survey of historical references to the musical structure of the imayō and a discussion of their interpretation in musicological terms, see Shida Nobuyoshi, *Nihon kayō-en shi* [*A History of the Realm of the Japanese Song*] (Tokyo, 1958), 504–518.

[66] Tanabe, *Nihon no ongaku*, p. 159.

[67] Three theories have been proffered. First, Shida Yoshihide has suggested that "shirabyōshi" may have been the name of a musical mode; see his article, "An Investigation of the Shirabyōshi," *Nōgaku*, VII, no. 2 (February, 1909), 13–19. Second, Takano Tatsuyuki has stated that the word denoted "plain, or ordinary, rhythm," and that it specified a type of rhythm used in shōmyō; see his *Nihon kayo shi*, pp. 278–279. And,

third, Nose Asaji has suggested that it was probably a name for a dance in which rhythm was the sole accompaniment; see his article, "Concerning the Shirabyōshi," *Kokugo kokubun*, I, no. 3 (December, 1931), 1–35.

⁶⁸ *Tsurezuregusa, dan* 225, in *Nihon koten zensho* (5th ed.; Tokyo, 1958), LXIII, 249. Both Shizuka and Kamegiku were shirabyōshi dancers; Shizuka is well known in history as the faithful consort of Yoshitsune. *Nyūdō* refers to a "secular priest," or a man who has taken the Buddhist tonsure but continues to lead a normal secular life in most respects.

⁶⁹ Ogata, *Chūsei geinō-bunkashi ron*, pp. 448–449.

⁷⁰ Sugawara Kazunaga (1460–1529) is the author of the text; the illustrations are by Tosa Mitsunobu (1434?–1525?). A reproduction is available in *Gunsho ruijū*, XVIII (Tokyo, 1904), 65–207; or XXVIII (rev. ed.; Tokyo, 1933), 464–606.

⁷¹ The entry for the 10th day, Fifth Month, 1427, in the *Manzai jugō nikki* [*The Diary of the Jugō Manzai*]; see *Zoku gunsho ruijū noi*, 2 vols. (2nd ed.; Tokyo, 1931–1932), I, 432. *Jugō* is an abbreviation of *junsankō*, an ecclesiastical title which denoted a status equal to that accorded the empress, the empress-mother, and the empress-grandmother.

⁷² *Zeami jūrokubu shū*, II, 75.

⁷³ Takano Tatsuyuki noticed this description in a variant text of the *Heike monogatari;* see his *Nihon engeki no kenkyū* [*A Study of the Japanese Theater*], II (Tokyo, 1928), 141–142.

⁷⁴ This description of Shizuka's dance is given in the kōwaka titled *Shizuka;* see *KBS*, II, 359.

⁷⁵ *Zeami jūrokubu shū*, II, 400.

⁷⁶ P. G. O'Neill, "The Structure of the Kusemai," *Bulletin of the School of Oriental and African Studies*, XXI (1958), 100–110.

⁷⁷ *Nihon engeki no kenkyū*, II, 146–148.

⁷⁸ *Zeami jūrokubu shū*, I, 614–615. The *issei* (literally, "first call") in the nō is a five-line verse—with lines, respectively, of 5, 7, 5, 7, and 5 morae—which is intoned by the *shite* as he first appears on the stage. The term *sanjū* (literally, "third layer"), as used in the shōmyō at least, refers to a song which is pitched at the uppermost level of the tonal range.

⁷⁹ *Zeami jūrokubu shū*, II, 386.

⁸⁰ An English translation of the kusemai in *Hyakuman* is available in P. G. O'Neill, *Early Nō Drama* (London, 1958), pp. 150–152.

⁸¹ *Tō Yashū kikigaki*, in *Gunsho ruijū*, X, 867; or see *KBS*, I, 27. The author, Tō Tsuneyori, was a poet of some renown; Yashū was his style-name.

⁸² *Yasutomi ki*, in *Shiryō taisei*, XXIX (Tokyo, 1936), 209; or see *KBS*, I, 27–28.

⁸³ Cited in *KBS*, I, 28.

⁸⁴ This passage, from the *Go-Hōkōin ki* [*The Diary of the Later Hōkōin*], is cited in Iwahashi, *Nihon geinō shi*, p. 56.

⁸⁵ Cited in *KBS*, I, 24–25.

86 *Yasutomi ki,* in *Shiryō taisei,* XXXI (Tokyo, 1936), 151 and 232; or see *KBS,* I, 25.

87 Cited in *KBS,* I, 25.

88 Cited in *KBS,* I, 29.

89 *Kakitsu ki,* in *Gunsho ruijū,* XIII (Tokyo, 1904), 317; or see *KBS,* I, 25.

90 Origuchi Shinobu stated that the *shōmonji* occupied the status of slaves and were restricted to the Buddhist temples which they served in a semiclerical capacity; see his *Nihon geinō-shi nōto,* pp. 180–181. This contradicts the view, first proffered by Yanagida Kunio, that the *shōmonji* were magico-religious performers who drifted about from place to place and who became the dancers and entertainers of the Muromachi and Edo periods; see Yanagida, "The Types of So-Called Segregated Communities (*tokushu buraku*)," *Kokka gakkai zasshi,* XXVII, No. 5 (1913), 91–120. Hayashiya Tatsusaburō accepted Yanagida's view but added that the *shōmonji* were associated with tax-exempt areas called *sanjo,* which were inhabited by those who performed various mean services; see chapter 2 "Medieval Era," *Buraku no rekishi to kaihō undō [History of the Buraku and the Movement for Its Emancipation],* ed. Naramoto Tatsuya (Kyoto, 1955).

91 *Kabuki izen [Before Kabuki]* (Tokyo, 1954), pp. 114–118.

92 Origuchi believed that the kusemai was developed by *senzu-manzai* performers in order to add entertainment to their magico-religious function. He stated: "The *senzu-manzai* were attached to Buddhist temples, and what they performed were 'dances' (*mai*); that which was vocalized during the dance was gradually transformed to become the essential element—that is, the narrative verse—of the kusemai." See his *Nihon geinō-shi nōto, pp.* 180–181. Sasano Ken cited references in the *Tokitsu-gu-kyō ki [The Diary of Yamashina Tokitsugu]* to fourteen occasions, between 1533 and 1570, in which both *senzu-manzai* and kusemai pieces were performed by the same troupe, and he opined that "a corrupted form" of the *senzu-manzai* came to be called kusemai. See *KBS,* I, 75–76.

93 *Kabuki izen,* pp. 26–28 and 114–118. The author's recent publication, *Chūsei geinō-shi no kenkyū [A Study of the History of the Performing Arts in the Medieval Era]* (Tokyo, 1960), should be consulted for his most current statements of facts and opinions.

94 The most objective, as well as competent, studies were made by Kida Teikichi, who pioneered the investigation of this subject; see his articles in *Tokushu-buraku kenkyū [A Study of the Segregated Communities],* a special number of *Minzoku to rekishi,* II, No. 1 (July, 1919). Recent investigators have been able to add little to Kida's studies, although they have contributed toward exposing the cruelties imposed on the oppressed class. For an English-language summary and evaluation of studies by the Japanese, see S. Ninomiya, "An Inquiry Concerning the Origin, Development, and Present Situation of the Eta in Relation to the History of Social Classes in Japan," *TASJ,* ser. 2, X (December, 1933), 49–154.

95 *Zeami jūrokubu shū*, II, 75.

96 *Tokitsugu-kyō ki;* cited in *KBS*, I, 31. *Hyōgo no tsukishima* is a variant title for the kōwaka *Tsukishima.*

97 *Tokitsugu-kyō ki;* cited in *KBS*, I, 31. *Shochi-iri* is not among the pieces known today.

98 *Tokitsugu-kyō ki;* cited in *KBS*, I, 75.

99 *Intoku Taikeiki*, in *Tsūzoku Nihon zenshi*, XIII (Tokyo, 1913), 296–297; or see *KBS*, I, 31. Kagawa Masanori, the author of this work, lived in the seventeenth century. "The kōwaka style" may have been a designation that was current during the author's time, but not during the earlier era which he wrote about.

100 *Tokitsugu-kyō ki;* cited in *KBS*, I, 32. The kōwaka *Soga jūbangiri* is better known by the title *Jūbangiri.*

101 *Shōjo-shōnin nikki* [*The Diary of the Eminent Shōjo*]; cited in *KBS*, I, 31. *Yoriwaka Tarō* is a variant title for the kōwaka *Yuriwaka daijin.*

102 *Tokitsugu-kyō ki;* cited in *KBS*, I, 31. *Tosa Shōshun* is probably a variant title for the kōwaka *Horikawa yo-uchi.*

103 See his article, "The Kōwaka and the Maimai," *Kokugo to kokubungaku*, XXXIV, no. 8 (August, 1957), 35–43. The author does not, however, recognize any qualitative difference between the kōwaka and the earlier kusemai.

104 Takano, *Nihon kayō shi*, p. 591.

105 Origuchi, *Nihon geinō-shi nōto*, pp. 191 and 206.

106 Iwahashi, *Nihon geinō shi*, p. 45.

107 Fujita, "Concerning the Founder of the Kōwaka and Its Repertoire," *Kokugo to kokubungaku*, VI, no. 9 (September, 1929), 48–49.

108 Muroki, "The Kōwaka and the Maimai," pp. 41–43.

109 A man named Kandayū, a performer of the kōwaka during the 1580's, is referred to in the diary of Matsudaira Ietada (1555–1600) as a *maimai* performer; for the pertinent entries see *KBS*, I, 35–37. This is the only recorded instance of a performer of *maimai* performing pieces from the kōwaka repertoire. This person usually performed in the provincial area of Mikawa, and he may have been a *maimai* performer who had learned the kōwaka. That *maimai* performers were members of a mean occupational group, and that they did not perform kōwaka pieces, is suggested by data presented in Gotō Hajime's *Chūseiteki geinō no tenkai* [*The Development of Medieval Performing Arts*] (Tokyo, 1959), pp. 161–183.

III: THE KŌWAKA TODAY

1 Matsuura Seizan, *Kasshi yawa zokuhen* [*Sequel to the Kasshi-Night Tales*], *maki* 21, in *KKKS*, ser. 2:11 (Tokyo, 1911), I, 325.

2 The genealogical record of the Daigashira School (reproduced in *KBS*, I, 284–293) is retained in Ōe Village by the present master, Esaki

Ushio. The oral traditions were acquired principally from Mr. Esaki and Mr. Matsuo Rikizō, the previous master.

³ This statement in the genealogical record with respect to the fate of the Kamachi may be inaccurate. The Kamachi, according to reliable chronicles, acknowledged the suzerainty of either the Ōtomo or the Ryūzōji, both of whom were allies of Hideyoshi during the campaign against the Shimazu.

⁴ The text of the Ōe Village version is available in *Kinko shōsetsu shinsan* [*A New Collection of Tales of Near Antiquity*], ed. Shimazu Hisamoto (Tokyo, 1928), pp. 367–381. The text of the second version appears in *KBS*, I, 335–345, but with the title of *Hidehira*.

⁵ See *KBS*, I, 79–96.

⁶ Casual observers of folk art have often "sensed" a relationship between the kōwaka and performing arts in other regions of Japan. But in all instances, what they have noticed is a resemblance in one, perhaps two, of the many features of performance. If we understand "related" to mean being temporally equidistant from a common antecedent, or sharing a significant number of common elements of performance, then we would have to say that none of the arts so frequently mentioned in this connection (*daimokutate, ennen* of Mōtsuji, and *Yamato manzai*) are closely related to the kōwaka. The *daimokutate,* a rudimentary dance-drama performed at Kami-Fukagawa in Nara Prefecture, is primarily a passing rite for the youths of the village. A dance in it, called *fusho-mai,* resembles the *coro risoluto (tsume)* of the kōwaka inasmuch as the dancer struts about the stage, stamping his feet loudly. Its songs are predominantly in the three-note scale (E-G-A) which is very common in Japanese folk songs. The *ennen-nō* that is still performed at the monastery of Mōtsuji at Hiraizumi in northern Japan is basically a nō drama. Its songs would, therefore, resemble those melodies in the kōwaka that are governed by the melodic principles of the nō song. The *ennen* program also includes other unsophisticated pieces in which the songs are either bitonal chants or repetitions of a few simple motifs in a pentatonic scale (A-C-D-E-G). Artistically, the *Yamato manzai* of Nara Prefecture can in no way be compared to the kōwaka. Its performers sing in a pentatonic scale (D-E-G-A-B) to the accompaniment of the *tsuzumi* drum. However, the rhythmic pattern of the drumbeat is reminiscent of that heard in the *coro risoluto* of the kōwaka.

⁷ According to the genealogy of the Kōwaka Yajirō family, the given name of the founder of this branch of the Kōwaka family was not Naoshige, but Yasuyoshi. See *KBS*, I, 274.

⁸ *KBS*, I, 192–193. The document is dated 1706. This account inaccurately cites Shōkō as the reigning emperor, and Go-Hanazono as the retired emperor. Go-Hanazono was actually the successor of Shōkō.

⁹ The term "nuclear tone" was first applied to the study of Japanese music by Kishibe Shigeo. Koizumi Fumio employs a similar term in his analysis, on the basis of the tetrachord, of scales and motifs in tradi-

tional Japanese music; but his *kakuon* (an adaptation of "nuclear note" or *Kernton*) denotes the gravitational tonal centers of the nō song, as well as the principal stable tones in a graduated musical scale. See his *Nihon dentō ongaku no kenkyū* [*A Study of Traditional Japanese Music*] (Tokyo, 1958).

10 There are two styles of melodies in the nō: *yowagin*, or "weak melody," and *tsuyogin*, or "strong melody." The rules stated here apply to the "weak melody," which is the older of the two. The "strong melody," which utilizes only the middle and lower tonal levels, is believed to have been developed during the Edo Period. See Miyake Kōichi, *Kanze-ryū fushi no seikai* [*A Detailed Explanation of the Kanze-School Melodies*] (rev., 4th ed.; Tokyo, 1955), pp. 4–6 and 81–86.

11 See, for example, the melodies of "Daisan" in Taki Dōnin and Yoshida Tsunezō, *Tendai shōmyō taisei* [*Compendium of Tendai Shōmyō*], 2 vols. (Hieizan, 1935), I, 122–127, and "Fudō kango" in Iwahara, *Nanzan-shinryū*, II, 66–67.

IV: THE CHARACTERISTICS OF
KŌWAKA TEXTS

1 That the *Tale of the Heike* was originally written to be recited by bards to the accompaniment of the *biwa* is the conclusion presented by Atsumi Kaoru in the most recent and comprehensive study of this work. See her *Heike monogatari no kisoteki kenkyū*, pp. 1–59.

2 For the text, see *KBS*, II, 208; or *Mai no hon* ed. Ueda Kazutoshi (Tokyo, 1900), p. 221.

3 For the text, see *KBS*, II, 12; or *Mai no hon*, pp. 229–230.

4 *Iliad*, translated by A. H. Chase and W. G. Perry, Jr. (New York, 1960), p. 75.

5 See *NK*, XXXIV, 51, 101–102. These passages are available in English translation in Helen C. McCullough, *The Taiheiki, No. LIX of the Records of Civilization, Sources and Studies* (New York, 1959), pp. 22–23, 73–74.

6 For the text, see *KBS*, II, 441.

7 *Iliad*, edition cited, p. 325.

8 See *Heike monogatari, maki* 5, in *NB*, ser. 1, IX, 267–280; and *Gempei seisui ki, maki* 18 and 19, in *KS*, VII, 553–603.

9 See *Heike monogatari, maki* 9, in *NB*, ser. 1, IX, 499–501; and *Gempei seisui ki, maki* 38, in *KS*, VIII, 402–405, 409–412.

10 For the text of the entire *michiyuki*, see *KBS*, II, 310–312.

11 For the text, see *KBS*, II, 355.

12 This translation is of a manuscript libretto used by the performers of Ōe Village. Cf. corresponding passages in the versions available in *KBS*, II, 399–411 (see, particularly, p. 410), and in *Kinko shōsetsu shinsan*, pp. 367–381 (see, particularly, pp. 379–380).

13 For an English translation of the section of the *Azuma kagami* in which events concerning Yoshitsune are recorded, see Minoru Shinoda, *The Founding of the Kamakura Shogunate 1180–1185* (New York, 1960).

14 Yoshitsune's meeting Fujiwara Hidehira is mentioned in the *Azuma kagami* in the entry of the 21st day of the Tenth Month, 1180 (see *KT*, XXXII, 53).

15 See *Gikeiki, maki* 3 (*NK*, XXXVII, 119–128). This theme is treated in several otogi-zōshi tales and in the nō play *Hashi-Benkei* [*Benkei* (*at the Gojō*) *Bridge*]. In most versions, however, this encounter takes place when Yoshitsune is still a small child.

16 Only the general fact of victory is noted in the *Azuma kagami,* in the entry of the 20th day of the First Month, 1184 (see *KT*, XXXII, 97). Details of the battle are given in the *Heike monogatari, maki* 9 (see *NB*, ser. 1, IX, 444–455); the Kamakura forces totaled 60,000 men —25,000 under Yoshitsune and 35,000 under his elder brother Noriyori.

17 The entry in the *Azuma kagami* of the 20th day of the Sixth Month, 1184 states: "The list of official appointments was issued on the fifth day [of this month], and the notice of the official appointments arrived [in Kamakura] today. The appointees were precisely those whom the Military Guard [Yoritomo] had stipulated." The entry for the day following mentions that "although Master Gen Kurō [Yoshitsune] sought persistently to be recommended for an official post, the Military Guard would not hear of it." See *KT*, XXXII, 118.

18 Entry of the 17th day of the Eighth Month, 1184 (see *KT*, XXXII, 121).

19 This piece is known also as *Fushimi-ochi* [*Escape to Fushimi*]. Tokiwa's suffering in her travels and the kindness of her hosts in Fushimi are described in the *Heiji monogatari* [*Tale of the Heiji* (*Turbulence*)], *maki* 3 (see *KS*, V, 88–92). The high point of the piece is the imaginative sequence of the singing and dancing by the five women, and the story of Tokiwa's adversity seems more or less a device for introducing this sequence. Structurally, this piece is reminiscent of such nō dramas as *Utaura*, in which all plot elements are subordinate to the kusemai dance. In the kōwaka this sequence represents a structural feature of the text alone and does not affect the usual scheme of performance; the actions of the five women are, of course, described only by narrative.

20 *Nabiki Tokiwa* was not one of the standard pieces. It is included in only one of the fifteen collections of kōwaka texts listed in the *Kōwaka bukyoku shū* (see *KBS*, I, 441–446). Its theme is treated in both the *Heiji monogatari, maki* 3 (see *KS*, V, 98–102) and the *Gikeiki, maki* 1 (see *NK*, XXXVII, 37–39). The kōwaka is closer to the version of the *Gikeiki.*

21 This piece is known also as *Kurama Tokiwa* [*Tokiwa at Kurama* (*Temple*)]. That Yoshitsune spent his childhood at Kurama Temple is cited in the *Azuma kagami,* in the entry of the 21st day, Tenth Month,

1180 (see *KT*, XXXII, 53); his activities at the temple are described in the *Gikeiki, maki* 1 (see *NK*, XXXVII, 39–41). The episode of Tokiwa visiting the temple is fictional.

22 That Ushiwaka received instructions from the *tengu* is cited in the *Heiji monogatari, maki* 3 (see *KS*, V, 110). This theme is treated also in the nō drama *Kurama tengu*.

23 The greater portion of this text concerns Kūkai's travels in his quest of the wisdom of the bodhisattva Mañjuśrī. The nō drama titled *Fue no maki* treats the same theme, but the emphasis is on the adventures of Ushiwaka. The legend of this flute is not included in the *Gikeiki* or the romantic chronicles of war.

24 The meeting of Ushiwaka and the merchant Kichiji is described in detail in the *Gikeiki, maki* 1 (see *NK*, XXXVII, 47–56; Ushiwaka is referred to as Shanaō, his clerical name); the encounter with Sekihara, however, is not mentioned. The nō drama *Sekihara Yoichi* is based on the same theme, but the setting is in Mino Province, which is several days' travel to the northeast from Kyoto.

25 The incident of the *eboshi* is not mentioned in the *Gikeiki* or the romantic chronicles of war. His initiation into adulthood and his spirited fight with the bandits are described in both the *Heiji monogatari, maki* 3 (see *KS*, V, 111) and the *Gikeiki, maki* 2 (see *NK*, XXXVII, 58–65); the year is given as 1174 rather than 1175. The *Heiji monogatari* states that Yoshitsune performed the initiation rites himself at Kagami, and his encounter with the bandits is merely mentioned in passing. The *Gikeiki* lists the two events in reverse order; Yoshitsune combats the thieves in Kagami, and later he is initiated into adulthood by the director of the Atsuta Shrine in Owari Province. The nō drama *Eboshi-ori* contains the same plot elements as the kōwaka; another nō, *Kumasaka*, treats Yoshitsune's encounter with the bandit chief. The incident of the *eboshi* is the central theme of *Genji eboshi-ori* (first performed in 1699), Chikamatsu's drama for the puppet theater.

26 This does not seem to have been among the standard kōwaka, for it is included in only two of the fifteen collections of texts (see *KBS*, I, 441–446). The story is imaginary. After Kiyomori's affections cooled (see synopsis no. 2), Tokiwa married a court noble, bore him several children, and presumably died a natural death.

27 The incident of Koshigoe is recorded in the *Azuma kagami*. The text of his letter of appeal generally corresponds to the versions cited in the *Azuma kagami* (see entries for the 15th and 24th days of the Fifth Month, 1185, in *KS*, XXXII, 155–157), the *Gikeiki, maki* 4 (see *NK*, XXXVII, 147–148), and the *Heike monogatari, maki* 11 (see *NB*, ser. 1, IX, 628–630).

28 This piece is known also by the titles *Horikawa* and *Shōzon*. The events are related approximately as they are described in the *Heike monogatari, maki* 12 (see *NB*, ser. 1, IX, 648–652) and the *Gikeiki, maki* 4 (see *NK*, XXXVII, 149–170). The basic historical facts are recorded in the *Azuma kagami*, in entries of the 9th, 17th, and 26th days of the

Tenth Month, 1185 (see *KT*, XXXII, 171–172, 179). The plot of the nō drama *Shōzon* is similar to that of the kōwaka. This theme is treated elaborately in the puppet drama *Goshozakura Horikawa yo-uchi* [*The Palace amidst Cherry Blossoms: The Night Attack on the Horikawa (Mansion)*] (first performed in 1737) written by Bunkōdō (active 1716–1740) and Miyoshi Shōraku (active 1736–1771). It also occurs as a subplot in the celebrated puppet drama *Yoshitsune sembonzakura* [*Yoshitsune and the Thousand Blossoming Cherry Trees*] (first performed in 1746) written jointly by Takeda Izumo (1691–1756), Namiki Senryū (1695–1751), and Miyoshi Shōraku.

29 This piece is known also by the title *Yoshitsune Shikoku-ochi*. The treatment of this theme in the *Gikeiki, maki* 4 (see *NK*, XXXVII, 170–188) differs considerably. The historical circumstances which influenced Yoshitsune's decision to sail to Shikoku and the account of his disastrous voyage are recorded both in the *Azuma kagami*, in entries of the 29th day of the Tenth Month and the 2nd to 8th days of the Eleventh Month, 1185 (see *KT*, XXXII, 179–180), and in the *Gyokuyō*, in entries for the Tenth Month of 1185 (see *KKKS*, ser. 1:10, III, 103–110). The sequence of the tempest has been dramatized in the nō *Funa-Benkei* [*Benkei on the Ship*] and also has been adapted for the kabuki stage. The encounter with ghosts of the Heike is an important motif in *Yoshitsune sembonzakura*.

30 This account of Shizuka is generally similar to the account in the *Gikeiki, maki* 6 (see *NK*, XXXVII, 274–297), but the motif of the maid's betrayal is unique to the kōwaka. The kōwaka version furthermore contains episodic references to the literary classics *Genji monogatari* and *Ise monogatari*. A variation on the theme of Kajiwara's attempt to tear out Shizuka's fetus is the basis for Chikamatsu's puppet drama *Futari-Shizuka tainai saguri* [*Searching the Wombs of the Two Shizuka*] (first performed in 1713).

31 This piece is known also by the titles *Ataka* and *Kanjinchō*. The theme has been a perennial favorite in traditional theater. The story is enlarged in the nō drama *Ataka;* the entire party is interrogated by Togashi, and Benkei thrashes Yoshitsune in order to allay Togashi's suspicion. The kabuki play *Kanjinchō* (first performed in 1840), one of the "eighteen kabuki specialties" (*kabuki jūhachiban*), is similar to the nō version. But two other versions performed on the kabuki stage, *Ataka* and *Ataka no seki* [*The Ataka Barrier*] (first performed in 1769 and 1904), are closer in plot to the kōwaka. There are a number of other kabuki and also puppet dramas on this theme. The encounter between Benkei and Togashi and the thrashing of Yoshitsune both are described in the *Gikeiki, maki* 7 (see *NK*, XXXVII, 336–343), but as separate episodes.

32 The incident at the port of Naoe and the perilous voyage are described in the *Gikeiki, maki* 7 (see *NK*, XXXVII, 343–349), but there are some differences in the details. The storm, for instance, is ascribed to an angry sea god and abates only after gift offerings are cast into the sea.

³³ This piece is known also as *Yashima*. Sato Tsuginobu's heroic death is described in both the *Heike monogatari, maki* 11 (see *NB*, ser. 1, IX, 584–588) and the *Gempei seisui ki, maki* 42 (see *KS*, VIII, 225); it is also mentioned in the *Azuma kagami*, in the entry of the 19th day of the Second Month, 1185 (see *KT*, XXXII, 138). The nō drama *Settai* [*The Reception*] is similar in content to the kōwaka. This theme has been incorporated into a number of later works, among which the best known is the puppet drama *Gaijin Yashima* [*The Triumphal Return from Yashima*], which is usually attributed to Chikamatsu but which may have been written by the novelist Saikaku; see Tsunoda Ichirō, "Miscellaneous Thoughts on the Problem concerning the Author of *Gaijin Yashima*," *Saikaku kenkyū*, no. 10 (December, 1957), 186–194.

³⁴ This piece does not appear to have been in the standard kōwaka repertoire; it is included in only one of the fifteen collections described in the *Kōwaka bukyoku shū* (see *KBS*, I, 441–446). This theme is treated also in the *Gikeiki, maki* 8 (see *NK*, XXXVII, 362–366).

³⁵ This episode is fictitious. This theme is given a similar treatment in the nō drama *Kiyoshige*.

³⁶ This piece is known also by the titles *Hidehira* and *Shōbuwake* [*A Draw Match*]. The nō drama *Nishikido* treats this theme in a similar fashion. The final act of the puppet play *Gaijin Yashima* is a dramatization of this theme. The slaying of Izumi by his brothers is mentioned only in passing in the *Gikeiki, maki* 8 (see *NK*, XXXVII, 369). The incident is recorded in the *Azuma kagami*, but as an occurrence of the Sixth Month of 1189, or two months after the death of Yoshitsune (see *KT*, XXXII, 333).

³⁷ The attack on the Takadachi Mansion is described similarly in the *Gikeiki, maki* 8 (see *NK*, XXXVII, 373-382). The ko-jōruri *Takadachi godan* is an adaptation of the kōwaka text for the puppet theater; for the text, see *Tokugawa bungei ruijū*, VIII (Tokyo, 1925), 1–17. The puppet drama *Yoshitsune shin-Takadachi* [*Yoshitsune: The New Takadachi*] (first performed in 1719) by Ki no Kaion (1663–1742) is actually a dramatization of the war in 1615 in which remnants of the Toyotomi clan were annihilated by the Toyugawa Shogunate. The story was placed in a twelfth-century setting, however, in order to circumvent the convention prohibiting the dramatization of events relating directly to the Tokugawa family.

³⁸ The *Azuma kagami* states that Yoshitsune's "child" was a four-year-old girl. See the entry of the 30th day, Intercalary Fourth Month, 1189, in *KT*, XXXII, 326.

³⁹ Yoshitsune's death is described similarly in the *Gikeiki, maki* 8 (see *NK*, XXXVII, 382–388), and is noted in the *Azuma kagami, loc. cit.*

⁴⁰ See entries for the 28th day of the Fifth Month to the 2nd day of the Seventh Month, 1193 (in *KT*, XXXII, 490–493).

⁴¹ The edition consulted is in *KS*, Vol. IV.

⁴² This piece is known also as *Ichiman Hakoō*. This episode is described at great length in the *Soga monogatari, maki* 3 (see *KS*, IV, 82–102). This theme is treated also in the nō drama titled *Kirikane Soga*.

43 These two episodes are described in the *Soga monogatari,* but there are some differences in the details of the story (see *KS,* IV, 106–111, 114–117).

44 This piece is known also by the titles *Wada* and *Wada no en* [*Wada's Feast*]. The kōwaka version differs slightly from the description of this episode in the *Soga monogatari, maki* 6 (see *KS,* IV, 177–178, 184–192). Many kabuki plays are based on this theme; they are mostly choreographic pieces (*shosagoto*), and the titles usually contain the word *kusazuri* ("hip plate") or the phrase *kusazuri-biki* ("hip-plate pulling"). The well-known *Ya no ne* [*The Arrowhead*], one of the "eighteen kabuki specialties," is a choreographic number depicting Gorō rushing forth to the rescue. The ko-jōruri *Fūryū Wada sakamori* [*The Popular Wada sakamori*] is much closer to the version in the *Soga monogatari;* for the text, see *Tokugawa bungei ruijū,* VIII, 106–124.

45 This piece is known also as *Kosode-goi* [*Begging for a Kosode*]. The episode is described in the *Soga monogatari, maki* 7 (see *KS,* IV, 207–222). The nō drama *Kosode Soga* is similar in content to the kōwaka, and the ko-jōruri *Kosode Soga* is an adaptation of the kōwaka text for the puppet theater. For the text of the latter, see *Tokugawa bungei ruijū,* VIII, 34–44.

46 This account of the legend of the sword is generally similar to that given in the *Soga monogatari, maki* 8 (see *KS,* IV, 237–240). The legend of the Demon-cutter appears also in the *Taiheiki, maki* 32 (see *KS,* IV, 232–234).

47 The account of the vendetta runs to some length in the *Soga monogatari* (see *maki* 8 and 9, in *KS,* IV, 242–285). The nō drama *Yo-uchi Soga* also describes the killing, but it proceeds further with the story and tells of Jūrō's death and Gorō's capture. Many puppet and kabuki dramas have been written on this theme; a representative work is *Youchi Soga kariba no akebono* [*The Night Attack by Soga: The Dawn at the Hunting Ground*] by Furukawa Mokuami (1816–1893).

48 These sequences are described in detail in the *Soga monogatari, maki* 9 to 11 (see *KS,* IV, 285–308, 335). Events described in the last two kōwaka are combined in one of Chikamatsu's better-known historical dramas, *Soga Kaikeizan* [*The Soga's Hui-chi Mountain*].

49 Yoshitomo's death is described similarly in the *Heike monogatari, maki* 2 (see *KS,* V, 73–78). This theme is treated also in the nō drama *Kamada,* which is not among the better-known pieces; for the text, see *Shin yōkyoku hyakuban* [*A New Selection of One Hundred Yōkyoku*], ed. Sasaki Nobutsuna (Tokyo, 1912), 98–103.

50 This piece is known also as *Ibuki-ochi* [*Escape to (Mount) Ibuki*]. This account of Yoritomo differs considerably from that given in the *Heiji monogatari, maki* 2 and 3 (see *KS,* V, 78–79, 88–96).

51 This piece is known also by the title *Shunkan.* The tragedy of Shunkan is one of the important themes in the *Heike monogatari* (see *maki* 2 and 3, in *NB,* ser. 1, IX, 116–134). The nō drama *Shunkan* is also based on this theme.

52 The instance of these auspicious dreams is cited in the *Gempei seisui ki, maki* 18 (see *KS*, VII, 552–553). A similar account appears also in the *Soga monogatari, maki* 2 (see *KS*, IV, 64–65).

53 Mongaku actually spent his period of exile on Izu Peninsula in an area not far from Yoritomo's residence.

54 This piece is known also as *Mongaku shōnin* [*The Eminent Mongaku*]. Mongaku's life and his relationship with Yoritomo are described in considerable detail in both the *Heike monogatari, maki* 5 (see *NB*, ser, 1, IX, 267–280) and the *Gempei seisui ki, maki* 18 and 19 (see *KS*, VII, 553–603). Mongaku is a frequent subject of puppet and kabuki dramas. Particularly well known is *Mongaku kanjinchō* [*Mongaku's Subscription Tablet*], which is included among the "new eighteen kabuki specialties" (*shin kabuki jūhachiban*).

55 This piece is known also by the titles *Hyōgo* and *Hyōgo tsukishima*. The construction of the island receives only brief mention in *maki* 6 of the *Heike monogatari* (see *NB*, ser. 1, IX, 320–322).

56 This theme appears to be unique to the kōwaka.

57 This incident is described similarly in the *Heike monogatari, maki* 7 (see *NB*, ser. 1, IX, 344–350). The version of the kōwaka was apparently taken from the *Heike monogatari*, for there are many parallels in passages. This theme is treated quite differently in the *Gempei seisui ki, maki* 29 (see *KS*, VIII, 101–104).

58 The tragedy of Atsumori and Kumagae is described both in the *Heike monogatari, maki* 9 (see *NB*, ser. 1, IX, 499–501) and in the *Gempei seisui ki, maki* 38 (see *KS*, VIII, 402–405, 409–412). The kōwaka version is closer to the account in the *Gempei seisui ki*. The nō drama *Atsumori* also treats this theme, but its basic plot structure is quite different from that of the kōwaka.

59 This event is set forth in both the *Heike monogatari, maki* 11 (see *NB*, ser. 1, IX, 588–591) and the *Gempei seisui ki, maki* 42 (see *KS*, VIII, 544–550). The kōwaka contains a number of lyrical passages and exhibits a literary quality not found in the romantic war chronicles.

60 This piece is known also by the titles *Hōraisan* [*Mount Hōrai*] and *Hōraijima* [*Hōrai Island*]. This text is included in the anthology of medieval tales, *Otogi-zōshi;* it appears with the title *Hamaide no sōshi* [*Hamaide Booklet*].

61 This piece is known also as *Kaitori* [*Shellfish Hunting*]. According to Shimazu Hisamoto, the title may have been derived from the legend that the flesh of an abalone with nine holes in its shell serves as an elixir of life.

62 Plot elements derived from a number of diverse sources are embodied in this kōwaka. The winding plot and the many bizarre elements remind one of Edo Period *yomihon* that were inspired by the story of the *Shui-hu-chuan*. One of Kagekiyo's many attempts at assassination is dramatized in the nō *Daibutsu kuyō* [*Services for the Great Buddha (of Nara)*]. The story told in the kōwaka is given a different ending in the nō *Kagekiyo*. Of the many puppet and kabuki dramas based on the

legend of Kagekiyo, the best known are Chikamatsu's *Shusse Kagekiyo* [*Kagekiyo's Success in Life*] (first performed in 1686), which is similar in plot to the kōwaka, and *Dannoura kabuto gunki,* a later revision of Chikamatsu's work. The *Kagekiyo* which is one of the "eighteen kabuki specialties" is a dramatization of his escape from prison.

63 The legend of Chang Liang and Huang-shih-kung is related in Chang's biography in both the *Shih-chi* and the *Han-shu* (see the K'ai-ming edition, I, 171a and 458b). The nō drama *Chōryō* is similar in plot to the kōwaka.

64 The power struggle between Kamatari and Iruka has been dramatized frequently in the puppet theater. Many of the plot elements of this kōwaka were incorporated into Chikamatsu's *Taishokan* (first performed ca. 1713).

65 The nō drama *Ama* [*Woman Diver*] is similar in plot to the kōwaka. This theme is treated also in Chikamatsu's *Taishokan*.

66 This piece is known also by the titles *Daijin* and *Yuri*. The many parallels between this kōwaka and the *Odyssey* were first pointed out by the novelist and scholar, Tsubouchi Shōyō (1859–1935) in his article, "The Original Source of the Legend of Yuriwaka," *Waseda bungaku,* n.v. (January, 1906), 134–143. Cf. Esther Lowell Hibbard, "The Ulysses Motif in Japanese Literature," *Journal of American Folklore,* LIX (1946), 221–246.

67 The nō drama titled *Manjū* (known also as *Nakamitsu*) is similar in plot to the kōwaka. The kabuki play *Nakamitsu* is included among the "new eighteen kabuki specialities." The theme of a samurai sacrificing his own son in order to save the life of his lord is not uncommon, nor is it considered bizarre, in the puppet theater. The famous "Temple School" (*terakoya*) scene in *Sugawara denju tenarai kagami* [*The Exemplar for Brush-Writing Transmitted by Sugawara*] (first performed in 1746) may have been inspired by the legend of Manjū and Nakamitsu; for an English version of this play, see *Three Japanese Plays from the Traditional Theater,* ed. Earle Ernst (London, 1959), pp. 53–128.

68 The nō drama *Shinoda* is a dramatization of the sequence in which Kotarō, having been captured by Oyama, escapes with the help of a former retainer of his father; for the text, see *Shin yōkyoku hyakuban,* pp. 393–396.

69 This is the only standard kōwaka to treat a theme from a period later than the twelfth century. It is actually an excerpt from the *Taiheiki, maki* 18 (see *KS,* III, 642–657), and the title itself suggests that it was added later to the standard repertoire. This same story is related in a Muromachi Period fable, *Chūshoō monogatari.*

70 The historical events recounted in *Miki* and *Honnōji,* the two kōwaka treating episodes in the life of Hideyoshi, are described in the various biographies of Hideyoshi. The Kōwaka family record states only that these pieces were set to melodies by orders of Hideyoshi (see *KBS,* I, 202).

71 The episode of *Honnōji* is the main theme of the celebrated puppet

drama *Ehon Taikō ki* [*The Picture-Book Chronicle of the Great Feats of the Taikō (Hideyoshi)*] (first performed in 1799).

V: A NARRATIVE: *Atsumori*

1 See *KBS, II,* 203–218.

2 See *Mai no hon,* ed. Ueda Kazutoshi, pp. 209–243. This text is based on a manuscript copy of the Kan'ei Period (1623–1643).

3 There are several nō dramas which treat this theme. *Atsumori,* written by Zeami, is still one of the more frequently performed pieces today. *Ikuta Atsumori* is a story woven about a forgotten son of Atsumori, describing his meeting with Kumagae, who had become a Buddhist monk in order to pray for the deliverance of Atsumori's soul. This story is retold in the medieval fable *Ko Atsumori* [*Child of Atsumori*]. Two other nō dramas treating Atsumori, titled *Katami Atsumori* and *Kōya Atsumori,* are no longer performed.

4 Entries for the 5th and 7th days of the Second Month, 1184 (see *KT,* XXXII, 100). According to the romantic war chronicles, Yoshitsune led an army of only 10,000 men.

5 In the romanticized versions, Yoshitsune has 3,000 men with him.

6 *Somosomo,* which is rendered as "to begin," is an introductory phrase that serves to prepare the reader for an extended tale or exposition to follow; it is a vestige of the tradition of oral literature.

7 A more faithful rendering of this passage would read, ". . . of the samurai commanders of the clan, sixteen in all were of the unblest group." *Saburai-taishō,* or "samurai commander," normally referred to a warrior who commanded a sizable military force. Later, particularly in the late Muromachi Period, it often denoted the leader of a small band of warriors. *Taishō* (literally, "great marshal") was originally the title of the highest commander of the guards of the Imperial Court; but the term, as employed among the samurai, denoted anything from the supreme commander down to the leader of a minimal unit of warriors.

8 "Sad reflections" is a rendering of *mono no aware,* a phrase which, if taken literally in modern Japanese, would mean "the pity of things." The term *aware* denotes a subtle but complex aesthetic mood which might be described in English with the word "melancholy" in its earlier usage, ". . . a quality that inspired pensiveness or sad reflection or awakened mournful thoughts or recollections which were not only not necessarily painful or disagreeable, but often agreeable, especially to the poetic or thoughtful mind" (*Webster's Dictionary of Synonyms*). The source of *aware* was the notion of the ephemeral nature of life— a notion implicit in the seasonal changes of nature, and explicit in the teachings of Buddhism—which imbued the thoughts of the Japanese strongly, particularly in the era of religious pessimism which encompassed the late Heian and Kamakura periods.

9 *Taifu,* or "grandee," was a title accorded nobles of the Fifth Grade

at the Imperial Court; grandees who were without a specific post, owing usually to their youth, were called *mukan no taifu,* or "grandee-without-post."

¹⁰ *Shōkoku* (or *sōkoku*), or "nation's overseer," is a Chinese loan-word (from *hsiang-kuo*) which was used as a sobriquet for the supreme official of the government, the prime minister *(dajō-daijin). Hsiang-kuo,* in the Ch'in and Han dynasties, referred to the highest office in the empire. Taira no Kiyomori became prime minister in 1167 and was known as *Hei-shōkoku,* or the Heike Grand Minister. In literature, *shōkoku* is usually synonymous with Kiyomori, just as the title *hōgan* is synonymous with Yoshitsune, and *taikō* with Hideyoshi.

¹¹ The silk *hitatare* served as the ordinary garment of the samurai. The color denoted the rank of the wearer, and brocade was customarily worn only by generals. The *hitatare* was derived from the normal plebeian costume and differed from the costume of the court nobles *(kuge)* mainly in the fact that the shirt had a surplice front like the present-day kimono and was tucked tightly into the trousers; the *kuge* wore loosely hanging shirts with round collars. The *hitatare* worn with battle gear had sleeves that were much narrower; it was called *yoroi-hitatare,* or "armor *hitatare.*"

¹² *Nerinuki,* or "soft silk," is a luxurious fabric that was used ordinarily for ceremonial attire. The weave consists of vertical strands of regular silk thread and horizontal strands of silk thread that has been given a softer texture through a special boiling process.

¹³ *Kisenaga* (literally, "worn long") refers to a suit of armor. Arms and weapons of noble personages were frequently referred to by the manner in which they were worn or used. Other examples of this kind are *mitorashi,* or "that which is grasped," for "bow" and *mihakase,* or "that which is worn," for "sword."

¹⁴ *Murasaki-susogo,* literally "purple, with dark hem," describes a garment of purple hue that is deep-toned at the hem and lightens (increases in brilliance) gradually into white. When referring to a suit of armor consisting of a number of leather plates surfaced with silk braid, the phrase implies that each plate is colored in this manner.

¹⁵ "Courtier" is a rendering of *jōrō* (literally, "high merit"), a term which originally denoted a female court attendant of high rank but later came to be used as a general designation for any courtier of high rank.

¹⁶ "Grand vessel" is a rendering of *gozabune* (literally, "ship for the exalted"), which referred to a large boat used by courtly personages. The name did not imply a specific style of architecture, although the *gozabune* frequently had a superstructure with a Chinese-style gabled roof.

¹⁷ Shioya is a settlement which was situated on the coast, a short distance west of Ichinotani.

¹⁸ The Shi Band *(Shi no tō)* was a band of warriors of the Kisaichi clan of Musashi Province, and we may assume that Kumagae was a

member of this clan. Shi represents the Sino-Japanese pronunciation of the first graph in the clan name.

¹⁹ The "reverse plate" (*sakaita*) is suspended from the back-shoulder plate. The "tasseled cord" (*agemaki*) is an ornamental cord which is tied in a bow knot and suspended from a metal ring in the reverse plate.

²⁰ *Ikani,* which is rendered as "come back," is perhaps closest in meaning to the colloquial "how about it?"

²¹ Kadowaki refers to Taira no Norimori (1129–1185), a younger brother and favorite of Kiyomori. Because Norimori was given a residence located beside the main gate of Kiyomori's Rokuhara Mansion, he came to be known as Kadowaki, literally "beside the gate." Norimori is referred to here as Kadowaki-*dono*. When *dono* is affixed to the name or title of an eminent person, it may be rendered as "lord"; in an address of a formal nature, it is convenient to render it as "the esteemed" —for example, "the esteemed Kumagae" for Kumagae-*dono*. It is used also in addressing intimates or inferiors; for example, a mother may address her own son as "Gorō-*dono*." In such instances, —*dono* is better left untranslated.

²² The Wicked Shichibyōe (Aku-Shichibyōe) refers to Taira no Kagekiyo, whose prowess as a warrior is eulogized in the kōwaka titled *Kagekiyo* and in a number of nō and kabuki dramas. Kagekiyo styled himself Shichirobei of Kazusa Province but was called the Wicked Shichibyōe because he murdered his own uncle, the monk Dainichi.

²³ This passage reads literally, ". . . [alternately] surfacing and sinking, he swam his horse."

²⁴ "Seasoned warrior" is a figurative meaning for *rōmusha* (literally, "aged warrior"). *Wakamusha* (literally, "young warrior"), in the sentence following, is used similarly to denote the "inexperienced warrior."

²⁵ "Middle-inserted" (*nakazashi*) is a term for arrows in a quiver. If a quiver were designed to hold sixteen arrows, the slots for the individual arrows would be arranged in a rectangular pattern of four rows with four slots each. Usually there were at least two additional slots for inserting special-purpose arrows, such as the fork-tipped arrow or one with a humming head. These extra slots were outside the rectangular pattern, and the special arrows were called *uwazashi,* or "above-inserted [arrows]."

²⁶ This is the *kabura,* a name which is homonymous with the word for "turnip." Its hollow wooden head is shaped like a turnip, and there are three small airholes that make it hum during its flight. A deadly forked point is usually affixed to the tip.

²⁷ "Bow-handler" is an epithet for a warrior. The attributive phrase "with a [prudent] mind" (*kokoro aru*) denotes a personal attribute that might be rendered as "circumspect." It is the quality which enables one to handle any predicament of a trying nature with acumen and grace.

²⁸ *Saru aida,* rendered as "now," is an archaic phrase that may be compared to "erstwhile" in English. It is a stock introductory phrase

in the kōwaka. Since it bears no semantic significance in the context, its function being a structural one, it is rendered in all instances as "now." Here it serves to mark the beginning of a new sequence.

29 *Yoroi no sode,* or "armor sleeves," refer to rectangular flaps suspended from the shoulders in order to protect the upper arm.

30 The term used here is *tenjōbito* (literally, "persons [allowed] in the palace"), which referred to courtiers who were permitted to enter the Seiryōden in the imperial quarters. Normally included in this category were courtiers of the Fifth Grade or higher and the *kurōdo,* officials of the Sixth Grade who handled affairs of immediate concern to the emperor.

31 *Unkaku,* or "dwellers amidst the clouds," refers to the same category of courtiers as *tenjōbito.*

32 *Shika-kangen* denotes "Chinese poetry (*shih*), Japanese poetry (*uta*), and the music of gagaku."

33 The images are borrowed from Chinese literature. Blossoms and moon viewing are conventional images of spring and autumn. "Half day" is a figurative expression for "a short while." The "moon viewed from a tower" alludes to a well-known theme in Chinese poetry (see note 84 below).

34 *Zense no koto* is, literally, "a thing of the previous world" and refers to events in a previous existence that have resulted in retributions in this existence.

35 "In my faithfulness to serve you" is a literal rendering of *hōkō no sono chū ni,* a phrase which is rather awkward in this context.

36 The main branch of the Heike was descended from the second son of Emperor Kammu (737–806; reigned 781–806). Descendents of three other sons of Kammu also took the surname of Taira and were included in the Heike clan.

37 This clause reads literally "if that arm is a serious matter."

38 *Kamuro* (or *kaburo*), literally "bald," is used figuratively to denote old age and is, therefore, rendered as "thin-haired."

39 *Fuchise no kawaru* (literally, "changing depths and shallows") is a literary cliché that expresses the temporality and fickleness of life. It alludes possibly to this well-known poem by an anonymous poet in the *Kohinshū* (complied in 905):

Yo no naka wa	In this world,
nani ka tsune naru	What things are permanent?
Asukagawa	In the Asuka River [of
kinō no fuchi wa	morrow],
kyō no se to naru.	The deeps of yesterday
	Are the shallows of today.
	(Poem no. 933 in the *Kokka taikan*)

40 A more literal rendering would read, "the fluttering twin moths resembled the moon over distant mountains." "Moth" (*ga*) is used here figuratively for "eyebrow"; long, arching brows were often praised as

gabi, or "moth brows." In this instance the metaphorical images are poorly matched, and the comparison is an awkward one.

[41] "A face of blooming fairness is a rendering of *kōgan* (literally, "crimson face"), a term that describes youthful freshness and beauty.

[42] This is the *yotsume-nui* (literally, "four eyes joined"), a diamond-shaped crest that is composed of four smaller diamonds. It was the crest of the Uda Genji, or those members of the Genji clan who were descended from Emperor Uda (867–931; reigned 887–897).

[43] The term *onzōshi* originally denoted the son of a court noble but later came to refer exclusively to a scion of the Genji. By the same token, the term *kintachi* (literally, "fellow lords") came to refer specifically to a scion of the Heike.

[44] "Treason" is a rendering of *futagokoro,* literally "two-hearted."

[45] The "icefish" (*hio*) is a small fish that is almost translucent in its whiteness. In former times fishermen trapped the icefish as it swam out of Lake Biwa and down the Seta River by setting up a "barrier net" (*ajiro*), an elaborate screen of embedded pegs that spanned the entire width of the river.

[46] *Me yori takaku,* literally "higher than the eyes," figuratively denotes "high above the head."

[47] "Helplessly" is a rendering of *tōzai o shirade,* literally "not knowing east from west," which is expressive of a state of utter confusion or helplessness.

[48] The verb "inserted" (*sasaretari*) is modified by an adverbial clause *shitan no ie ni hichiriki soete,* the meaning of which is not entirely clear.

[49] "Inspectors" (*azechi*) were instituted in the early eighth century as official overseers of provincial governors, but the post was quickly reduced to one that was merely titular. During the Heian Period, great councilors (*dainagon*) and middle councilors (*chūnagon*) were often appointed *azechi* even though they never left the capital.

[50] *Kyūka,* or "nine [ten-day periods of] summer," refers to the ninety days of the summer season.

[51] *Shiran* is a combined form of *reishi* (usually translated as "touchwood") and *ran* ("orchid"). The *reishi* is the *Fomes japonicus,* a dark, lustrous mushroom that is prized as an ornament. The *ran* is the *Orchis japonica.*

[52] "Deer on mountains high" (*onoe no shika*) is an image of autumn that was employed as a cliché by poets of the Heian Period. The treatment in this poem by Fujiwara Toshiyuki (d. 907?) is typical:

> *Aki-hagi no*   The autumnal bush clovers
>   *hana sakinikeri*   Have blossomed.
> *takasago no*   Lofty peaks:
>   *onoe no shika wa*   The deer on mountains high
>   *ima ya nakuramu.*   Should cry anon.
>
>   (*Kokinshū,* Poem no. 218, in *Kokka taikan*)

⁵³ The Tatsuta River flows southward into the Yamato River at a point not far from the Hōryūji monastery in Nara. The area of the confluence is famed for its autumnal colors, the beauty of which has been immortalized in poetry by the Buddhist priest Nōin (998–1050):

Arashi fuku	The maple leaves
Mimuro no yama no	Of the windswept
momijiba wa	Mimuro Mountain
Tatsuta no kawa no	Form brocades
nishiki narikeri.	On Tatsuta River.

(*Goshūishū*, Poem no. 316, in *Kokka taikan*)

⁵⁴ The *hagi,* or "bush clover," has been a favorite autumnal plant among the Japanese since antiquity. The graph for representing *hagi* was selected by the ancient Japanese because it contains, quite appropriately, the radicals for "grass" and "autumn." The *hagi* is the *Lespedeza bicolor Turcz.* var. *japonica Nakai* and is not related to the Chinese *ch'iu* plant, which is represented by the same graph.

⁵⁵ "I saw disappear in the distance the treetops" is a rendering of *kigi no kozue o misutetsutsu,* which is literally "forsaking the branches of tree [upon] tree."

⁵⁶ *Uzumoruru,* literally "buried," is used figuratively to mean "forgotten."

⁵⁷ Takakura was the sobriquet of Prince Mochihito (1151–1180), a son of the Emperor Go-Shirakawa (1127–1192; reigned 1155–1158); because his mother was lowborn, he was not considered a prince of the blood (*shinnō*). He attempted to organize a general uprising against the Heike in 1180, but the effort was abortive. He sought refuge in Mii Temple and then tried to escape to Nara but was killed en route.

⁵⁸ Iga no Heinaizaemon was a trusted vassal of Kiyomori's third son, Tomomori. His given name was Ienaga. *Jō,* which may be rendered as "lieutenant," was the title of his rank in the Palace Guards. According to the *Heike monogatari, maki* 11, he died at Dannoura; but in the *Gempei seisui ki, maki* 38, he is listed among the important Heike commanders killed at Ichinotani.

⁵⁹ *Namimakura* and *kajimakura* are, literally, "wave-pillow" and "tiller-pillow." They are ornamental epithets used in poetic descriptions of sea travel. Since they are extragrammatical appendages to the sentence, their lyrical implications have been paraphrased.

⁶⁰ This passage contains wordplays which produce a double level of meaning, as diagrammed in the following:

Inochi mo shiranu	*Matsurabune*
Uncertain of life,	[we] linger in our boats;
Uncertain of life,	[in] the Matsuura boat,

kogarete	mono ya omōran.
tormented,	our thoughts shall be melancholy.
[as we are] rowed,	our thoughts shall be melancholy.

The upper line of the translation conveys the primary meaning of this passage. *Matsurabune* refers to boats which set sail from the port of Matsuura in northwestern Kyushu, and is irrelevant to the context of the sentence; it is inserted as a pun, for its first two morae *matsu* constitute the word "to linger." However, it serves to introduce *kogarete* "tormented," with which it is verbally associated inasmuch as *kogarete* may also mean "rowed."

61 "Minister (ōi) refers to Taira no Munemori (1147–1185), who after Kiyomori's death, assumed leadership of the Heike. He held the post of "inner minister" (*naidaijin*), which in this era was immediately below that of the Minister of the Right.

62 *Mappō*, or "end of the Law," refers to the final period of the Buddhistic world—an era of mounting chaos and declining morality. The belief was widespread that the *mappō* would begin 1,500 years after the death of Gautama Buddha, a time which in Japan corresponded to the late Heian Period. The religious pessimism that prevailed is evident especially in the literature of that era; there are constant reminders of the ephemeral nature of life on this earth and expressions of abiding faith in the power of Amitābha to deliver men's souls.

63 The *katabira* worn by the samurai of the Kamakura Period was an unlined shirt made of hemp fabric; white was customarily worn during the winter, and crimson during the warmer months. *Hikichigae*, which is rendered simply as "wore," means literally "to pull [either side] across the other" and describes the process of donning a shirt with a surplice front.

64 *Kachin*, an extremely deep shade of blue, was the conventional color for samurai armor. For a description of the *hitatare*, see note 11 above.

65 The weave called the *yōbaitōri*, or "[hues of the blossoms of] the arbutus, peach, and plum," was a decorative combination of many brilliant hues.

66 "Ankle" is a paraphrasing of *aguchidaka*, literally "the height of the [trouser] opening." Trousers worn under the armor were laced at the bottom so that they could be wound tightly about the ankles.

67 The "right-side guard" (*waidate*) is a protective leather plate that was fitted against the right side; it was worn under the suit of armor.

68 "Hour of the serpent" (*mi no toki*), which precedes the noon hour, is metaphorically associated with freshness or newness.

69 'Armor-piercer" (*yoroidōshi*) is a dagger that was used in hand-

to-hand fighting; it was also called *metezashi*, litterally "inserted in the steed-hand [side]," since it was always worn in the right side. The Japanese "foot" (*shaku*) is approximately the same length as the U.S. foot, but it is divided into ten "inches" (*sun*). Hence this blade was actually nearly a foot long.

70 *"Slashing blade"* (*uchigatana*) referred to the shorter of the two swords worn by the samurai. During the Muromachi Period, however, this term came to denote the longer sword, and the shorter sword came to be called *wakizashi*, literally "inserted at the side."

71 The "soft *eboshi*" (*nashiuchi eboshi*) was made of a soft fabric so that it could be worn under a helmet. Most *eboshi* were made of paper pulp or silk and stiffened with black lacquer. *Nashiuchi* is thought to be an abbreviation of *nayashiuchi*, or "softly made."

72 "Female official" (*nyokan*) was the general term of designation for women who served as palace attendants. The mother of an emperor was customarily addressed as *nyoin*, a title which might be rendered as "Dame-sanctum." The suffix *-in* "sanctum" was used in names of palatial buildings in ancient Japan and, later, in titles taken by retired emperors and mothers of emperors. Many such personages took the Buddhist tonsure, but *in* as a term had no explicit religious significance. The *nyoin* in this instance was Tokuko, a daughter of Kiyomori; her title at this time was Kenreimon'in (literally, "Sanctum of the Kenrei Gate"). She was to become a nun after the fall of the Heike in the following year.

73 "Enter Nirvana" (*nyūmetsu*) is a euphemism for the death of a person of high Buddhistic attainment; it is usually associated with the death of Gautama Buddha.

74 An "arhat" (*rakan*) is one who, in Hinayana Buddhism, has attained the state of enlightenment. The Sixteen Arhats were entrusted by Gautama Buddha with the task of staying in this world in order to help others enter Nirvana.

75 This clause reads *takumi o rakuseki ni megurashi*. *Takumi* and *rakuseki* are not meaningful words, and probably represent phonetic corruptions in the text. This clause has been replaced with *tada mi o rakusei ni megurashi*, the reading in the text of *Atsumori* contained in the *Mai no hon*, p. 235.

76 *Sese-bamban*, which is rendered as "countless," seems to be a phrase expressing the passage of time and the repetition of events. *Sese* can mean "successive worlds," a phrase which refers figuratively to the succession, or turn, of events; *bamban* possibly connotes the repetition of actions or events.

77 "Accursed bond" is a rendering of *gyakuen*, which refers to a bond between two persons that is predestined to be an accursed one due to the influence of karma. *Gyakuen* is used also as the opposite of *jun'en*, a term which means the achieving of ties with the Buddha through the natural, ordained course; *gyakuen* in this case would mean

the achieving of salvation through the intercession of some extraordinary force.

⁷⁸ *Bodai o tomurau* is, literally, "pray for [his] bodhi." *Bodai,* or bodhi in Sanskrit, is interpreted to mean "way" or "enlightenment" and implies salvation.

⁷⁹ "Demon of Naraka" is a rendering of Avo-rākṣasa *(Abō-rasetsu),* the demon who tortures the souls of the dead in the Buddhist hell.

⁸⁰ "Defiled land" *(edo)* refers to man's present world as opposed to the "Pure Land" *(jōdo),* the Buddhist heaven. The concept of the world as a sinful, defiled realm was emphasized and popularized by the Pure Land Sect of Buddhism, which promised salvation through the grace of Amitābha.

⁸¹ *Bompu,* rendered as "unworthy one," is used here as a humble expression in referring to one's own child. As a Buddhist term, *bompu* refers to one who has not yet attained spiritual enlightenment.

⁸² This passage, expressing figuratively the infinite bounds of his gratitude, has been translated literally since the meanings of the figures are not entirely clear. The verb "to respond" is modified by the word *shimusoku* ("god's speed"?), which has been left untranslated.

⁸³ *Saru hodo ni,* rendered as "now," is another of the stock introductory phrases employed to indicate a new sequence. It is an archaic phrase and is similar in meaning to the English "erstwhile."

⁸⁴ This passage possibly alludes to the opening stanza of the enkyoku titled *Kinkoku o omou* ["Thoughts of Chin-ku"] contained in the *Shūkashū* (see *Nihon kayō shūsei,* V, 112):

> On a spring morn at Chin-ku,
> The wind entices the fading blossoms;
> In the South Tower, all through the night,
> We admire the moon that is low.

Chin-ku, located in the southwest of Lo-yang Prefecture *(hsien)* in Honan Province, was famed for its Chin-ku-yüan, the villa of Shih Ch'ung of the Chin Dynasty (for his biography, see the *Chin-shu, ch.* 33, in the K'ai-ming ed., II, 1176d–1177d); it was the scene of many an extravagant party. "Flourishing blossoms" *(eiga)* denotes figuratively either prosperity or those who are prosperous. The "South Tower" *(Nan-lou)* was the scene of a moon-viewing feast held by Yü Liang (289–340), a brother-in-law of the Emperor Ming-ti of Eastern Chin (for Yü's biography, see the *Chin-shu, ch.* 73, in the K'ai-ming ed., II 1272b–1273b); this event was celebrated in poetry and provided the theme for the Ming drama *Nan-lou yüeh [South-Tower Moon]* by Hsü Ch'ao. "Secreted amidst the clouds" is a euphemism for death.

⁸⁵ *Jōdo no hashi ni watashi,* literally "laid [it] as a bridge to the Pure Land," expresses metaphorically the idea of inaugurating a life dedicated to Buddhism. In the description of Kurodani in the *Dekisai kyōmiyage [Dekisai's Presents from the Capital]* (1677), there is mention of a

stone bridge named *Jōdobashi* ("Pure-Land Bridge") which, according to tradition, was originally made from the pieces of Kumagae's bow; see *Kyōto sōsho* [*Compendium of Books on Kyoto*], VII (Kyoto, 1914), 71–72.

⁸⁶ Higashiyama, literally "eastern mountains," refers to the series of hills bordering the eastern side of the city of Kyoto. There are two Kurodani in Kyoto. The one referred to here is usually called Shin-kurodani, or "New Kurodani," and is located at the foot of Higashi-yama, between Shishigadani and the Ginkakuji.

⁸⁷ Hōnen (1133–1212) founded the Pure Land Sect of Buddhism in Japan. Although his proselytizing was directed in the main toward the plebeian populace, his disciples were to be found among all the social classes. He preached at Shin-kurodani and hence came to be known as Kurodani-shōnin, or "Eminence of Kurodani." *Shōnin*, literally "eminent one," was a title of respect accorded Buddhist monks of high religious attainment; it did not refer to any formal rank in the Buddhist hierarchy.

⁸⁸ The name Renshō means literally "lotus grows." The suffix *-bō*, meaning "bonze," is derived from its primary meaning of "bonzes' quarter."

⁸⁹ These temples date back at least to the early Heian Period. The Yasaka Temple, of which only the five-storied pagoda remains today, dates back to the Nara Period.

⁹⁰ The Kiyomizu Temple was actually built in 805 by the famed general Sakanoue no Tamuramaro (758–811). This was four years prior to Emperor Saga's accession to the throne.

⁹¹ Kumagae here extols the Buddha of Kiyomizu Temple. The principal Buddha of Kiyomizu Temple is actually the Eleven-faced Avalokiteśvara. The Thousand-armed Avalokiteśvara is the Buddha worshipped in the Seikanji.

⁹² *Tani-no-dō Mine-no-dō*, or "Hall of the Valley and Hall of the Peak," was a popular cognomen for the Hokkesanji, which was destroyed by fire in 1332; it was situated in the locality called Shimoyamada on the western fringe of Kyoto, approximately a mile west of the Katsura River. Tamba is the name of this general area, and *Oi-no-yama* (should be *Oi-no-saka*), or "Mountain of the Aged," rises to its west. For a description of this temple, see *Miyako meisho zue shūi* [*Collected Illustrations of Famed Sites of the Capital, a Supplement*] (published 1780–1787), in the *Kyōto sōsho*, I (1916), 270–271 and 277.

⁹³ The site of the original Imperial Palace of Kyoto was later called Uchino, literally "Inner Wilds." The palace was first destroyed by fire in 960, and after that it was repeatedly rebuilt and burned. The site was especially desolate during the years following the great fire of 1177, which is described graphically in the *Hōjōki* [*Record of the Ten-foot-square Hut*] of Kamo no Chōmei (1153–1216). Rendaino is a cemetery in the northern sector of Kyoto, and Funaokayama is a hillock situated to the east of Rendaino.

⁹⁴ Tōji and Saiji, or "East Temple" and "West Temple," were located

just inside the Rashōmon (the main gate of the capital) on the east and west sides of Suzaku Street, formerly the main thoroughfare that led from the Rashōmon to the Imperial Palace. Only the East Temple remains today. The Rashōmon was destroyed in the late tenth century; the area of its former site is called Yotsuka (or Yotsuzuka), literally "four mounds."

⁹⁵ Kumagae is traveling in a southwesterly direction from Kyoto, along the Yodo River, toward present-day Osaka. Yamazaki lies on the west bank of the river, approximately ten miles from Kyoto; Takara Temple (known today as Hōshakuji) and the Sekido Cloister (Sekido-no-in) are in this vicinity. The Yahata Hill is situated directly across the river from Yamazaki, and the area which was known as the "wilds of Katano" lies several miles to its south. Prince Koretaka (844–897) was the son of Emperor Montoku (827–858; reigned 850–858).

⁹⁶ Udono is adjacent to the Yodo River and is noted for the "Udono rush," from which reeds for the *hichiriki* are made. Having traversed the fields of Itoda, Kumagae arrives finally in Osaka. The "King-Child" (*Ōji*) of Kubotsu probably refers to the Shinto deity of this locality. The Tennōji, better known as Shitennōji, was built by Prince Shōtoku in 586 in an area nearer the bay; it was transferred to its present location in 592. Shitennōji is, literally, "Temple of the Four Celestial Kings."

⁹⁷ The *Kame-i*, or "Turtle Well," is located within the Golden Hall (*Kondō*) of the Shitennōji.

⁹⁸ Amano, situated on the western side of Mount Kōya, is the site of the Shinto shrine which deifies the goddess Niu-tsu-hime, a younger sister of Amaterasu. Known also as the "Amano Luminous-Deity" (*Amano myōjin*), she is regarded as the tutelary goddess of Mount Kōya.

⁹⁹ Parts of this sentence cannot be analyzed into meaningful segments. *Shihakuri, teisei,* and *munimujō* are rendered somewhat arbitrarily as four hundred *ri*," "Imperial pale," and "deserted ground." Calculated by the "short" *ri,* the distance of 400 *ri* would be equivalent to approximately 165 miles. Mount Kōya is actually situated less than 80 miles south of Kyoto.

¹⁰⁰ "Eightfold peaks" describes the topography of the summit of Mount Kōya—a flat ground that is encircled by eight peaks. "Eightfold" also alludes to the petals of the lotus, of which there are eight.

¹⁰¹ The "Portrait Hall" (*Mieidō*) is a small edifice in which a portrait of Kūkai (774–835), founder of the temple grounds, is enshrined. The plan of the temple grounds is described in terms of the mandala, which is a device in Esoteric Buddhism to represent the cosmos graphically in diagrams that depict two realms—the Vajradhātu (*Kongōkai*) and the Garbha-kośa-dhātu (*Taizōkai*), or "Metal-hard Realm" and "Womb-store Realm." The Garbha-kośa Mandala depicts Mahāvairocana (*Dainichi*) seated on a red, eight-petaled lotus and with manifold groups of deities arrayed about him.

¹⁰² The principal Buddha of the Golden Hall is actually Bhaiṣajyaguru (*Yakushi*), or "Teacher of Medicine," who is worshipped for his power

to heal the sick; the statue is purportedly a work of Kūkai. "Great Teacher" (*daishi*) refers to Kūkai, who is better known among the Japanese by his posthumous title of Kōbō daishi.

103 *Nanten*, or "Southern Celestial [Region]," actually refers to southern Indian, *-ten* being an abbreviation of *Tenjiku* "India." Little is known about the fabled "Iron Tower" aside from the fact that it is said to have been constructed of iron.

104 "Tuṣita Heaven" (*Tosotsuten*) is one of six celestial realms of desire. It is divided into two spheres—the inner sphere, which serves as the resting place for bodhisattvas who are about to become Buddhas and which is ruled by Maitreya (*Miroku*), and the outer sphere which is the playground for celestial beings. *Hanri*, the meaning of which cannot be determined, is presumably the name of one of the many glittering edifices that fill the Tuṣita Heaven.

105 The "Twenty-eight Followers" and the "Twelve Deities" refer to the sets of Buddhist deities that are subservient to Avalokiteśvara and Bhaiṣajyaguru.

106 The "Three Venerated [Buddhas]" of Amidism are Amitābha and his two attendant bodhisattvas, Avalokiteśvara and Mahāsthāmaprāpta (*Seishi*).

107 Arghya (*aka*) is water that contains fragrant flowers; it is prepared as a Buddhist offering.

108 *Ōjō*, a Buddhist euphemism for death, implies being reborn in Amitābha's Pure Land. *Daiōjō*, or "magnificent *ōjō*," is used to describe the stately death of a person of extreme age.

VI: A LIBRETTO, *Izumi's Fortress*

1 See *Kinko shōsetsu shinsan*, pp. 367–381.

2 See *KBS*, II, 399–411.

3 This text is available in the library of the Faculty of Literature, Kyoto University; it has not been published. The signature of the copyist, Sugiwara Kambei, is inscribed at the end, but the date of transcription is not indicated. Other pieces in this collection of texts transcribed by the same copyist are dated between 1624 and 1628.

4 A "capped name" (*kanjamei*) was taken when a youth was "capped," or formally initiated into adulthood. There was no prescribed age for this initiation, but it was normally conducted during adolescence.

5 Historians doubt that they were related. In a recent survey of the Chūsonji, the temple in Hiraizumi which houses the mummified remains of four generations of Fujiwara, much attention was given to anthropological observations to determine whether or not the Fujiwara were of Ainu stock; see *Chūsonji to Fujiwara yondai* [*The Chūsonji and the Four Generations of Fujiwara*], ed. Asahi Press (Tokyo, 1950). According to the *Sompi bummyaku*, a compendium of genealogies compiled in the 15th century by descendants of Tōin Kinsada (1340–1399), the Fujiwara

of the north trace their ancestry through Fujiwara Hidesato (fl. early 10th century), the militant governor of Musashi and Shimotsuke provinces, back to Fujiwara Uona (721–783), who was a high-ranking courtier in Kyoto; see *Kojitsu sōsho,* LXXXVII (Tokyo, 1903), 65a.

⁶ The Ainu Pacification Office (*Chinjufu*) was established in the early ninth century at the Izawa Fortress, which lay a short distance north of Hiraizumi. The head of the office was termed *kami* (see note 13 below); his full title was *chinjufu-shōgun.*

⁷ The rich beauty of the temples—the Chūsonji built by Kiyohira, the Mōtsuji built by his son Motohira, and the Muryōkōin which Hidehira built as a copy of the famed Phoenix Hall (Hōōdō) of the Byōdōin south of Kyoto—are described in detail in the entry for the 17th day of the Ninth Month, 1189, in the *Azuma kagami* (see *KT,* XXXII, 353–354).

⁸ In *maki* 41; see *KS,* VIII, 526–527.

⁹ This episode is described in detail in the *Gempei seisui ki, maki* 21 (see *KS,* VII, 642–646).

¹⁰ Entry for the 21st day of the Fourth Month, 1185 (see *KT,* XXXII, 150).

¹¹ "Now" is a rendering of the stock introductory phrase, *saru aida* (see note 28 to Chapter V).

¹² *Kinō kyō to wa omōedomo* is, literally, "although it seemed that it were [only] yesterday or today." *Omōedomo* (transliterated *OMOHU-WEDOMO*) is normally pronounced and written *omoedomo* (*OMOHE-DOMO*). The insertion of the extra mora, changing the second syllable from short to long (-*mo-* > -*mō-*), occurs several times in this text; this may reflect the vocal recitational style or, possibly, a dialectal idiosyncrasy.

¹³ Hōgan, which became a popular sobriquet for Yoshitsune, was actually the title of the post in the Criminal Investigation Board (*Kebiishichō*) to which he was appointed in 1184 by the retired Emperor Go-Shirakawa. The term *hōgan* means literally "adjudicating official," but it was primarily the designation for the third-ranking officer, or *jō,* in this government office. The Chinese graphs that were used to represent *hōgan* were, in fact, more commonly read *jō.* The chief official of a government office was usually called *kami* ("head"); he was assisted by the *suke* ("assistant"); and subordinate to the *suke* were several *jō* ("lieutenant").

¹⁴ "Palace" is a rendering of *gosho* (literally, "emperor's place [of residence]"). Although the term originally denoted the emperor's residence, it was later applied to the residences of other members of the imperial family and, from the Kamakura Period, of the shogun and his immediate family.

¹⁵ Actually, Yoshitsune had been in Hiraizumi less than nine months. In the *Azuma kagami,* the date of his arrival in Hiraizumi is given as the 10th day of the Second Month, 1187; the date of Fujiwara Hidehira's death is given as the 29th day of the Tenth Month, 1187 (see *KT,* XXXII, 252 and 281).

¹⁶ *Nyūdō* (literally, "an entrant into the [Buddhist] Way") refers to a

man who has taken the Buddhist tonsure but continues to lead a normal secular life in most respects although his head may be shaved and his garb be that of a priestly order. Owing to his ambiguous status, the *nyūdō* is usually described in English as "lay monk," a rendering which is misleading to the extent that "monk" implies monastic living. As opposed to the *nyūdō*, one who takes the tonsure and leaves his secular domicile to enter a monastery is called a *shukke* (literally, "one who leaves the home").

[17] Ōshū, or the Interior Region, referred to the northern one-third of Honshū—the sector which is known today as the Ōu District. The barrier of Shirakawa, which was situated approximately one hundred miles north of present-day Tokyo, was regarded traditionally as the gateway to the Interior Region. Hiraizumi lay 140 miles north of this barrier.

[18] *Hiban tōban hima mo nashi / itsuki kashizuki tatematsuru.* A very literal translation would read, "[Guards] off-duty and on-duty, there were no vacant moments; they stood by him and watched over him."

[19] The term *gekō*, literally "go down," indicates travel in a direction away from the imperial capital of Kyoto. Yoshitsune in this instance had journeyed from Kyoto northward to Hiraizumi.

[20] Mongaku (dates unknown) was the chief priest of Jingoji, a Shingon Sect monastery situated on the summit of Mount Takao outside the northwest limits of Kyoto. Mongaku first met Yoritomo when both were living in Izu Province as political exiles. He influenced Yoritomo's decision to rise against the Heike, and he served as the link between Yoritomo and the retired Emperor Go-Shirakawa in Kyoto. Because of this association, Mongaku at this time had considerable influence with Yoritomo.

[21] Tōkōbō, or "Tōkō Cloister," was a sobriquet of Rennin of the temple known as Kuramadera (the "official" pronunciation is Ambaji). The temple is located on Mount Kurama, which is several miles to the north of Kyoto. Yoshitsune had spent his childhood at this temple under the guardianship of Tōkōbō.

[22] "Karma Master" is a rendering of *tokko* (or *tokugō*), literally "[he who has] acquired karma." It was an academic degree conferred on monks who had attended a prescribed series of lectures or seminars on Buddhist sutras. "Karma Master of Nara" refers to Shōkō (dates unknown) of Kōfukuji, who was known also as Kanjubō. He befriended the fugitive Yoshitsune (see *Gikeiki, maki* 6, in *NK*, XXXVII, 255 ff.), and for this was to answer personally to Yoritomo. The *Azuma kagami,* in the entry of the 5th day of the Third Month, 1187, states: "Shōkō, the Karma Master of Suō of the Southern Capital [Nara], arrived in accordance with the summons. The reason [for this summons] was his master-disciple [relationship] with [the former governor of] Iyo Province [Yoshitsune]." (See *KT*, XXXII, 253.)

[23] *Kami wa goittai nareba* is, literally, "since [those] above are of one body." The intended meaning of "above" (*kami*) is not entirely clear.

²⁴ Watanabe and Fukushima were situated on the Yodo River estuary in the Province of Tsu (or Settsu), which is the present-day Osaka-Kobe area.

²⁵ *Chōbuku,* or "imprecation," was a magical rite to effect a curse in order to subjugate or destroy persons whom one could not counter physically. See note 31 below for the details.

²⁶ "Monk superior" is a rendering of *sōjō,* the highest ecclesiastical rank in the Buddhist hierarchy; the literal meaning of *sōjō* is "monk righter." The title *bettō,* which is rendered as "superintendent," applied to offices both religious and secular. In Buddhist institutions, the *bettō* was the superintendent monk of a temple. The *bettō* of a Shinto shrine was, however, an official of minor importance. The two highest administrative officers of the Kamakura Shogunate were also called *bettō.* The "superintendent of Wakamiya" cannot be identified. Wakamiya, or "young shrine," refers to a subsidiary Shinto shrine built usually within the precincts of the parent shrine. Here Wakamiya refers to the Hachiman Shrine which was newly built in Tsurugaoka in Kamakura; its parent shrine is the Usa-Hachiman Shrine in Kyushu. A Dual-Shintoist institution, it was served in former times by both Shinto priests and Buddhist monks.

²⁷ Text A has here "garments" (*ishō*); Texts B and C have "a place" (*issho*), which is more in context.

²⁸ *Goma,* homa in Sanskrit, refers to ritualistic burning in Esoteric Buddhism. The shape of the fireplace and the type, size, and shape of the wood used for burning varied according to the nature of the rite being conducted (see note 31 below).

²⁹ This passage begins with the stock introductory phrase, *somosomo,* which is rendered as "now." (See note 6 to Chapter V.)

³⁰ This clause in Text A reads *jōdan wa shidan nari,* or "the upper atlar is four altars." It should probably read, as in Texts B and C, *ijō dan wa shidan nari,* literally "as for altars, there are these four altars."

³¹ These four rites in Esoteric Buddhism are described as follows in Oda's *Bukkyō daijiten:* (1) Śāntika (*sokusai*) is the rite for warding off adversity that one is fated to encounter. It is performed in the early evening hours during the first eight days of the lunar month. The fireplace for the homa burning is circular, and the devotee performs the rite facing north, a direction that symbolizes winter and the withering of life. (2) Puṣṭika (*zōyaku*) is the rite for bringing prosperity, wisdom, official rank, and affection. It is performed at dawn, during the ninth to fifteenth days of the month. A square fireplace is used, and the direction faced is east, which symbolizes spring and the growth of life. (3) Vaśīkaraṇa (*keiai*) is the rite through which one expresses spiritual devotion, and is performed in the predawn hours, during the 16th to 22nd days of the month. A lotus-shaped fireplace is used, and the direction faced is west, which is symbolic of fruition. (4) Abhicāraka (*chōbuku*) is the rite for subjugating or destroying one's enemies. It is performed either at

noon or midnight, between the 23rd day and the end of the month. The fireplace is triangular, and the direction faced is south, which symbolizes heat and radiance of destructive intensity.

³² The directions indicated are at variance with those stated in the note above.

³³ The Chinese graphs for *gumotsu* in Text A indicate the meaning "implements," whereas those in Text C indicate the meaning "offerings," which is more in context. In Text B, the word is rendered syllabically.

³⁴ *Nare* (Text A), to which no significant meaning can be attached, should probably be *tare* "dripped" (Texts B and C).

³⁵ The bodhisattva Kṣitigarba, known widely in Japan as *Jizō*, is noted for his great benevolence in guiding and enlightening those who dwell in non-Buddhistic realms.

³⁶ The *boshi-* of *boshioroshite* (Text A) cannot be identified as a morpheme; the word should probably be *oshioroshite,* as in Texts B and C. *Oshi-* is possibly the continuative form (*ren'yōkei*) of the verb *osu* "to eat"—in which case *oshioroshite* would mean, literally, "ate and downed [it]," or "swallowed [it]."

³⁷ *Naibaku-gebaku* is, literally, "bind [the victim both] within and without."

³⁸ *Ususana* (Text A) should be *Ususama* (Texts B and C), the Buddhist deity (Ucchuṣma in Sanskrit) who is customarily enshrined in latrines because of his power to cleanse defilement. Vajrakumāra (*Kongō-dōji*), or "Vajra Boy," is a deity who in Esoteric Buddhism is regarded as a separate manifestation of Amitābha. He is depicted as a child of ferocious appearance, wielding a vajra, a hand weapon that is gripped in the middle and has sharp points on either end.

³⁹ *Tokko* denotes the ordinary vajra, which has a single sharp point at either end. Among the other types of vajras, the most common were the "three-pronged vajra" (*sanko*) and the "five-pronged vajra" (*goko*).

⁴⁰ *Moayuru,* which is rendered here as "flowed," may be a corruption of *moyuru,* which means "to blaze" or "to shoot forth, or sprout."

⁴¹ Yamāntaka (*Dai-itoku*) is one of the five "luminous-kings" (*myōō*), the ferocious protectors of Buddhism; he is often depicted riding a great white ox. The "Ox of the Wise" refers to the ox of the bodhisattva Mañjuśrī (*Monju*). In Esoteric Buddhism, each of the five great Buddhas is regarded as having two other manifestations—one as a bodhisattva, and the other as a luminous-king. The luminous-king Yamāntaka and the bodhisattva Mañjuśrī were regarded as the two other manifestations of Amitābha.

⁴² Some of the methods mentioned here seem to be fictitious; most of the titles appear to be those of dhāraṇi (magical formulas for incantation) of one sort or another. *Emmei* "round-bright" should be *emmei* "life prolongation," which is a ritual associated with Acala (*Fudō*), the luminous-king who is regarded as a manifestation of Mahāvairocana.

⁴³ For a description of the *hitatare,* see note 11 to Chapter V.

⁴⁴ Sahā (*shaba*) is the Buddhist realm in which the inhabitants must endure the woes of mortal passions; it refers to man's present world. "Dusky Circuit" (*meido*) is the Buddhist equivalent of Hades. "Yellow Spring" (*kōsen*) is the Confucian concept of a subterranean realm which one enters after death.

⁴⁵ Nishikido no Tarō is referred to in the text as *chakushi,* a term which denotes "eldest son by a formal wife."

⁴⁶ *Kanja,* which is rendered as "son," is literally "a capped person"— that is, one who has been initiated into adulthood. The term was usually applied to young adults. (See note 4 above.)

⁴⁷ *Utemairase* consists of the stem *ute-* "to slay" and the perfect form (*izenkei*) of *mairasu.* If *mairasu* were considered a potentially free form, it would be analyzed as an inflectional formation of the verb *mairu* "to come, or go." During the Muromachi Period, however, it was used as a respectful suffix (a bound form), a derivational formation of *mairu.*

⁴⁸ This clause occurs in Texts B and C, but is omitted in Text A.

⁴⁹ The *kishō* (rendered erroneously as *kisho,* or "documentary record" in Text A) is a formal oath made to Buddhist and Shinto deities as an attest of one's resolutions. The samurai customarily inscribed these oaths on "Goō charm slips" (see note 51 below).

⁵⁰ *Mōshiorosu,* which is rendered as "obtain," is a variant form of *mōshiuku;* the latter comprises the two verbs *mōsu* "to speak or petition" and *uku* "to receive."

⁵¹ This Kami, whom the Fujiwara considered their clan god, was worshipped in a shrine which today is called Murasaki-jinja and located in the coastal town of Matsushima; the deity is identified with "the Master of Heaven's Center" (*Ame-no-minaka-nushi*). Goō, an abbreviation of *Goō-hōin* (literally, "Ox-King's treasure-seal"), is the name of a charm slip that was carried to all parts of Japan by "Goō peddlers." These charm slips were first issued by the Dual-Shintoist Kumano Shrine, but they were later issued by Buddhist temples as well.

⁵² Minamoto no Yoshiie (1041–1108) was the most illustrious among the early Genji generals. Hachiman Tarō was his "capped name." It was due largely to the success of his campaigns against the rebellious Abe and Kiyohara clans in the north that the Genji became a political power in the eastern half of Japan.

⁵³ Kiyohira was actually appointed *ōryōshi* (literally, "territory-subduing emissary"), the title being that of a Heian Period local administrator. The provincial administrator called the *shugo,* or "constable," was created formally in 1185 by the Kamakura Shogunate. The term *shugo* is seen in the *Azuma kagami* in an entry for the year 1180 (see *KT,* XXXII, 53); but the compilers, chronicling events of earlier years, may have used the term mistakenly. Mitachi (literally, "Honored Residence") was a sobriquet of Kiyohira. *Gon-taifu* ("acting grandee")—and not "Gontarō" as in the text—was his official rank.

⁵⁴ *Shikashinagara* is used here in its original denotation of "all" or "entirely" rather than its usual meaning of "however."

⁵⁵ The verb stem *itoshi-* in Text A should be *hitoshi-* "is equal" as in Texts B and C.

⁵⁶ Brahmadeva (*Bonten*), or "Brahman Heaven," is a Buddhist realm of purity and quietude, far apart from worlds in which desires exist. *Bonten*, in this instance, probably refers to *Dai-Bonten-ō*, or "King of Mahābrahman."

⁵⁷ *Taishaku* is an abbreviated translation into Japanese of Śakra devānām Indra, or "Lord of the Śakra Heaven." This Buddhist deity dwells atop Mount Sumeru, the central hub of the universe, and reigns over Trāyastrimśa (*Tōriten*), one of the six realms of desire.

⁵⁸ The "Four Celestial Kings" (*Shitennō*) are subordinate to the lord of the Śakra Heaven. They occupy four peaks on the slope of Mount Sumeru whence they command the four celestial realms of Dhritarāṣṭra (*Jikoku*) in the east, Virūḍhaka (*Zōchō*) in the south, Virūpākṣa (*Kōmoku*) in the west, and Dhanada (*Tamon*) in the north.

⁵⁹ The Sun Goddess, Amaterasu.

⁶⁰ Hachiman, a bodhisattva of Japanese invention, was the clan god of the Genji. A product of Dual Shinto, in which all native Kami were regarded as local manifestations of Buddhist deities, Hachiman was considered a manifestation of Amitābha.

⁶¹ The clause which occurs here, *nyūdō o odorokashitatematsuru tokoro o*, cannot be analyzed so as to be placed in context. Its substitution with the line, "May their wrath be visited upon us," is entirely arbitrary.

⁶² Padma (*Guren*), or "Scarlet-Lotus hell," and Mahāpadma (*Daiguren*), or "Great Scarlet-Lotus hell," are names of the two coldest of the eight frigid hells. The names are purportedly derived from the legend that because of the cold the bodies of the damned would burst like blossoms of the scarlet lotus.

⁶³ *Mi no ke yodatsu*, or "the hair on the body stand on end," is, in modern Japanese just as it is in English, an expression of great horror. But in the Medieval Era, this expression usually described the sensation of mysteriousness brought on by the observation of some supernatural occurrence; this has been indicated by the annotators of the Iwanami edition of the *Heike monogatari*. (See *NK*, XXXII 445.)

⁶⁴ *Gogōden* (Text A) should be *Gohōden* "Treasure Hall" (Texts B and C).

⁶⁵ *Gotai*, literally "five bodies," refers to the head and the four limbs— i.e., " a body." Text C has here *gonin*, or "five persons."

⁶⁶ *Shidai shidai ni nondarishi* is, literally, "[they] drank it very gradually."

⁶⁷ The second, third, and fourth lines of this *coro melos pastorale* passage are not contained in Texts B and C.

⁶⁸ This first sentence of the quotation is omitted in Text A.

⁶⁹ Benkei, whose strength and military prowess are legendary, had lived at one time in the West Tower of the Enryakuji monastery on

Mount Hiei. He was more commonly known by the sobriquet Musashibō, or "Monk of Musashi [Province]."

70 "War commissioner" (*ikusa-bugyō*) is a command position that was instituted by the Kamakura Shogunate. The superintendent (*bettō*) of the Sumurai Office (*samuraidokoro*) assumed this post in times of war.

71 *Kurogane* "black metal" referred to iron.

72 The *Azuma kagami* gives the date of Hidehira's death as the 29th day of the Tenth Month, the Third Year of Bunji, or 1187 (see *KT*, XXXII, 281). The *Gikeiki*, which is not a reliable historical source, states that Hidehira died on the 21st day of the Twelfth Month, 1188 (see *NK*, XXXVII, 368).

73 Hidehira was actually in his 66th year at the time of his death. The figure ninety-eight does not refer specifically to his age; perhaps it has some other significance.

74 *Kahō*, or "karmic results," refers to the rewards or retributions one may receive in life as the consequence of the workings of karma (*gō*), the principle of moral causality. *Kahō* usually suggests "rewards" rather than retribution. For suggesting karmic retribution, the term *gōka* (literally, "karmic fruits") is normally used.

75 *Nobe no okuri*, or "escorting to the edge of the wilds," is an expression which possibly reflects archaic burial customs; it referred to either funeral processions or simply the funeral rites. Actually, Hidehira's body was enclosed in a coffin and placed in the Golden Hall of Chūsonji, where it has lain in a mummified state to the present day.

76 *Emma no chō*, or "Court of Yama-rāja," is the Buddhist version of the court of judgment for the dead. It is located in the subterranean Yama-loka Realm and is presided over by the king-adjudicator Yama-rāja.

77 The 49th day after one's passing is termed *chūin* (literally, "middle darkness"). It is regarded as the day on which the soul is midway between the existence whence it has come and the one it is about to enter. The day is an occasion for elaborate memorial services.

78 Matsushima probably refers to the Matsushima Temple, which was built originally in 838 on the coast of Matsushima Bay, which is famed as one of the "Three Scenic Sights of Japan." The temple was destroyed in the late Kamakura Period and was rebuilt in the early Edo Period by the daimyo Date Masamune (1567–1636). At that time the name of the temple was changed to Zuiganji.

79 This paragraph is omitted in Text A.

80 *Hyakkanichi*, or the one hundredth day after a person's death, is in Buddhism a prescribed day for conducting memorial services.

81 The word used here is *mikyōsho* (literally, "august missive of instruction"), which originally denoted a document issued by a retired emperor or an imperial regent. In later times, the term applied also to those issued by a shogun.

82 This section is labeled *irokatakiri* in the libretto used by the per-

formers of Ōe Village. The melodic pattern is, however, identical with that of the *irokakari*, Type I, or *solo pastorale*. It may be the name of a melodic pattern that has been lost.

83 *Oku no ittō*, or "the band of the Interior [Region]," refers to the Fujiwara clan of northern Japan.

84 These five provinces constitute the major part of the entire Kantō area. If these were added to the territory already under their control, the Fujiwara domain would then have covered almost the entire eastern half of Honshū.

85 *Shuryō* (Text A has *shūryō*) is presumably to be read with a voiced initial. *Juryō* (or *zuryō*) is a title which might be rendered as "provincial provost." It referred to the governor of a province and was synonymous with *kuni no kami*, or "provincial protector."

86 *Yo ni mo*, literally "even in [this] world," is an adverbial phrase which functions to intensify descriptive adjectives, and may be rendered as "indeed," "very," "beyond anything in this world," and so forth.

87 The term *temmei*, or "decree of Heaven," in Confucian ethics referred to the *li*, or the operating principle of the universe; its observance was held vital to the achieving of order in society. The term *tembatsu*, "or retribution of Heaven," would have been more appropriate here.

88 *Zashiki*, which is rendered as "matted room," originally denoted a room in which mats or cushions were placed on the wooden floor; it was usually the best room in the house. During the Muromachi Period, it became customary to cover the floor of all rooms with mats (*tatami*); the term *zashiki* then came to denote the more elegant rooms of a house.

89 "Only this" is a rendering of *sara sara betsu no shisai ni te sōrawazu*, literally "furthermore, it is not a special matter." This is a stock expression for prefacing a statement of an explanatory nature.

90 The expression here is *zashiki o ketatete tatsuru*, literally "left the matted room, stomping," which is like "slamming the door."

91 This sentence is omitted in Text A.

92 The four paragraphs which follow are omitted in Text A. This omission probably represents the loss of a leaf in the manuscript text.

93 *Mune no hitohashi* is, literally, "a fragment of the significance."

94 As a title of a post in the Imperial Court, *taishō* would be rendered literally as "great marshal." As a term used among the samurai, however, "commander" would be a more appropriate rendering (see note 7 to Chapter V).

95 "Main gate" is a rendering of *ōte*, literally "great hands." *Ōte* "great hands" is said to be derived from *ōte* "pursuing hands" (see *Daigenkai*). It referred to the front-center of a fortress or a battle position and, by extension, to the main gate.

96 *Sendo*, literally "the path ahead," refers to the ultimate extent, or end, of one's path in life. It is used figuratively to mean "death which is imminent."

97 The linear distance of a *chō* is about 119 yards. Eighteen *chō* would thus be slightly less than one and one-quarter miles.

98 *Te ni toru yō ni kikoeru* is an idiomatic expression which, rendered literally, is "was heard [as if it were so close] as to be graspable by the hand."

99 The passage "Such is to be the fate of this Yoshitsune!" is omitted in Text A.

100 The word *iza* is an exclamation which expresses a determination to embark on a task or action; it is also uttered in a situation where one is attempting to lead others in concerted action. It is manifested in the translation with the exclamation point.

101 *Michi yori mo hikikaesu* is, literally, "turned back [while] on the way."

102 Takanao (not Takano, as in Text A) was the given name of Terui no Tarō.

103 "Clashing swords" is a rendering of *shinogi o kezuru,* literally "shave the blade-ridges," a stock phrase in depictions of furious sword-play.

104 *Taisei* (Text A) should read *mōsei* "surging vigor" (Texts B and C).

105 *Kogusoku,* which is rendered as "brief-armor," refers to an ensemble consisting only of guards over the limbs, the throat, and the right side of the torso.

106 This line and the line preceding it are omitted in Text A.

107 "Death-journey Mountain (*shide no yama*), originally a metaphorical symbol of the agonies of death, came to be regarded in popular Japanese belief as a physical mountain that rises at the boundary of the subterranean Yama-loka Realm. "Three-way River" (*sanzu no kawa*), which symbolizes the three evil paths, is in the same way regarded popularly as a physical river—one which, like the Styx, must be crossed in order to arrive at the realm of the dead.

108 The last four lines of this section vary with the text. The version of Text B has been translated.

109 Although this section is labeled *solo recitativo* (*iro*) in the libretto, in performance the melody is actually that of the *solo pastorale* (*irokakari,* Type I).

110 "One-space room" is the *hitomadokoro,* or a room measuring one *ma* square. During the Heian Period, a *ma* was the distance between two pillars in a house, not a fixed unit of measure. But in the Muromachi Period, *ma* designated an area six feet square.

111 The *haramaki,* literally "belly-girder," was a lightweight and close-fitting armor that was worn about the torso and laced together at the back. It was the normal battle wear for the common foot soldier. Samurai of higher rank also wore the *haramaki* when in the rear echelons, but they always donned a full suit of armor for actual combat. For a detailed description with illustrations, see Sekine Masanao, *Shōzoku zukai [Pictorial Explanation of Dress],* 2 vols. (enl. ed.; Tokyo, 1916), II, 25–29.

112 The Governor of Noto Province, Taira no Noritsune (1160–1185) was a warrior and archer of great repute. When he shot at Yoshitsune

during the height of the Battle of Yashima in 1184, Satō Tsuginobu used his own body as a shield and died by the arrow that was intended for his master. This episode is described in detail in the *Heike monogatari, maki* 11 (see *NB*, ser. 1, IX, 584–588).

113 "Renowned" is a rendering of *kakure mo naki,* literally "wholly without concealment."

114 The word *aware,* when used as an interjection, is expressive of a variety of emotions depending on the situation, and may be compared to the English "oh" or "ah." *Appare,* which appears in Texts B and C, represents a phonetic intensification of *aware* and is an interjection to be used in enthusiastic praise of a person or his actions.

115 Texts B and C have here *niguru mono,* or "those who fled." Text A has *nikushi,* or "the detested [ones]."

116 *Nagifusu* "cut down" is modified by the adverbial phrase *te no shita ni te,* literally "to [a place] below her hands," which connotes either "to the ground" or "to the floor." It is actually redundant since *nagifusu* implies cutting down to the ground or floor.

117 The translation of this paragraph is based on Text B, since the version of Text A contains a number of omissions.

118 The *tsukedake,* literally "[fire-] lighting bamboo," was similar to the old European "match"—a slender material dipped in melted sulfur to make it ignitable by tinder.

119 *Shōji,* or "partition," is a name of a class that includes both sliding screens and portable standing screens. In its recent usage, *shōji* refers specifically to the framed, paper-covered sliding door, or what has been called the *akari-shōji* (literally, "light [-giving] partition").

120 *Tenka kasumi to* is an adverbial phrase which, translated literally, is "so that [all] beneath the heaven became hazy."

121 This sentence is omitted in Text A.

122 According to the *Azuma kagami,* the two events occurred in reverse order. The death of Yoshitsune is noted in the entry for the 30th day of the Intercalary Fourth Month, 1189; the slaying of Izumi by his elder brother Yasuhira is listed as an occurrence of the 26th day of the Sixth Month (see *KT*, XXXII, 326 and 333).

123 For pertinent entries in the *Azuma kagami,* see *KT*, XXXII, 332, 333, 335–350.

APPENDIX

1 According to the *Bugaku yōroku* [*A Record of Important Facts on Bugaku*] (12th century?), a piece called "sarugaku" was included in a program of bugaku as early as the year 936. The edition consulted is in *Gunsho ruijū,* XII, (Tokyo, 1904), 149–174.

2 Such programming is described in the *Shōyūki,* the diary of Fujiwara Sanesuke (957–1046); see *Shiryō tsūran,* I, 199 and 339, and II, 272–273 and 365.

3 The contents of fifteen bugaku programs presented during sumō-

wrestling festivals held between the years 936 and 1158 are described in the *Bugaku yōroku;* "sarugaku" is listed as one of the numbers presented in twelve of these programs (*Gunsho ruijū,* XII, 162–166).

4 Nose, *Nōgaku genryū kō,* p. 6.

5 Hayashiya, "The Genesis of the Sarugaku-nō," in *Chūsei bungaku kenkyū to shiryō* [*Medieval Literature: Research and Material*] (Tokyo, 1958), p. 43.

6 The *Gōke shidai* written by Ōe Masafusa (1041–1111) describes the various rites and ceremonies of the Imperial Court in the late Heian Period. See *Zōtei kojitsu sōsho,* XVII (Tokyo, 1929), 257.

7 See *Nihon koten zenshū,* ser. 5, XX, 891.

BIBLIOGRAPHY

****

BIBLIOGRAPHY

KŌWAKA TEXTS

Kinko shōsetsu shinsan [*A New Collection of Tales of Near Antiquity*], ed. Shimazu Hisamoto (Tokyo, 1928). This anthology contains partly annotated texts of three kōwaka, *Izumigajō, Kuketsu no kai,* and *Nihongi* (see synopses 18, 39, and 41 in Chapter IV). The only other kōwaka to have been published with annotations is *Hamaide* (see synopsis 38), which is contained in the anthology, *Otogi-zōshi,* ed. Ichiko Teiji, *NK,* XXXVIII, 307–311.

Ko-jōruri oyobi Mai-no-hon shū [*Anthology of Ko-jōruri and Texts for (Kōwaka) Dances*], Vol. II of *Kindai Nihon bungaku taikei* (Tokyo, 1928). This anthology contains 25 kōwaka printed in the style of ordinary prose. This is a convenient edition for reading, for the text is fully punctuated and, furthermore, Chinese graphs have been supplied for many of the words which are written in the kana syllabary in the original librettos.

Kōwaka-bukyoku shū [*KBS*], ed. Sasano Ken, 2 vols. (Tokyo, 1943); available also in a single-volume edition. This represents an achievement in thoroughness as a compendium of sources on one research topic. The editor has attempted to gather all available data on the kōwaka, so that future students may be relieved of this tedious step in research procedure. He indulges in a few interpretive comments but in the main goes no further than to suggest possible avenues of approach to problems which might be solved with the use of this material. Volume I consists of relevant material ferreted from innumerable volumes of primary-source documents. Volume II is an antholgy of kōwaka texts; many of the pieces appear in the original format of the libretto, even with musical neumes reproduced with specially-cast types.

Mai no hon, ed. Ueda Kazutoshi (Tokyo, 1900). The fifteen
kōwaka texts in this collection are reproductions of manuscript copies from the early seventeenth century. Recitative
instructions are given in the text.

Nihon kayō shūsei [Compendium of Japanese Songs], ed. Takano
Tatsuyuki, Vol. V, *Kinko [Near Antiquity]* (Tokyo, 1928).
This volume contains collections of *kōwaka-kayō,* which are
particularly favored passages from kōwaka texts.

Shin gunsho ruijū, Vol. VIII, *Bukyoku,* ed. Kōda Rohan (Tokyo,
1906). Most of the 41 pieces contained are versions which were
printed in the seventeenth century as prose fiction rather
than librettos.

Tokugawa bungei ruijū, Vol. VIII, *Jōruri* (Tokyo: Kokusho
kankō kai, 1915; or Hirotani kokusho kankō kai, 1925). This
anthology contains two ko-jōruri, *Takadachi godan* and
Kosode Soga, which are almost identical with the kōwaka
Takadachi and *Kosode Soga* (see synopses 19 and 24 in
Chapter IV).

JAPANESE WORKS OF THE
PREMODERN PERIOD

(Authors, when known, are listed after the titles)

Azuma kagami [Mirror of the East] (late 13th century), ed. Kuroita Katsumi. *KT,* Vols. XXXII and XXXIII (Tokyo,
1932–1933).

Bugaka yōroku [A Record of Important Facts on Bugaku] (12th
century?). In *Gunsho ruijū,* XII (Tokyo, 1904), 149–174.

Chūyūki [The Diary of the Minister of the Right, Nakamikado]
by Fujiwara Munetada (1032–1114). *Shiryō tsūran,* Vols. IV-X
(Tokyo, 1915–1916).

Dekisai Kyō-miyage [Dekisai's Presents from the Capital] (published 1677). In *Kyōto sōsho [Compendium of Books on
Kyoto],* VII (Kyoto, 1914), 1–165.

Enkyoku shū and other anthologies of enkyoku compiled by
Meikū (ca. 1240–1306). In *Nihon kayō shūsei,* V (Tokyo,
1928), 23–171.

Gakkaroku [A Record of Music Houses] (1690) by Abe Suehisa.
Nihon koten zenshū, ser. 5, Vols. XVIII-XXII (Tokyo, 1935–
1936).

*Gempei seisui ki [Chronicle of the Flourish and Decline of the
Genji and the Heike]* (13th century). *KS,* 3rd ed., Vols. VII
and VIII (Tokyo, 1918).

Gikeiki [*Annals of (Minamoto no) Yoshitsune*] (ca. 1400), ed. Ichiko Teiji. *NK*, Vol. XXXVII (Tokyo, 1959).

Gōke shidai [*Proceedings of the Ōe House*] (1111) by Ōe Masa-fusa (1041–1111). *Zōtei kojitsu sōsho,* Vol. XVII (Tokyo, 1929).

Gyokuyō [*Gem Leaves*], the diary of Kujō Kanezane (1149–1207). *KKKS,* ser. 1:10, 3 vols. (Tokyo, 1907).

Heiji monogatari [*Tale of the Heiji (Insurrection)*] (12th century), *KS,* 14th ed., Vol. V (Tokyo, 1918).

Heike monogatari [*Tale of the Heike*] (13th century), ed. Mozume Takakazu. *NB,* ser. 1, Vol. IX (Tokyo, 1927).

Intoku Taiheiki (17th century) by Kagawa Masanori. *Tsūzoku Nihon zenshi,* Vol. XIII (Tokyo, 1913).

Kaei sandai ki [*Chronicle of Three Generations in the Floral Quarters*] (15th century). In *Gunsho ruijū,* XVI (Tokyo, 1904), 744–820.

Kakitsu ki [*Chronicle of the Kakitsu (Period)*] (15th century). In *Gunsho ruijū,* XIII (Tokyo, 1904), 308–317.

Kangin shū, a collection of *kouta* compiled in 1518. In *Nihon kayō shūsei,* V (Tokyo, 1928), 375–395.

Kasshi yawa zokuhen [*Sequel to the Kasshi-Night Tales*] (1892), a miscellany written originally during 1821–1828 by Matsuura Seizan. *KKKS,* ser. 3, Vols. VII and VIII (Tokyo, 1910).

Kawasumi Taikō ki [*The Kawasumi Annals of Taikō (Hideyoshi)*] (17th century). *Kaitei shiseki shūran,* Vol. XIX (Tokyo, 1901).

Kiyū shōran (1830) by Kitamura Nobuyo (Tokyo: Ryokuen shobō, 1958).

Koji ruien [*Encyclopedia of Classical Matters*], Vols. XLIII and XLIV, *Gakubu-bu* [*Volumes on Music and Dance*] (2nd reduced-size ed.; Tokyo, 1931, 1933).

Kyōkunshō [*Selections for Instruction and Admonition*] (1233) by Koma Chikazane (1177–1242). In *Zoku gunsho ruijū,* 5th ed., XIX:1 (Tokyo, 1931), 172–373.

Manzai jugō nikki [*The Diary of the Jugō Manzai*] by Manzai (1378–1455). *Zoku gunsho ruijū hoi,* 2 vols. (2nd ed.; Tokyo, 1931, 1932).

Meigō ōrai [*Correspondences with Akihira*] (known also by the title *Unshū shōsoku* [*News for Izumo Province*]) by Fujiwara Akihira (989–1066). In *Gunsho ruijū,* VI (Tokyo, 1904), 1042–1091.

Miyako meisho zue [*Collected Illustrations of Famed Sites of the Capital*] (published 1780–1787). *Kyōto sōsho,* Vol. IV (Kyoto, 1916).

Murasaki Shikibu nikki [*The Diary of Murasaki Shikibu*] (1010) by Murasaki Shikibu (975?–1016?). In *NK*, XIX (Tokyo, 1958), 405–520.

Nimaze no ki [*Potpourri of Records*] (1811) by Takizawa Bakin (1767–1848). In *Nihon zuihitsu zenshū*, III (Tokyo, 1929), 373–473.

Nobunaga-kō ki [*Annals of the Lord Nobunaga*] (17th century). *Kaitei shiseki shūran*, Vol. XIX (Tokyo, 1901).

Ryōjin hishō [*Secret Selection of Songs*], compiled by Emperor Go-Shirakawa (1127–1192; reigned 1155–1158). The extant portion (*maki* 2) in *Nihon kayō shūsei*, II (Tokyo, 1928), 473–513.

Ryōjin hishō kuden shū [*Secret Selection of Songs: The Collection of Oral Traditions*] (1169) by Emperor Go-Shirakawa. The extant portion in *Nihon kayō shūsei*, II (Tokyo, 1928), 514–532.

Sandai jitsuroku [*A Veritable Record of Three (Imperial) Eras*] (901), compiled by Sugawara Michizane (845–903) *et al. KT*, Vol. IV (Tokyo, 1934).

Shichijūichi-ban shokunin uta-awase [*Matched Poems on the Seventy-one Occupations*] (ca. 1500) by Sugawara Kazunaga (1460–1529) and illustrated by Tosa Mitsunobu (1434?–1525?). In *Gunsho ruijū*, XVIII (Tokyo, 1904), 65–207; or XXVIII (rev. ed.; Tokyo, 1933), 464–606.

Shin sarugaku ki [*Record of the New Sarugaku*] by Fujiwara Akihira (989–1066). In *Gunsho ruijū*, VI (Tokyo, 1904), 991–1002.

Shinzei kogaku zu [*Shinzei's Illustrations of Ancient Performing Arts*], attributed to Fujiwara Michinori (d. 1159). *Nihon koten zenshū*, ser. 2, Vol. XIX (Tokyo, 1927).

Shoku Nihongi. Vol. IV of *Rikkokushi* [*The Six National Histories*] (Osaka: Asahi Press, 1929).

Shōyūki [*The Diary of the Minister of the Right, Prince Ono*] by Fujiwara Sanesuke (957–1046). *Shiryō tsūran*, Vols. I and II (Tokyo, 1915).

Soga monogatari [*Tale of the Soga (Brothers)*] (ca. 1400). *KS*, 10th ed., Vol. IV (Tokyo, 1918).

Sompi bummyaku, a compendium of genealogies compiled by Tōin Kinsada (1340–1399) *et al. Kojitsū sōsho*, Vols. LXXXIII–XCIV (Tokyo, 1903–1904).

Taiheiki [*Chronicle of the Grand Pacification*] (ca. 1370). *KS*, 10th ed., Vols. III and IV (Tokyo, 1918).

Bibliography 257

Tō Yashū kikigaki [*Memos of Tō Yashū*] by Tō Tsuneyori (1401–1494). In *Gunsho ruijū*, X (Tokyo, 1904), 859–888.
Tokitsune-kyō ki [*The Diary of the Noble Tokitsune*] by Yamashina Tokitsune (1543–1611). *Dai-Nihon kokiroku*, part II, 2 vols, to date (Tokyo, 1959——).
Yasutomi ki [*The Diary of Nakahara Yasutomi*] (1457) by Nakahara Yasutomi (1399–1457). *Shiryō taisei*, Vols. XXIX–XXXII (Tokyo, 1936).
Zeami jūrokubu shū hyōshaku [*Sixteen-Part Anthology of Zeami, Annotated*], ed. Nose Asaji, 2 vols. (5th ed.; Tokyo, 1960).

BOOKS IN JAPANESE

Atsumori Kaoru. *Heike monogatari no kisoteki kenkyū* [*A Fundamental Study of the Tale of the Heike*] (Tokyo, 1962).
Bukkyō ongaku no kenkyū [*A Study of Buddhist Music*] (*Tōyō ongaku kenkyū*, combined numbers 12 and 13 [September, 1954]).
Buraku no rekishi to kaihō undō [*History of the Buraku (Segregrated Community) and the Movement for Its Emancipation*], ed. Naramoto Tatsuya (Kyoto, 1955).
Chūsei bungaku kenkyū to shiryō [*Medieval Literature: Research and Material*], ed. Hisamatsu Sen'ichi (Tokyo, 1958).
Chūsei bungei to minzoku [*The Literary Arts and Folk Society in the Medieval Era*], ed. Wakamori Tarō *et al. Minzoku bungaku kōza*, Vol. V (Tokyo, 1960).
Chūsei kinsei kayō shū [*Anthology of Songs of the Medieval and Recent Eras*], ed. Shimma Shin'ichi *et al. NK*, Vol. XLIV (Tokyo, 1959).
Chūsonji to Fujiwara yondai [*The Chūsonji and the Four Generations of Fujiwara*], ed. Asahi Press (Tokyo, 1950).
Ellis, A. J. *On the Musical Scales of Various Nations.* Published in Japanese translation, with the title *Shominzoku no onkai* (Tokyo, 1951). Published originally in *Journal of the Society of Arts* (1885).
Fujita Tokutarō. *Kodai kayō no kenkyū* [*A Study of the Song of the Ancient Era*] (Tokyo, 1934).
Gotō Hajime. *Chūseiteki geinō no tenkai* [*The Development of Medieval Performing Arts*] (Tokyo, 1959).
Haino Shōhei. *Dai-Nihon engeki shi* [*History of Japanese Drama*] (Tokyo, 1932).
Hayashiya Tatsusaburō. *Chūsei geinō-shi no kenkyū* [*A Study of*

the History of the Performing Arts in the Medieval Era]
(Tokyo, 1960).

———. *Kabuki izen* [*Before Kabuki*] (Tokyo, 1954).

———. *Nihon engeki no kankyō* [*The Circumstances (of Development) of the Japanese Theater*] (Kyoto, 1947).

Hirade Kōjirō. *Kinko shōsetsu kaidai* [*Explanatory Bibliography
of Tales of Near Antiquity*] (Tokyo, 1909).

Ichiko Teiji. *Chūsei shōsetsu no kenkyū* [*A Study of Medieval
Fiction*] (Tokyo, 1955).

Ihara Toshirō. *Nihon engeki shi* [*History of the Japanese
Theater*] (Tokyo, 1904).

Inoura Yoshinobu. *Nihon engeki shi* [*History of the Japanese
Theater*] (Tokyo, 1963).

Iwahara Teishin. *Nanzan-shinryū shōmyō kyōten* [*Canon of the
Shingon-Sect Shōmyō*], 2 vols. (Kōyasan, 1938).

Iwahashi Koyata, *Nihon geinō shi* [*A History of the Performing
Arts of Japan*] (Tokyo, 1951).

Kana-zōshi, ed. Mizutani Yumihiko (Tokyo, 1919).

Kawatake Shigetoshi. *Nihon engeki zenshi* [*A Comprehensive
History of the Japanese Theater*] (Tokyo, 1959).

Kida Teikichi. *Tokushu-buraku kenkyū* [*A Study of the Segregated Communities*]. *Minzoku to rekishi,* II, No. 1 (July,
1919).

Kishibe Shigeo. *Tōdai ongaku no rekishiteki kenkyū* [*A Historical
Study of the Music of the T'ang Period*], 2 vols. to date
(Tokyo, 1960, 1961———).

Koizumi Fumio. *Nihon dentō ongaku no kenkyū* [*A Study of the
Traditional Japanese Music*] (Tokyo, 1958).

Konakamura Kiyonori. *Kabu onkagu ryakushi* [*A Condensed
History of the Song, Dance, and Music*], 2 vols. (Tokyo, 1888).

Minzoku geinō [*Folk Performing Arts*], ed. Honda Yasuji. *Dentō
geijutsu kōza,* Vol. IV (Tokyo, 1954).

Miyake Kōichi. *Kanze-ryū fushi no seikai* [*A Detailed Explanation
of the Kanze-School Melodies*] (rev., 4th ed.; Tokyo, 1955).

Morisue Yoshiaki. *Chūsei no jisha to geijutsu* [*Temples and
Shrines and the Arts in the Medieval Era*] (Tokyo, 1942).

Nagashima Nobuko. *Nihon ifuku shi* [*The History of Japanese
Attire*] (Kyoto, 1932).

Nishitsunoi Masayoshi. *Kagura kenkyū* [*A Study of the Kagura*]
(Tokyo, 1934).

Nogami Toyoichirō. *Nō kenkyū to hakken* [*Nō: Studies and
Discoveries*] (Tokyo, 1930).

Nose Asaji. *Nogaku genryū kō* [*An Investigation of the Origin of the Nō*] (Tokyo, 1938).
——. *Nōgaku kenkyū* [*A Study of the Nō*] (Tokyo, 1952).
Ogata Kamekichi. *Chūsei geinō-bunkashi ron* [*A Thesis on the Cultural History of Medieval Performing Arts*] (*Tokyo,* 1957).
Origuchi Shinobu. *Nihon geinō-shi nōto* [*Notes on the History of the Performing Arts of Japan*] (Tokyo, 1957).
Reifuku chakuyō zu [*Illustrations on the Wearing of Ceremonial Attire*]. *Zōtei kojitsu sōsho,* Vol. XXXV (Tokyo, 1928).
Sasaki Nobutsuna. *Ryōjin hishō no kenkyū* [*A Study of the Ryōjin hishō*] (Tokyo, 1948). This study is appended to the *Gempon fukusei Ryōjin hishō* [*Reproduction of the Original Text of the Ryōjin hishō*], of which Sasaki is the editor.
Sasano Ken. *Kōwaka-bukyoku shū* (Tokyo, 1943), Vol. I, *Introduction* (see bibliographic entry under "Kōwaka Texts").
Sekine Masanao. *Shōzoku zukai* [*Pictorial Explanation of Dress*], 2 vols. (enl. ed.; Tokyo, 1916).
Shida Nobuyoshi. *Nihon kayō-en shi* [*A History of the Realm of the Japanese Song*] (Tokyo, 1958).
Shimoosa Kan'ichi. *Nihon min'yō to onkai no kenkyū* [*A Study of Japanese Folk Music and Scales*] (Tokyo, 1954).
Takahashi Kenji. *Rekisei fukushoku zusetsu* [*Pictorial Explanations of Attires of Historical Eras*], 2 vols. (Tokyo, 1929).
Takano Tatsuyuki. *Jōruri shi* [*A History of the Jōruri*] (Tokyo, 1900).
——. *Kabu ongyoku kōsetsu* [*A Study of the Song, Dance, and Music*] (Tokyo, 1915).
——. *Nihon engeki no kenkyū* [*A Study of the Japanese Theater*], Vol. II (Tokyo, 1928).
——. *Nihon engeki shi* [*A History of the Japanese Theater*], 3 vols. (Tokyo, 1947–1949).
——. *Nihon kayō shi* [*A History of the Japanese Song*] (Tokyo, 1926).
Taki Dōnin and Yoshida Tsunezō. *Tendai shōmyō taisei* [*Compendium of Tendai Shōmyō*], 2 vols. (Hieizan, 1935).
Taki Ryōichi. *Tōyō ongaku shi* [*A History of Oriental Music*] (Tokyo, 1953).
Tanabe Hisao. *Nihon no Ongaku* [*Japanese Music*] (3rd ed.; Tokyo, 1957).
Tōa ongaku ronsō [*A Collection of Treatises on the Music of East Asia*], ed. Kishibe Shigeo (Tokyo, 1943).
Uehara Rokushirō. *Zokugaku senritsu kō* [*An Investigation of the*

Scales of Popular Music] (Tokyo, 1892). Available also in an
    Iwanami bunko ed. (Tokyo, 1927).
Wakatsuki Yasuji. *Ningyō-jōruri shi kenkyū [A Study of the His-*
    tory of Puppet Jōruri] (Tokyo, 1943).
Watanabe Sesuke. *Azuchi jidai shi [History of the Azuchi Period]*
    (Tokyo, 1956).
Watsuji Tetsurō. *Kabuki to ayatsuri-jōruri [Kabuki and Puppet*
    Jōruri]. *Nihon geijutsu shi kenkyū,* Vol. I (Tokyo, 1955).
Yuzawa Kōkichirō. *Muromachi jidai gengo no kenkyū [A Study*
    of the Language of the Muromachi Period] (Tokyo, 1955).

ARTICLES IN JAPANESE

Agō Toranoshin. "Chūsei kayō" ["Songs of the Medieval Era"],
    Iwanami kōza Nihon bungaku shi, Vol. IV (Tokyo, 1958),
    pamphlet no. 5.
Araki, J. T. "Kōwakamai kenkyū no ichi-hōhō" ["A Methodo-
    logical Approach to the Study of the Kōwaka"], *Chūsei*
    bungaku no janru of the Chūsei bungaku kenkyūkai, no. 1
    (1960), 7–8.
Atsumi Kaoru. "Kōwaka-bukyoku no kayōteki seikaku" ["The
    Songful Characteristics of the Kōwaka-bukyoku"], *Kiyo* of the
    Aichi Kenritsu Joshi Tanki Daigaku, no. 5 (1954), 20–33.
Fujita Tokutarō. "Kōwakamai no ryūso to kyokumoku ni tsuite"
    ["Concerning the Founder of the Kōwaka and Its Reper-
    toire"], *Kokugo to kokubungaku,* VI, no. 9 (September, 1929),
    28–53.
Hayashi Kenzō. "Gigaku-kyoku no kenkyū" ["A Study of Gigaku
    Music"], *Nanto bukkyō,* no. 8 (1960), 75–99.
———. "Sangaku ni-kō" ["An Investigation of Two Items Per-
    taining to Sangaku"], *Tōyō ongaku kenkyū,* no. 9 (March,
    1951), 27–46.
Hayashiya Tatsusaburō. "Sarugaku-nō no seiritsu" ["The Genesis
    of the Sarugaku-nō"], *Chūsei bungaku kenkyū to shiryō* (see
    bibliographic entry under "Books in Japanese"), pp. 34–72.
Inoura Yoshinobu. "Daigashira-ryū kōwakamai no keifu to geifū"
    ["The Lineage and the Artistic Style of the Daigashira School
    of Kōwaka"], *Kokugo to kokubungaku,* XXXV, no. 4 (April,
    1958), 51–62.
———. "Nihon engeki-shi kenkyū no kadai" ["An Issue in the
    Study of the History of Japanese Drama"], *Kokugo to koku-*
    bungaku, XXXIX, no. 6 (June, 1962), 1–11.

Iwahashi Koyata. "Kusemai," *Geibun*, XI, nos. 1, 2, and 3 (January, February, and March, 1920), 52–70, 32–46, 39–54.

Matsuda Osamu. *"Chikusai no seiritsu"* ["The Genesis of *Chikusai*"], *Kokugo kokubun*, XXVI, no. 3 (March, 1957), 1–10.

Muroki Yatarō. "Kōwaka to maimai" ["The Kōwaka and the Maimai"], *Kokugo to kokubungaku*, XXXIV, no. 8 (August, 1957), 35–43.

Nakagawa Zenkyō. "Nanzan-shinryū shōmyō gaisetsu" ["An Outline of the Shingon-Sect Shōmyō"], *Bukkyō ongaku no kenkyū* (see bibliographic entry under "Books in Japanese"), pp. 101–140.

Nose Asaji. "Kirokurui yori mitaru kōwaka" ["The Kōwaka as Seen in Historical Sources"], contained in his monograph *Nōgaku kenkyū [A Study of the Nō]* (Tokyo, 1952), pp. 296–315.

———. "Nō no senkō geijutsu" ["The Antecedent Arts of the Nō"], *Nōgaku zensho*, ed. Nogami Toyoichirō (Tokyo, 1935), II, 1–41.

———. "Shirabyōshi ni tsuite" ["Concerning the Shirabyōshi"], *Kokugo kokubun*, I, no. 3 (December, 1931), 1–35.

Shida Yoshihide. "Shirabyōshi kō" ["An Investigation of the Shirabyōshi"], *Nōgaku*, VII, no. 2 (February, 1909), 13–19.

Takano Tatsuyuki. "Ennen-shidai chū" [Notes on the Ennen-shidai"], *Bungaku*, I, no. 1 (January, 1932), 40–59.

———. "Introduction" to Vol. V of *Nihon kayō shūsei* (see bibliographic entry under "Kōwaka Texts").

———. "Kōwaka-bukyoku kenkyū" ["A Study of the Kōwaka-bukyoku"], *Nihon bungaku kōza* (Tokyo: Shinchōsha, 1932), VII, 171–244.

Tomikura Tokujirō. "Biwa-hōshi ra no yakuwari" ["The Role of Biwa-playing Monks"], *Kokubungaku kaishaku to kanshō*, XXV, no. 13 (November, 1960), 76–79.

———. "Chūsei no monogatari" ["Tales of the Medieval Era"], *Kokubungaku kaishaku to kanshō*, XXV, no. 6 (May, 1960), 80–88.

———. "Katarimono bungei" ["The Recitative Literary Arts"], *Iwanami kōza Nihon bungaku shi*, Vol. V (Tokyo, 1958), pamphlet no. 2.

Tsubouchi Shōyō. "Yuriwaka densetsu no hongen" ["The Original Source of the Legend of Yuriwaka"], *Waseda bungaku*, n.v. (January, 1906), 134–143.

Tsunoda Ichirō. *"Gaijin Yashima no sakusha mondai zakkan"* ["Miscellaneous Thoughts on the Problem concerning the

Author of *Gaijin Yashima*"], *Saikaku kenkyū*, no. 10 (December, 1957), 186–194.

————. "Jōruri-ayatsuri sōsei no engekiteki igi" ["The Implications of Drama in the Beginnings of the Jōruri Puppet Play"], *Nihon bungaku*, no. 51 (March, 1957), 11–21.

————. "Ko-jōruri," *Iwanami kōza Nihon bungaku shi*, Vol. VII (Tokyo, 1958), pamphlet no. 4.

————. "'Sate mo sono nochi' hassei kō" ["An Inquiry into the Origin of 'sate mo sono nochi' "], *Kinsei bungei*, no. 5 (May, 1960), 1–10.

Yamanoi Motokiyo. "Fūzoku no onkai" ["The Scale of the Fūzoku"], *Geinō*, new ser. 3, X (October, 1961), 11–13.

————. "Gagaku ni okeru ryo ritsu no sempō" ["The Ryo and Ritsu Modes in Gagaku"], *Geinō, new ser.* 3, XII (December, 1961), 5–8.

Yanagida Kunio. "Iwayuru tokushu-buraku no shurui" ["The Types of So-called Tokushu-buraku (Segregated Communities),"] *Kokka gakkai zasshi*, XXVII, no. 5 (1913), 91–120.

Yoshida Tōgo. "Nihon ongaku shi no kodai ni tsuite" ["Concerning the Ancient Era in the History of Japanese Music"], *Shigaku zasshi*, XVI, nos. 9 and 10 (September and October, 1905), 1–18, 21–38.

————. "Nōgaku no genryū oyobi hensen no ippan" ["The Origin of the Nō and a Phase of Its Evolution"], *Nōgaku*, III, no. 3 (March, 1905), 29–33.

Yoshida Tsunezō. "Shōmyōgaku gairon" ["An Outline Study of Shōmyō"], *Bukkyō ongaku no kenkyū* (see bibliographic entry under "Books in Japanese"), pp. 5–100.

WORKS IN WESTERN LANGUAGES

Abercrombie, Lascelles. *The Epic* (London, 1914).

Ancient and Oriental Music, ed. Egon Wellesz, *The New Oxford History of Music*, Vol. I (London, 1957).

Araki, James T. "*Kōwaka:* Ballad-Dramas of Japan's Heroic Age," *Journal of the American Oriental Society*, LXXXII, no. 4 (December, 1962), 545–552.

Bake, Arnold. "The Music of India," in *Ancient and Oriental Music* (see bibliographic entry above), pp. 195–227.

Bonneau, Georges. "Le problème de la poésie japonaise: Technique et traduction," *Monumenta Nipponica*, I, no. 1 (January, 1938), 20–41.

Bowra, C. M. *The Greek Experience* (London, 1957).

Finney, Theodore M. *A History of Music* (rev. ed.; New York, 1949).

Flickinger, Roy C. *The Greek Theater and Its Drama* (Chicago, 1918).

Haigh, A. E. *The Attic Theater* (Oxford, 1889).

Harich-Schneider, Eta. "The Earliest Sources of Chinese Music and Their Survival in Japan," *Monumenta Nipponica*, XI, no. 2 (1955), 85–103.

——. "The Remolding of *Gagaku* under the Meiji Restoration," *Transactions of the Asiatic Society of Japan*, ser. 3, V (December, 1957), 84–105.

——. "Rōei, The Medieval Court Songs of Japan. Part II: Musical Analysis," *Monumenta Nipponica*, XIV, nos. 3 and 4 (January, 1959), 73–109.

Haydon, Glen. *Introduction to Musicology* (New York, 1941).

Hibbard, Esther Lowell, "The Ulysses Motif in Japanese Literature," *Journal of American Folklore*, LIX (1946), 221–246.

Iliad, translated by A. H. Chase and W. G. Perry, Jr. (New York, 1960).

Japanisches Theater, ed. Curt Glazer (Berlin, 1930).

Katre, S. M. *Introduction to Indian Textual Criticism* (Bombay, 1941).

Ker, W. P. *Epic and Romance: Essays on Medieval Literature* (2nd ed.; London, 1908).

Kimotsuki Kanekazu. "The Analysis of Sound Wave [sic]," *Bukkyō ongaku no kenkyū* (see bibliographic entry under "Books in Japanese"), pp. 11–46.

Kishibe Shigeo. "The Origin of the *k'ung-hou* (Chinese Harp)," in *Shamisen no kenkyū* [*A Study of the Samisen*] (*Tōyō ongaku kenkyū*, combined numbers 14 and 15 [December, 1958]), pp. 1-52.

——. "The origin of the *p'i-p'a*, with particular reference to the five-stringed *p'i-p'a* preserved in the Shōsōin," *Transactions of the Asiatic Society of Japan*, ser. 2, XIX (December, 1940), 259–304.

McCullough, Helen C. *The Taiheiki*, No. LIX of the *Records of Civilization, Sources and Studies* (New York, 1959).

Malm, William P. *Japanese Music and Musical Instruments* (Rutland and Tokyo, 1959).

Ninomiya, S. "An Inquiry Concerning the Origin, Development, and Present Situation of the Eta in Relation to the History of

Social Classes in Japan," *Transactions of the Asiatic Society of Japan,* ser. 2, X (December, 1933), 49–154.

O'Neill, P. G. *Early Nō Drama: Its Background, Character and Development 1300–1450* (London, 1958).

———. "The Structure of the Kusemai," *Bulletin of the School of Oriental and African Studies,* XXI (1958), 100–110.

Phillimore, J. S. *Some Remarks on Translations and Translators,* The English Association pamphlet no. 42 (Oxford, 1919).

Pickard-Cambridge, A. W. *Dithyramb Tragedy and Comedy* (Oxford, 1927).

Postgate, J. P. *Translation and Translations* (London 1922).

Sachs, Curt. *The Rise of Music in the Ancient East and West* (New York, 1943).

Shinoda, Minoru. *The Founding of the Kamakura Shogunate 1180–1185,* No. LVII of the *Records of Civilization, Sources and Studies* (New York, 1960).

Three Japanese Plays from the Traditional Theater, ed. Earle Ernst (London, 1959).

GLOSSARY OF
JAPANESE AND CHINESE WORDS

✳✳✳✳✳✳✳✳✳✳✳✳✳✳✳✳✳✳✳✳✳✳✳✳

GLOSSARY OF JAPANESE AND CHINESE WORDS

Abe Suehisa	安倍季尚
aguchidaka	開口高
Akizuki monogatari	秋月物語
Akushichibyōe	悪七兵衛
Ama	海士
Amano	天野
Ataka no seki	安宅の關
Atsumori	敦盛
Azuma kagami	吾妻鏡
bamban	盤盤
Baramon	婆羅門
Bokkai	渤海
bugaku	舞樂
Bugaku yōroku	舞樂要錄
bukyoku	舞曲
Butokuraku	武德樂
Chang Liang	張良
chang-nei san-yüeh	仗內散樂
chi (chih)	徵
Chikusai	竹齋
Chin-ku-yüan	金谷園
Chin-shu	晉書
ch'iu (see hagi)	
chōbuku	調伏
Chōryō	張良
Chu-ju	侏儒
chūkyoku	中曲
Ch'un-kuan	春官
chūsei	中世
Chūshoō monogatari	中書王物語
Chūsonji	中尊寺
Chūyūki	中右記
Daibutsu kuyō	大佛供養

Daigashira	大頭
Daijōin jisha zōji ki	大乘院寺杜雜事記
Daiko	大狐
Dai-Nihon kokiroku	大日本古記錄
Daisan	大讃
Dannoura kabuto gunki	壇浦兜軍記
Dekisai Kyō-miyage	出來齋京土産
dengaku	田樂
Eboshi-ori	烏帽子折
edo	檅土
Ehon Taikō ki	繪本太功記
ei (ying)	嬰
Emman'i	圓滿井
engeki	演劇
enju (huai)	槐
Enkyoku shū	宴曲集
ennen	延年
Esaki Ushio	江崎潮
Fan K'uai	樊噲
Fudō kango	不動漢語
Fue no maki	笛之卷
Fujiwara Akihira	藤原明衡
Fujiwara Hidehira	藤原秀衡
Fujiwara Michinori	藤原通憲
Fujiwara Munetada	藤原宗忠
Fujiwara Nakamitsu	藤原仲光
Fujiwara Sanesuke	藤原實資
Fujiwara Tadahira	藤原忠衡
Fukumijō	含狀
Funa-Benkei	船辨慶
Fūryū Wada sakamori	風流和田酒盛
Fushimi Tokiwa	伏見常盤
Futari-Shizuka tainai-saguri	礫靜胎內捃
Gaijin Yashima	凱陣八島
Gakkaroku	樂家錄
gakko	樂戶
gaku	樂
Geibun	藝文
geinō	藝能
Gembuku Soga	元服曾我

Gempei seisui ki	源平盛衰記
Genji eboshi-ori	源氏烏帽子折
gigaku	伎樂
Gikeiki	義經記
Go-Hōkōin ki	後法興院記
Gōke shidai	江家次第
Go-kō	吳公
Goshozakura Horikawa yo-uchi	御所櫻堀河夜討
gozabune	御座船
Gunsho ruijū	群書類從
Gyokuyō	玉葉
Gyōnen	凝然
hagi (ch'iu)	萩
hakase	墨譜
Hamaide	濱出
Hamaide no sōshi	濱出草子
Han-shu	漢書
Heiji monogatari	平治物語
Heike monogatari	平家物語
hen (pien)	變
Hidehira	秀平
Hiraizumi	平泉
Hōgan	判官
Honnōji	本能寺
Hōraisan	蓬莱山
Horikawa yo-uchi	堀河夜討
Hōshakuji	寶積寺
Hsin T'ang-shu	新唐書
Hsü Ch'ao	許潮
Hu Shih wen-ts'un	胡適文存
hu-yüeh	胡樂
huang-chung	黃鐘
Huang-shih-kung	黃石公
Hung-lou-meng	紅樓夢
Hyakuman	百萬
Hyōgo	兵庫
Ibuki	伊吹
ichikotsu	壹越
Ichiman Hakoō	一滿箱王
Iguchi Naokatsu	猪口直勝

Ikuta Atsumori	生田敦盛
Imagawa Ryōshun	今川了俊
imayō	今様
Intoku Taiheiki	陰徳太平記
Iōgashima	硫黄之島
Iruka	入鹿
Itchū	一忠
i-yüeh	夷樂
Izumi no Saburō	泉三郎
Izumigajō	和泉城
jo-ha-kyū	序破急
jōrō	上﨟
Jūbangiri	十番切
Kaei sandai ki	花營三代記
Kagawa Masanori	香川正矩
Kagekiyo	景清
kagura	神樂
Kaitei shiseki shūran	改定史籍集覽
Kaitori	貝取
Kakitsu ki	嘉吉記
kaku (chüeh)	角
kakuon	核音
Kakyō	花鏡
Kamachi Akimune	蒲地鑑連
Kamada	鎌田
Kan'ami	觀阿彌
kanejaku	曲尺
Kangin shū	閑吟集
Kanjinchō	勸進帳
Kankenki	管見記
Kantan	邯鄲
Karora	迦樓羅
Kasshi yawa zokuhen	甲子夜話續篇
Katami Atsumori	形見敦盛
Kawasumi Taikō ki	川角太閤記
keiai	敬愛
Keisei niga-byakudō	傾城二河白道
Kikkan	狤犿
Kindai Nihon bungaku taikei	近代日本文學大系
Kinko shosetsu shinsan	近古小說新纂

Kinsei bungei	近世文藝
Kirikane Soga	切兼曽我
Kisaichi	私市
Kiso gansho	木曽願書
Kitayama	北山
Kiyō	紀要
Kiyoshige	清重
Kiyū shōran	嬉遊笑覧
Ko-Atsumori	子敦盛
Kōchū kokubun sōsho	校註國文叢書
Koda	小田
Kojitsu sōsho	故實叢書
ko-jōruri	古淨瑠璃
Kokka gakkai zasshi	國家學會雜誌
Kokubungaku kaishaku to kanshō	國文學解釋と鑑賞
Kokugo kokubun	國語國文
Kokugo to kokubungaku	國語と國文學
Kokusho kankō kai sōsho	國書刊行會叢書
Koma Chikazane	狛近真
Komparu	金春
Konakamura Kiyonori	小中村清矩
Konju	胡飲酒
Konoe Masaie	近衞政家
Konron	崑崙
Konron hassen (*Korohase*)	崑崙八仙
Koshigoe	腰越
Kosode Soga	小袖曽我
kōwaka	幸若
Kōwaka-buyoku shū	幸若舞曲集
Kōwaka Hachirokurō	幸若八郎九郎
Kōwaka Yajirō Naoshige	幸若彌次郎直茂
Kōwaka Yasuyoshi	幸若安義
Kōwakamaru	幸若丸
ko-wu-hsi	歌舞戲
Kōya Atsumori	高野敦盛
Kujō Kanezane	九條兼實
Kuketsu no kai	九穴貝
Kumasaka	熊坂
k'ung-hou	箜篌

Kurama-de	鞍馬出
Kurama tengu	鞍馬天狗
Kurama Tokiwa	鞍馬常盤
Kurodani	黒谷
kusemai	曲舞
kyōgen	狂言
Kyōkunshō	教訓抄
Kyokuzuke no sho	曲附書
Kyōto sōsho	京都叢書
kyū (kung)	宮
lang-chung-ling	郎中令
Lü-li-chih	律曆志
Mai no hon	舞の本
Manjū	滿仲
Manzai jugō nikki	滿濟准后日記
Matsuo Masuoki	松尾増塊
Matsuo Rikizō	松尾力造
Matsuura Seizan	松浦静山
Meigō ōrai	明衡往来
Meikū	明空
Miki	三木
Ming-ti	明帝
Minzoku to rekishi	民俗と歴史
Miraiki	未来記
Mitachi	御館
Miyako meisho zue shūi	都名所圖會拾遺
Momonoi Naoaki	桃井直詮
Momonoi Naokazu	桃井直和
Momonoi Naotomo	桃井直知
Momonoi Naotsune	桃井直常
Momonoi Senshin	桃井詮信
Momonoi Yasunao	桃井安直
Mongaku	文覚
Mongaku kanjinchō	文覚勧進帳
Moriya	杜屋
Motomasa	元雅
Mōtsuji	毛越寺
Mukadeya Zembei	百足屋善兵衛
Murasaki Shikibu nikki	紫式部日記
Muryōkōin	無量光院

Nabiki Tokiwa	靡常盤
Nakahara Yasutomi	中原康富
Nakamitsu	仲光
Nakayama Yukinaga	中山行長
Nan-lou	南樓
Nanzan-shinryū shōmyō	南山進流聲明
Nasu no Yoichi	那須の與一
Nihon kayō shūsei	日本歌謠集成
Nihon kiryaku	日本記略
Nihon koten bungaku taikei	日本古典文學大系
Nihon koten zenshū	日本古典全集
Nihongi	日本記
Nimaze no ki	烹雜の記
Nishi-Tanaka	西田中
Nishikido	錦戶
Niu	丹生
Nobunaga-kō ki	信長公記
Nobutane-kyō ki	宣胤卿記
Nōgaku zensho	能樂全書
Nōsakusho	能作書
Ōe	大江
Ōe Masafusa	大江匡房
ōi	大臣
Oi-sagashi	笈さがし
Okayama	岡山
On'ami	音阿彌
on'yōshi	陰陽師
Ōsawa Yukitsugu	大澤幸次
Po-hai (see Bokkai)	
po-hsi	百戲
Po-kuan-chih	百官志
reishi	靈芝
Rennin	蓮忍
Rikishi	力士
Rikkokushi	六國史
Rin'yūgaku	林邑樂
ritsu	律
Rokudō kōshiki	六道講式
ryo	呂
Ryōjin hishō kuden shū	梁塵秘抄口傳集

Saikaku kenkyū	西鶴研究
Sakurai Jizaemon Naokuni	櫻井次左衛門直邦
Sandai jitsuroku	三代實錄
sangaku	散樂
sanjo	散所
sanjū	三重
san-yüeh (see *sangaku*)	
saru aida	去る間
sarugaku	猿樂
Sarugaku dangi	申樂談義
Sekido-no-in	關戸院
Sekihara Yoichi	關原與一
sendo	先途
senzu-manzai	千秋萬歲
Settai	攝待
Shanaō	遮那王
Shi no tō	私壽
Shichijūichi-ban shokunin uta- *awase*	七十一番職人歌合
Shida	信田
Shigaku zasshi	史學雜誌
Shih-t'ung	十通
Shih Ch'ung	石崇
Shikoku-ochi	四國落
Shin gunsho ruijū	新群書類従
Shin sarugaku ki	新猿樂記
Shin yōkyoku hyakuban	新謠曲百番
Shinkyoku	新曲
Shinoda	信田
Shinshaku Nihon bungaku *sōsho*	新釋日本文學叢書
Shintei-zōho kokushi taikei	新訂增補國史大系
Shinzei kogaku zu	信西古樂圖
shirabyōshi	白拍子
shiran	芝蘭
Shiryō tsūran	史料通覽
Shizuka	静
shō (shang)	商
Shōbuwake	勝負分
Shochi-iri	所知入

Shōjo-shōnin nikki	證如上人日記
Shōkō	聖弘
Shoku Nihongi	續日本紀
shōmonji	聲聞師
shōmyō	聲明
Shōyūki	小右記
Shōzon	正尊
Shūdōsho	習道書
Shui-hu-chuan	水滸傳
Shunkan	俊寬
Shusse Kagekiyo	出世景清
sōga	早歌
Soga Kaikeizan	曾我會稽山
Soga monogatari	曾我物語
sokusai	息災
Sompi bummyaku	尊卑分脈
Sugawara denju tenarai kagami	菅原傳授手習鑑
Sugawara Kazunaga	菅原和長
Sugiwara Kambei	杉原勘兵衛
Suiko	醉胡
sumō sechie	相撲節會
su-yüeh	俗樂
Tachibana	立花
Taiheiki	太平記
Taishaku	帝釋
Taishokan	大織冠
T'ai-yüeh-shu	太樂署
Takadachi	高館
Takadachi godan	高館五段
Tanaka Naotane	田中直穠
Tanchi	湛智
T'a-yao-niang	踏搖娘
Tenko	天鼓
Tō Tsuneyori	東常緣
Tō Yashū kikigaki	東野州聞書
Togashi	富樫
Tōin Kinsada	洞院公定
Tokitsugu-kyō ki	言繼卿記
Tokitsune-kyō ki	言經卿記
Tokiwa mondō	常盤問答

Tōkōbō	東光房
Tokugawa bungei ruijū	徳川文藝類聚
Tosa Mitsunobu	土佐光信
Tōsen	唐船
Tōyō ongaku kenkyū	東洋音樂研究
Ts'ao Chan	曹霑
Ts'ao Chih	曹植
Ts'ao Yin	曹寅
Tsukishima	築島
Tsurugi sandan	剣讃談
tsuyogin	剛吟
Tsūzoku Nihon zenshi	通俗日本全史
Tu Yu	杜佑
Tung-i chuan	東夷傳
T'ung-tien	通典
u (yü)	羽
Umazoroe	馬揃
Uno Mondo nikki	宇野主水日記
Unshū shōsoku	雲州消息
Uraminosuke	恨の介
Utaura	歌占
Wada sakamori	和田酒盛
Waseda bungaku	早稲田文學
Yamamoto Shirozaemon	山本四郎左衛門
Yamanaka Tokiwa	山中常盤
Yamashina Tokitsugu	山科言継
Yamashina Tokitsune	山科言經
Yamashita	山下
Yamauba	山姥
Yanagawa	柳河
Ya no ne	矢の根
Yashima	屋島
Yashima no ikusa	屋嶋軍
Yasutomi ki	康富記
yen-yüeh	燕樂
Yoshitsune sembonzakura	義經千本櫻
Yoshitsune shin-Takadachi	義經新高館
Yo-uchi Soga	夜討曾我
Yo-uchi Soga kariba no akebono	夜討曾我狩場曙

yowagin	柔吟
Yume-awase	夢合
Yuriwaka daijin	百合若大臣
Yuriwaka daijin nomori no kagami	百合若大臣野守鏡
Yūsaki	結崎
Yü Liang	庾亮
Zeami jūrokubu shū hyōshaku	世阿彌十六部集評釋
Zōami	增阿彌
Zoku gunsho ruijū	續群書類從
Zōtei kojitsu sōsho	增訂故實叢書
zōyaku	增益
Zuiganji	瑞巖寺

INDEX

****

INDEX

Akizuki monogatari, 65
Annals of Yoshitsune. See *Gikeiki*
Ashikaga, relation to Kōwaka family of, 19
Ashikaga Tadayoshi, 20
Ashikaga Takauji, 20
Ashikaga Yoshimasa, 26
Ashikaga Yoshimi, 26
Ashikaga Yoshimochi: favors *dengaku-nō,* 58
Atsumori, 118, 119, 150, 151, 152 ff.; structure of, 112; characterization in, 113–114; synopsis of, 142. See also Taira no Atsumori
Avalokiteśvara, 25; in kōwaka, 144
aware: defined, 227
Azuma kagami, 122, 133, 150, 151, 174; quoted, 124, 220, 240

Bakin. See Takizawa Bakin
Benkei, 112, 123; in kōwaka, 128–133 *passim*
Beowulf, 116
biwa: in *gagaku* and Buddhist music, 46–47; in recitation of *Heike monogatari,* 48–49; origin of, 211–212
biwa-hōshi, 46–47, 48
Bokkai. See Po-hai
Buddhism: motifs in *ko-jōruri,* 18; motifs in *nō,* 66–67; and *shōmonji,* 70; motifs in kōwaka, 112, 116–117, 141–147 *passim,* 162n, 167n, 168n, 169n
Buddhist liturgical music. See *shōmyō*
bugaku: described, 27n; sources of, 36, 43; social role of, 43; relation

to *nō,* 43–44; influence on *shirabyōshi,* 61–62; in kōwaka, 143; Dances of the Left and Right, 200–201
Bugaku yōroku, 213
bukyoku, 15
Butokuraku, 41

Canon for Learning the Way. See *Shūdōsho*
Canon for Melodizing. See *Kyokuzuke no sho*
Canon for Nō Composition. See *Nōsakusho*
Chang Liang, 144, 166n. See also *Chōryō*
Characterization in kōwaka, 113–114, 115–116
Chikamatsu Monzaemon, 17, 83, 207
China: music and morality in, 28; classical scale of, 31–32; early performing arts of, 36, 50–51; tonal theory of, 48, 209, 212; motifs in kōwaka, 145–146, 149, 163n, 166n
Chōryō, 73, 112; synopsis of, 144
Chronicle of the Grand Pacification. See *Taiheiki*
Chu-ju, 54
Cid, epic of the, 122
Costume: in kōwaka, 6, 9, 87–92; in *shirabyōshi,* 63, 65; in *kusemai,* 63–64, 65
Courtesan, 60, 61–62

Daigashira, 73, 80, 84, 85, 92
Daijōin jisha zōji ki, 68, 69